D1268286

TOOLS

TOOLS

EXTENDING OUR REACH

COOPER
HEWITT

This catalog is published in conjunction with the exhibition *Tools: Extending Our Reach* on view at Cooper Hewitt, Smithsonian Design Museum, December 12, 2014–May 25, 2015

TOOLS: Extending Our Reach is made possible by major support from

Generous support is also provided by Newell Rubbermaid, Dorit and Avi Reichental, and Esme Usdan.

Additional funding is provided by the August Heckscher Exhibition Fund, the Ehrenkranz Fund, and Smithsonian Institution funds from the Grand Challenges Consortia.

Copyright © 2014 by Cooper Hewitt, Smithsonian Design Museum

All rights reserved. No part of this publication may be reproduced, stored in a retrieval system, or transmitted in any form or by any means, electronic, mechanical, photocopying, recording, or otherwise, without prior consent of the publishers.

Published by:

COOPER HEWITT

Cooper Hewitt, Smithsonian Design Museum
2 East 91st Street
New York, NY 10128, USA
cooperhewitt.org

Smithsonian Design Museum

Distributed Worldwide by ARTBOOK | D.A.P.
155 Sixth Avenue, 2nd floor
New York, NY 10013, USA
artbook.com

Library of Congress Control Number: 2014947988

ISBN: 978-091-0503-77-8

Cooper Hewitt, Smithsonian Design Museum
Pamela Horn
Head of Cross-Platform Publishing

Matthew Kennedy
Image Rights & Cross-Platform Publishing Associate

Book and cover design: Gabriele Wilson
Font: Regular by A2-Type

On the front cover: Patent Model for a Clothespin, No. 76,547, 1868, made by A. L. Taylor

2014 2015 2016 2017 / 10 9 8 7 6 5 4 3 2 1

Printed in China

On the front endpaper: *RoboBee, August 2012, designed by Kevin Y. Ma and Robert J. Wood with Pakpong Chirarattananon, Sawyer B. Fuller, Harvard School of Engineering and Applied Sciences*

On the back endpaper: *Handaxe, 1.4 million years old*

Previous page: *Photograph (detail), Stahls Chain-nose Pliers, 1955*
Photograph by Walker Evans

CONTENTS

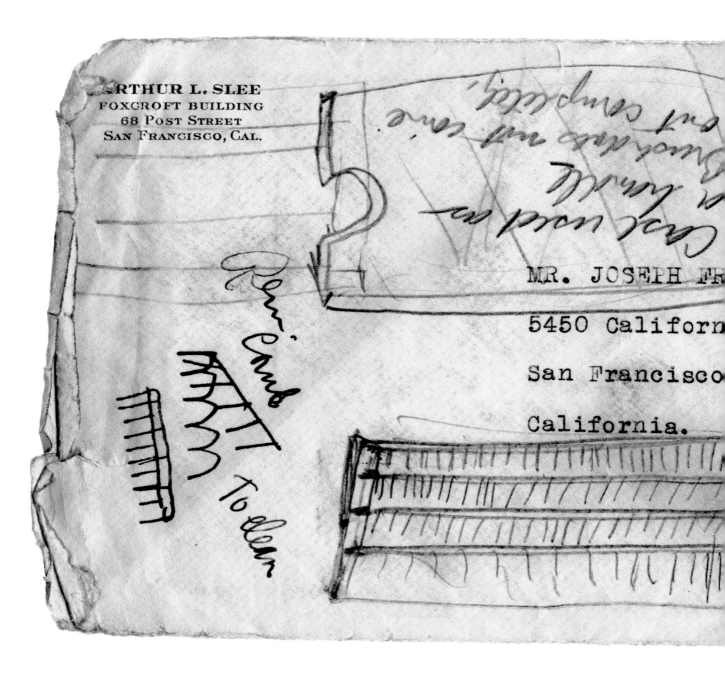

ARTHUR L. SLEE
FOXCROFT BUILDING
68 POST STREET
SAN FRANCISCO, CAL.

MR. JOSEPH FR

5450 Californ

San Francisco

California.

Sketch on Envelope for Pocket Brush, ca. 1935; Made by Joseph B. Friedman (American, 1900–1982); Pencil on paper; 10.5 x 24.1 cm (4⅛ x 9½ in.); Joseph B. Friedman Papers, Archives Center, National Museum of American History, Washington, DC, 2001.3031

Tellatouch Braillewriter, ca. 1945, designed by the American Foundation for the Blind

FOREWORD

Tools: Extending Our Reach is a fitting exhibition to inaugurate the new Cooper Hewitt, Smithsonian Design Museum. The 175 objects shown on these pages celebrate the ingenuity, innovation, and collaborative efforts underlying the devices that, throughout history, have helped us to survive, communicate, work, explore, and discover. The exhibition itself is the result of a remarkable pan-institutional collaboration, bringing together works from ten Smithsonian museums and research facilities along with other loans. *Tools* is the brainchild of Cooper Hewitt curators Cara McCarty and Matilda McQuaid, whose hard work and dedication brought this astounding array of objects together. I cannot thank them enough. I would also like to thank our Smithsonian colleagues for generously sharing their expertise and these treasures from their collections. Not only do these objects demonstrate connections among user, designer, scientist, anthropologist, engineer, and artist, they reinforce design itself as an invaluable tool that shapes our lives.

The exhibition experience features a new Cooper Hewitt tool: an interactive pen developed especially for Cooper Hewitt to make our collection and loan objects come alive for our visitors. Leading up to our opening, following an extensive renovation, we reconsidered the museum experience with designers Local Projects and architects Diller Scofidio + Renfro. Together, we conceived of a device that would allow visitors to access information about objects on view in our galleries. Similar to the examples of design process included in the *Make* chapter of this book, we brainstormed, sketched, studied, and tested many iterations of what such a device could be, do, and look like—and, of course, how it would work. Our new interactive pen, a global first, is the result of an inspiring collaboration between Cooper Hewitt, Undercurrent, GE Design Council, Tellart, SistelNetworks, and MakeSimply.

Upon arriving at the museum, a visitor will be loaned an interactive pen and may use it to collect information from the exhibition object labels and explore additional content available at digital tables in the galleries. By following a URL printed on the admission ticket, each visitor can recall the visit at home, learn more about the objects collected with the pen, and dig deeper into our collection. Cooper Hewitt's new museum experience is no longer just about looking; it is about interacting with design in revolutionary new ways, including ways that we may not have imagined.

From a beautifully simple fish hook fashioned by an unknown Iñupiat and the Polaroid SX-70 camera, to "Big Bertha," one of our nation's most ambitious engineering and infrastructure improvement works and Cooper Hewitt's new interactive pen, we celebrate the makers, designers, and users who create these remarkable tools that extend our reach and make the seemingly impossible possible.

Our sincere appreciation goes to GE, Newell Rubbermaid, Trustee Avi and Dorit Reichental, Trustee Esme Usdan, the August Heckscher Exhibition Fund, the Ehrenkranz Fund, and Smithsonian Institution's Grand Challenges Consortia, whose generous support made *Tools* a reality.

CAROLINE BAUMANN
DIRECTOR, COOPER HEWITT, SMITHSONIAN DESIGN MUSEUM

ACKNOWLEDGMENTS

Cooper Hewitt, Smithsonian Design Museum Board of Trustees
Barbara A. Mandel, Chairman; Nancy A. Marks, Vice Chairman; Enid W. Morse, Vice Chairman; Beth Comstock, President; Agnes C. Bourne, Vice President; Michael R. Francis, Vice President; Lisa S. Roberts, Vice President; Judy Francis Zankel, Secretary; Eric A. Green, Treasurer; Elizabeth Ainslie; Kurt Andersen; Carl Bass; Scott Belsky; Andy Berndt; Amita Chatterjee; Alberto Eiber, M.D.; Marilyn F. Friedman; Alice Gottesman; Paul Herzan, Chairman Emeritus; John R. Hoke III; Jon C. Iwata; Madeleine Rudin Johnson; Francine S. Kittredge; Claudia Kotchka; Harvey M. Krueger, Chairman Emeritus; David Lubars; John Maeda; Margery F. Masinter; Richard Meier; Henry R. Muñoz III; Karen A. Phillips; Avi N. Reichental; David Rockwell; Esme Usdan; Todd Waterbury; Kathleen B. Allaire, Chairman Emerita, Honorary; Joan K. Davidson, Honorary; Kenneth B. Miller, Chairman Emeritus, Honorary

Ex Officio—Smithsonian Institution
G. Wayne Clough, Secretary; Richard Kurin, Under Secretary for History, Art, and Culture

Cooper Hewitt, Smithsonian Design Museum is immensely grateful to colleagues at the Smithsonian who were integral to this pan-institutional endeavor, for lending their collections and sharing generously of their time and expertise, and for their collaborative spirit throughout this project. Many also contributed essays about specific objects and they are acknowledged separately as contributors. We would like to give special thanks to Jake Homiak, Andrew Johnston, Alison Oswald, and Katherine Ott.

SMITHSONIAN INSTITUTION
Claudine Brown, Barbara Rehm

Grand Challenges Consortia
Pierre Comizzoli, Michelle Delaney, Christine Forman, W. John Kress, Robert Leopold, Joanne Flores, Maggie Stone

Co-investigators, Level 1 Grand Challenges grant
Frederica Edelman, Jane Milosch, Diana N'Diaye, Sally Shuler, Barbara Stauffer, Mary Augusta Thomas

Archives of American Art
Liza Kirwin

Freer Gallery of Art and the Arthur M. Sackler Gallery
Julian Raby, Director; Becky Gregson, Tim Kirk

Harvard-Smithsonian Center for Astrophysics
Charles Alcock, Director; Jon Chappell, Mark Weber

National Anthropological Archives, National Museum of Natural History
Kirk R. Johnson, Director; Carrie Beauchamp, Jonathan Coddington, Susan Crawford, Aron Crowell, Doug Erwin, William Fitzhugh, Grethe Hansen, Igor Krupnik, Conrad Labandeira, Jane Norman, Felicia Pickering, Gina Rappaport, Ted Schultz, Shari Werb, Don Wilson, Melinda Zeder

National Museum of American History, Archives Center
John L. Gray, Director; Doris Bowman, Alicia Cutler, Janice Ellis, Margaret Grandine, Walter Hursey, Stephanie Joyce, Cathy Keen, Peter Liebhold, Shannon Perich, Suzanne Thomassen-Krauss, Susan Tolbert, Deborah Warner, Diane Wendt, Roger White

Lemelson Center
Art Molella, Director; Jeffrey Brodie, Eric Hintz, Monica Smith

National Air and Space Museum
John Dailey, Director; Paul Ceruzzi, Martin Collins, Malcolm Collum, Lauren Horelick, Melissa A. N. Keiser, Margaret Weitekamp, Lisa Young

National Museum of the American Indian
Kevin Gover, Director; Sharla Blanche, Victoria Cranner, Elizabeth Gordon, Marian Kaminitz, Patricia Nietfeld, Heather Shannon

National Museum of African Art
Johnetta Cole, Director; Clarissa Fostel, Karen Milbourne

Office of Exhibits Central
Susan Ades, Lora Collin, Rick Pelasara, Scott Schmidt, Seth Waite

Smithsonian American Art Museum
Elizabeth Broun, Director; Alison Fenn, Elaine Webster

Smithsonian Libraries
Nancy Gwinn, Director; Elizabeth Broman

The individuals, institutions, and manufacturers listed below lent work and provided assistance and support at various stages in the realization of this catalog and exhibition, and we want to express our sincerest gratitude to all.

ADDITIONAL LENDERS

AmiDov
Dov Ganchrow

CyArk
Elizabeth Lee

Eames Foundation
Eames Demetrios, Genevieve Fong, David Hertsgaard

Fine Science Tools
Christina Callanta

FLAG Art Foundation
Glenn and Amanda Fuhrman, Stephanie Roach

fuseproject
Yves Béhar, Jordan Felling

GE
Beth Comstock, Jenna Pelkey

The J. Paul Getty Museum, Los Angeles
Marc Harnley, Miriam Katz, Amanda Maddox

Given Imaging, A Covidien Company
Chantal Beaudry, Daniel Denofsky, Taylor Dobler

Gladstone Gallery
Barbara Gladstone, Damián Ortega, Esme Watanabe

Harvard School of Engineering and Applied Sciences
Kevin Ma, Rob Wood

Hitachi Zosen Corporation
Risa Hirano, Yukinobu Nakamoto, Ryo Nakamura

Leica Geosystems
Geoff Jacobs

Made in Space, Inc.
Jason Dunn, Alison Lewis, Grant Lowry

Del Ben
Michele Daneluzzo

MicroSystems Laboratory of the University of California, Irvine
Andrei M. Shkel

MoboSense
Logan Liu

MORROW SOUND
Charlie Morrow

Nanobiosym
Dr. Anita Goel

Nokia Sensing XCHALLENGE
Vivian Cabral

Seattle Tunnel Partners Joint Venture
Lindsey Gilchrist Burgess

Tangible Media Group and MIT Media Lab
Sean Follmer, Hiroshi Ishii, Daniel Leithinger, Mary Tran Niskala

Wyss Institute for Biologically Inspired Engineering, Harvard University
Donald E. Ingber

ADDITIONAL INDIVIDUALS

Special recognition is owed to Julian Beinart of MIT, whose expertise and critical advice were invaluable.

We also thank Chuck Hoberman, David Mindell, Danny Stillion; DS+R: Kumar Atre, Elizabeth Diller, and Ricardo Scofidio; Tellart: Andrew Haarsager.

External Publication
Editor: Alexandra Bonfante-Warren
Book design: Gabriele Wilson

Exhibition Design
Thinc: Bill Camp, Julie Chung, Tom Hennes, Aki Shigemori

COOPER HEWITT STAFF

Communications and Marketing
Laurie Bohlk, Jennifer Northrop

Conservation
Lucy Commoner, Kira Eng-Wilmot, Annie Hall

Curatorial
Amanda Kesner

Development and External Affairs
Deborah Fitzgerald, Kevin Hervas, Kelly Mullaney

Digital and Emerging Media
Aaron Straup Cope, Micah Walter

Education
Kimberly Cisneros, Sarah Freeman, Caroline Payson, Kim Robledo-Diga

Exhibitions
Jocelyn Groom, Matthew O'Connor, Mathew Weaver

Finance
Paula Zamora

Information Technology
Shamus Adams, Helynsia Brown

Operations
Nate Wilcox

Registrar
Kimberly Hawkins, Steve Langehough, Antonia Moser, Larry Silver

Interns
Steven Burges, Andrew Gardner

SPECIAL THANKS TO:

Kimberly Randall, Curatorial; Pamela Horn, Matthew Kennedy, Sara Rubinow in Cross-Platform Publishing; and former director, Bill Moggridge.

ACKNOWLEDGMENTS

11

"Technology is nothing. What's important is that you have a faith in people, that they're basically good and smart, and if you give them tools, they'll do wonderful things with them."

STEVE JOBS

INTRODUCTION

TOOLS: EXTENDING OUR REACH

Tools form our world and enable us to access and grasp it—sometimes literally. The word "tool" describes virtually anything that aids us in accomplishing a task. No matter where we live, from the moment we wake up until we go to bed, we use tools to get things done. The 175 objects chosen for this publication and accompanying exhibition represent a fraction of the ingenious creations humans have devised to engage with the world. Some are seemingly simple, beautiful poetic gestures; others save time and alleviate the toils of daily life; still others are game changers that have allowed us to achieve amazing feats that propel us as humans.

Tools are often equated with technology and engineering, but many acquire meaning through aesthetics, the economy of their design, the cultural significance of their materials, and the imagination of their designers. The objects have been organized into seven sections: *Work, Communicate, Survive, Measure, Make, Toolboxes,* and *Observe*. These categories reflect some of the reasons why tools are made, and each grouping includes a range of implements that address different ways people have solved analogous challenges.

Every tool has a primary function—a job to complete or an activity to assist—and most serve several applications. Some are iterations, improvements on existing, time-tested tools, others have been conceived for highly specialized users and professions. Many are made by individuals— an artisan, a doctor, or an independent inventor who customized a fit-for-purpose tool—while others required large teams of people with expertise in different aspects of design, engineering, and craftsmanship. Often, the maker goes beyond the purely functional to add beauty like the decorative stitching on an Aleut's translucent work bag, which gives meaning beyond its basic purpose. Rather than a survey of the history of tools or a hierarchy of the "best" implements from around the world, *Tools: Extending Our Reach* is an exploration of the very intimate relationship between human beings and the instruments we invent and employ.

Among the most ancient evidence of our humanness are the things we make and have made to survive. But tools are also the first examples of human design, and they have always been integral to the manifold ways in which we encounter our surroundings with the world. For the paleontologist Louis Leakey, whose pioneering work in Kenya unearthed some of the earliest tools, the act of designing these implements was key to the evolution of humans. As Leakey wrote, "[T]he most significant step that ever was taken in human history, the thing that turns animal into man was this step of making tools to a set and regular pattern."[1]

Choppers, the oldest known tools made by early humans, date back at least 2.6 million years. These were stone cores roughly modified for specific purposes, such as cutting, pounding,

[1] Martin Meredith, *Born in Africa: The Quest for the Origins of Human Life* (New York: PublicAffairs, 2011), 68.

and crushing; they were followed by the classic, teardrop-shaped handaxe technology, which predominated between 1.76 million and 150,000 years ago.[2] A mere five to six thousand years ago, bronze and then iron made possible the first metal implements, followed by the explosion of new tools in the industrial age of the nineteenth century and, more recently, in today's electronic age. The early use of handaxes led to an expansion of the available food and thus of nutrition, which played a critical part in the enlargement of the human brain. The making of food-storage tools such as pots also contributed to dietary improvements, and the social changes that ensued. Furthermore, recent research claims that the early development of more complex stone tools may have coincided with the first instances of human language.

Tools are intended to bring about change. They exist so that we may do more, see better, gather information, transform things, make decisions, investigate new frontiers, interact more fluidly and precisely, achieve higher forms of aesthetic satisfaction—extend our reach. During the sixteenth-century Age of Exploration, the need for greater precision in navigation led to more intricate instruments that were better at observing, measuring, and calculating—clocks, the astrolabe, the sextant—as well as to techniques by which sailors, scholars, and scientists evaluated ideas, improved construction techniques, and studied foreign cultures and environments. These scientific tools helped us apprehend and get closer to nature. As Steven Turner from the National Museum of American History has noted, they "were often called 'philosophical instruments' and their precision and unique properties were seen as revealing fundamental aspects of their physical world."[3] Gears, levers, and steam-driven machines slowly replaced hands and physical exertion, reducing strenuous, tedious labor for many people and making many lives more efficient and enjoyable. With the methods of inquiry that took hold during the eighteenth-century Age of Reason in Europe, research and science defined a new conception of what tools could do.

Informing most tools are the limitations and desires of the human body. Many tools are extensions of our physical selves, efficient surrogates filling in where humans lack capacity.[4] They leverage our ability to do more than we could without them: calculators extend the capacity of the brain to do computations, the mechanical finger helps astronauts pick up something beyond arm's length, and the temporary Jarvik-7 artificial heart enables our own survival. Before the twentieth century, human flight and travel to outer space were restricted to the shaman's spirit journeys, storytellers, and science fiction. As we designed new instruments, the universe proved to be very different from how it had appeared before. Now, more than ever, tools are opening up worlds to us, including those we cannot travel to in the flesh.

If we consider our eyes, ears, hands, and brains to be our original tools for investigation, then the telescope extended our ability to observe the universe. Invented in the early seventeenth century, it confirmed what had been outsider scientific and philosophical ideas about the Earth and its place in the solar system. More, of course, would be revealed. As David DeVorkin, of the National Air and Space Museum, has written:

[2] Richard Potts, email message to author, June 12, 2013.

[3] Steven Turner, email message to author, December 18, 2013.

[4] Katherine Ott, email message to author, November 17, 2013.

The eye is a sensitive qualitative detector, but it does not accumulate, or integrate, information over time. Photography does, and can render quantitative evidence about physical appearances and change over time. When photography was added to the telescopic toolkit, with ever-larger and more capable telescopes, it proved to be capable of resolving some of those distant patches of light and finding stars within them, showing that there were vast systems of stars we now call galaxies.[5]

Satellites and cameras are tools, but so are the images they send back to Earth. As instruments of observation, they detect, register, and communicate information. Today, as extensions of the eye, satellites and the latest advances in microscopy continue to uncover secrets, giving humans closer views into extreme environments and previously inaccessible regions, from the solar atmosphere to the innermost recesses of the human body, from the cosmic to the nano. At near nanoscale, in fact, the contemporary noninvasive PillCam® is a camera in an ingestible capsule that allows a doctor to view a patient's gastrointestinal tract. High-precision 3D laser-scanning "eyes," like Lidar, help us see and map remote terrains, archaeological sites, and objects, such as buried antiquities, that are otherwise impossible to access.

In the process of designing tools for people with disabilities, we have learned more about the body. A prosthetic, whether it is a limb, hearing aid, or artificial heart, is an extension designed to replicate a human ability. Initiated in large part by the military and for athletes, scientific advances, including new materials, are improving the dexterity of prosthetics. Recent innovations mimic the movement of natural limbs, even if the final manifestation bears little formal relation to the human body, as in the case of the Flex-Foot Cheetah® Xtend whose blade design is based on the rear leg of the eponymous cat. And, with the advent of implanted sensors, some aids will soon be further responsive when merged with our bodies.

Many of today's prosthetics are updates as well as replacements, which is true of other tools, too. For instance, the paper and handheld pencil traditionally used to sketch architectural drawings have been replaced by digital tools and electronic imaging. The new instruments serve the same objective—the design of a building. But what is the impact of a new medium on a traditional process? One answer to this question was offered by the media theorist Marshall McLuhan, who predicted the World Wide Web almost thirty years before it was invented. He stated, "The past went that-a way. When faced with a totally new situation, we tend always to attach ourselves to the objects, to the flavor of the most recent past. We look at the present through a rear-view mirror. We march backwards into the future."[6]

Stewart Brand's utopian *Whole Earth Catalog*, launched in 1968, was a compendium of knowledge- and a precursor to the World Wide Web. The Internet, an online tool with an international reach, now used by two billion people every day, is the "most powerful information network ever conceived!" in the words of the journalist Andrew Blum.[7] This global infrastructure has altered our sense of geography and distance, forming new kinds of community through social networking and other

[5] David DeVorkin, email message to author, September 18, 2011.
[6] Marshall McLuhan and Quentin Fiore, *The Medium Is the Message: An Inventory of Effects*, produced by Jerome Agel (New York: Bantam Books, 1967), 74–75.
[7] Andrew Blum, *Tubes: A Journey to the Center of the Internet* (New York: HarperCollins, 2012), 2.

worldwide conversations, with the constant free-flow of abundant information and images at our fingertips. It has redefined the ways in which we interact, as well as our understanding of the world and ourselves.

Interwoven throughout the history of tools is the story of materials and how we have transformed and improved them. For many societies, nature is the toolbox and repair kit—the hardware store. Whatever parts of the sea mammal the Yup'ik of Alaska did not consume for food they used to make garments, fishing tools, and other essential objects. The threads and knots of the quipu, the Incan recording system, remind us that fibers have often been important mediums for capturing and relaying information. The emergence of metallurgy made possible an onslaught of new types of tools and improvements to existing implements, such as the iron throwing knives of the Democratic Republic of the Congo and Central African Republic. A nascent technology often precedes the development of the materials required to fully execute an idea. Radio loop antennas, created of wire coils over a sphere, caused aerodynamic drag on airplanes, until the invention of the moldable composite plastic, Bakelite, made possible the improvement of these crucial instruments.[8]

It is still difficult for many of us to grasp the myriad applications of the microchip, itself a remarkable story of the convergence of science, technology, materials, and design. Once people figured out how to convert silicon into integrated circuits, a single tiny object and material replaced the mass of steel gears and other internal mechanisms of machines, thereby liberating design from many of its previous constraints. Form no longer necessarily followed function. Many tools got smaller. Embodying our perpetual drive toward increased precision, speed, and optimization, nearly every instrument in our postindustrial society has been informed by these microtools.

The ever-increasing power of chips has enabled us to integrate disparate handheld tools, machines, and entire systems into single, lightweight devices, "toolboxes" that fit in the palm of our hand, like command central. Today's ubiquitous tool kit is the computer. In the words of Steve Jobs, a computer "is the most remarkable tool that we have ever come up with. It's the equivalent of a bicycle for our minds."[9]

There is a long tradition of technical economy, of individual tools performing multiple tasks—the ancient handaxe is an elegant example. But there has never been a multipurpose instrument quite like the smartphone. Although called a "phone," it fulfills a plethora of functions, now compressed into one object. Actions that people performed on single-purpose tools for decades have been abstracted to the point that there is essentially no difference in the gestures required to make a phone call, take a photograph, file a folder, or even look up information in this hand-size "library." The smartphone has changed how we work, socialize, and otherwise collaborate. With this metatool, users, too, are tool makers, customizing their own applications to individual interests. Available all over the world and affordable for millions of people, it is a device with significant political implications.

[8] Roger Connor, email message to author, April 17, 2014.
[9] "Steve Jobs, 'Computers are like a bicycle for our minds.' - Michael Lawrence Films," YouTube video, 1:39, from the documentary film *Memory & Imagination: New Pathways to the Library of Congress*, directed by Julian Krainin and Michael R. Lawrence, posted by "Michael Lawrence," June 1, 2006, http://youtu.be/ob_GX50Za6c.

The physical movements associated with hand tools changed with automation. Today, user interfaces are no longer activated by muscle power—sewing, pounding, sawing, throwing, or the pulling of levers—but by intuitive microgestures on touch-sensitive displays. Akin to the dancing motion of fingers performing calculations on an abacus, the gentle tap on a button; scrolling, pinching, and releasing; or sliding a bar and swiping on glass are effortless motions with exponential outcomes. Even the terms for manipulating data—cut, copy, paste—are familiar metaphors borrowed from haptic actions associated with traditional hand tools. Good interactive design means that young children and those with little technological savvy can intuitively operate these extremely complex devices. The interfaces pair basic finger/hand gestures with multitouch sensors, but as the physical and virtual become increasingly seamless, and as researchers and designers work to engage other senses, we will soon bypass two-dimensional glass touchscreen devices. Touch-free gestural control systems—using eye movement, voice-activated input, and motion sensors such as inFORM's—will become normal ways to control our tools and perform some tasks.

A by-product of many tools is sound. It can provide important feedback for both the user and the observer, and is often our first indication that a tool is being employed. For the operator, it satisfies our psychological need for a sensorial response, offering encouraging reassurance that something is being achieved, like the gratifying sound and feel of a hammer when we hit a nail squarely on the head. Skilled telegraph operators could accelerate the transmission of messages by transcribing the sounds of the clicks. For people with visual impairment, white canes are aural as well as physical navigational devices. The users "look" with their white canes, but depend on the sound from the cane's tip to provide information about the terrain they are navigating. To the observers, the cane's white color and characteristic tapping convey its presence and significance.

Contemporary designers and marketers, recognizing the value of users' perceptions and of positive sensorial feedback, integrate sound into their products. The Polaroid SX-70 camera, a miniature factory, yields different aural cues as it progresses through each step of the "instant" picture-taking and self-developing process, heightening anticipation. The audible click of a mouse confirms we've successfully pressed it far enough. Designed into the experience of otherwise silent Apple products is the delightful whoosh or sound of crumpled paper that assures us that an email has been sent or an item dropped into the trash can.

Global health care is being dynamically shaped by portable diagnostic tools that give doctors and other medical personnel the ability to take their tool kits to the field, to carry their "offices," particularly in resource-poor areas. With the handheld Vscan™, for instance, a health-care practitioner in an underserved region can perform an ultrasound, collect and send a patient's data—often via smartphone—and receive a real-time diagnosis and treatment instructions from a doctor elsewhere in the world. A wearable amulet, the Kernel of Life, analyzes saliva, urine, drops of blood, and breath, and then transmits the results to a mobile application, allowing patients to be monitored remotely.

Tools are never neutral. They are defined by the actions they perform and the objects and effects they produce. Choosing one tool over another is a decision that excludes other options—other outcomes, experiences, insights, or even the use of certain skills. For instance, hammers not only assemble, they break things apart. They can foster uncertainty, be used in unintended ways, and forcefully destroy. Destruction, the unleashing of a process, is frequently an important part of the creative act.

It is easy to be seduced by the magic of the latest technology, but what we do with it is what matters. Tools are both the products and consequences of technology. There is also a darker, dystopian side. Smartphones are deployed for clandestine surveillance. USB flash drives, akin to miniature briefcases that enable us to conveniently store and transport massive amounts of data, are the currency of cyberespionage. In addition, the problem of the environmental harm from their mass disposal remains unsolved. And ethical questions made front-page headlines when blueprints for a 3D-printable gun were posted online in the US and downloaded by thousands before the government intervened.

The making of tools is about the making of society. Tools are fundamental to who we are. Their technology, aesthetics, and culture are inextricably linked, and their creation expresses the temper of their times. They demonstrate how design shapes experience and brings about change. When we consider that handaxes persisted for more than 1.5 million years, it is remarkable how rapidly new tools have emerged during the past 10,000 years, since the genesis of cities. We perpetually demand more from our tools, what we control with them, and the experiences we want them to give us.

Although we continue to manufacture physical tools such as screwdrivers and drills, many of our basic implements are now supplemented by "smart" or virtual components. They are interactive in more ways than one: they track our daily activities and our locations. They observe our patterns of behavior and analyze them. Not only do they multiply our capabilities, they detect and memorize our preferences, anticipate our wants, give feedback, and remind us of what not to forget. The future will be defined in part by the continued increase in the intelligence of tools that learn more from and about us, so they become more discerning partners. What is certain is that we will make new tools; what is hoped is that they will extend our reach to create a less divided and more con-nected, open, and generous society.

CARA McCARTY & MATILDA McQUAID

*(opposite) Copy of Patent for Drinking Tube, September 28, 1937;
Made by Joseph B. Friedman (American, 1900–1982); Ink on paper;
28.9 x 20 cm (11⅜ x 7⅞ in.); Joseph B. Friedman Papers, Archives Center,
National Museum of American History, Washington, DC, 2001.3031*

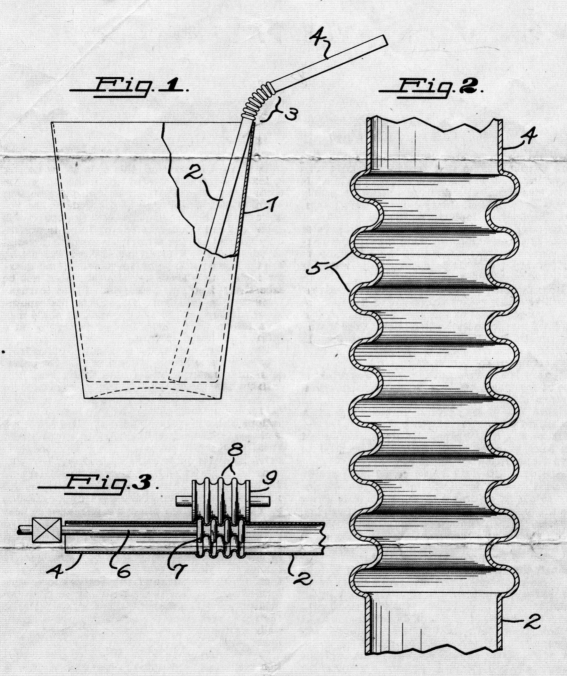

Fig.1.

Fig.2.

Fig.3.

INVENTOR,

JOSEPH BERNARD FRIEDMAN.

BY

Lippincott & Metcalf

ATTORNEYS.

Mary Jo Arnoldi
National Museum of Natural History
MJA

Joshua Bell
National Museum of Natural History
JB

Nicholas R. Bell
Smithsonian American Art Museum
NRB

Sebastian Chan
Cooper Hewitt,
Smithsonian Design Museum
SC

Judy Chelnick
National Museum of American History
JC

Sarah D. Coffin
Cooper Hewitt,
Smithsonian Design Museum
SDC

Roger Connor
National Air and Space Museum
RC

Aron Crowell
National Museum of Natural History
AC

David DeVorkin
National Air and Space Museum
DD

Joseph Gingerich
National Museum of Natural History
JAMG

Candace Greene
National Anthropological Archives,
National Museum of Natural History
CG

Jessica Gumora
MA Fellow, Cooper Hewitt,
Smithsonian Design Museum
JG

Hunter Hollins
National Air and Space Museum
HH

Barbara Janssen
National Museum of American History
BJ

Andrew Johnston
National Air and Space Museum
AJ

Adrienne Kaeppler
National Museum of American History
AK

Greg Kenyon
National Museum of American History
GK

Peggy Kidwell
National Museum of American History
PK

Jim Krakker
National Museum of Natural History
JK

Sarah Lake
National Museum of American History
SL

Mary Jane Lenz
National Museum of the American Indian
MJL

Cathleen Lewis
National Air and Space Museum
CL

Bonnie Campbell Lilienfeld
National Museum of American History
BCL

Ellen Lupton
Cooper Hewitt,
Smithsonian Design Museum
EL

Cara McCarty
Cooper Hewitt,
Smithsonian Design Museum
CM

Kelly McHugh
National Museum of the American Indian
KM

Matilda McQuaid
Cooper Hewitt,
Smithsonian Design Museum
MM

Alexander Nagel
Freer Gallery of Art
and the Arthur M. Sackler Gallery
AN

Valerie Neal
National Air and Space Museum
VN

Allan Needell
National Air and Space Museum
AAN

Alison Oswald
National Museum of American History, Archives Center
AO

Katherine Ott
National Museum of American History
KO

Junyao Peng
MA Fellow, Cooper Hewitt,
Smithsonian Design Museum
JP

Briana Pobiner
National Museum of Natural History
BP

Robert Pontsioen
National Museum of Natural History
RP

Nancy A. Pope
National Postal Museum
NP

Richard Potts
National Museum of Natural History
RPotts

Kimberly Randall
Cooper Hewitt,
Smithsonian Design Museum
KR

Ann M. Seeger
National Museum of American History
AMS

Alex Spencer
National Air and Space Museum
AS

Carlene Stephens
National Museum of American History
CS

Paul M. Taylor
National Museum of Natural History
PMT

Cynthia Trope
Cooper Hewitt,
Smithsonian Design Museum
CT

Steven Turner
National Museum of American History
ST

Stephen Van Dyk
Smithsonian Libraries
SVD

Harold Wallace
National Museum of American History
HW

Diane Wendt
National Museum of American History
DW

Henry "Trae" Winter III
Harvard-Smithsonian Center
for Astrophysics
HTW

POUNDING HERBS, GRASPING out-of-reach objects, and performing surgery all require tools that fit into our hand. How we hold them and use them often determines their particular shape and the tactility of the material that the designer or maker has chosen. A slight indentation in stone or a curved lip in stainless steel positions the thumb so the hand can cut more efficiently. Braided fiber or silicone rubber provides a secure and even pleasing surface for gripping. These and other ergonomic characteristics help us to work more effectively, and in the end enhance our performance and satisfy the desire to get a job done well.

Some tools, like the Tlingit halibut hooks, are born of specific needs and wants, while some are created for the solution of a singular problem but are then adapted to solve others. The flat-head screwdriver's multifarious functions, for example, have evolved with each user and have been passed on to the next person like an oral history.

Still other tools have been multipurpose from the beginning. The Acheulean handaxe, which persisted for more than 1.5 million years, has often been described as the Swiss Army knife of the Paleolithic era: a single object performing several actions. Woodworking, bone breaking (to obtain marrow), hide scraping, and butchery were the handaxe's primary functions.[1] It was portable and, along with a hammerstone and chopper—both used for knapping sharp stone flakes—made up the tool kit of early humans.

In the digital age, the multitasking smartphone's sleek rectangular body can be spotted in almost every hand. We dress it up like a fashion icon and wear it as an accessory, but these are personal disguises for its job of communicator and computer. No tool has fulfilled as many functions or been accessible to such a range of users. A simple tap of the finger is all that is required to activate the camera, radio, calculator, map, phone, and the hundreds of other apps inside.

All of the tools in this section are extensions of the hand. They augment our ability to catch fish, cultivate land, make precise cuts, or navigate a computer screen. Even when we scale up the job and its corresponding tools, the essence of the task does not change. What changes are the means of performing them. Big Bertha, for example, is a gigantic digging machine that places concrete tiles on the tunnel wall while it bores through thousands of tons of dirt and takes the rubble away. Where once a hoe, spade, and trowel accomplished such labor—given enough time and manpower—technical challenges of this proportion require new technologies.

As work continues to expand in complexity and scale our tools respond accordingly. Whether they become smaller or larger or are made from natural or synthetic materials, we will always, consciously or unconsciously, relate them to ourselves and the task at hand.

WORK

(opposite) *Radiograph image, Glove, MOL (MH-7), 2008*

---

[1] Kathy Diane Schick and Nicholas Patrick Toth, "The Role of Rock: Uses of Early Stone Tools," in *Making Silent Stones Speak: Human Evolution and the Dawn of Technology* (New York: Simon & Schuster, 1993).

Gloves:
Manned Orbiting
Laboratory (MOL)
Military Hamilton,
Version 7 (MH-7)
1968
→

Manufactured by United Aircraft
Hamilton Standard Division (USA)
Steel, anodized aluminum, brass, nylon,
HT-1 Nomex®, Velcro®, rubber / Neoprene
with flocked fiber coating, sharkskin, PVC
29.2 x 11.4 x 12.7 cm (11½ x 4½ x 5 in.)
Smithsonian National Air and Space Museum
Washington, DC, Transferred from NASA
1973.0860.003

AS A CONSEQUENCE OF USING TOOLS, humans have had to devise ways to protect their hands from those tools and the consequences of their work. Over the centuries, the function of the glove has at times expanded from mere protection to augmenting the capacities of the human hand, so that some gloves become tools themselves. Low-tech examples such as boxing, baseball, and hockey gloves not only shield the wearer from injury, but also increase grip strength in ways that contribute to the activity.

Similarly, spacesuit gloves protect astronauts' hands and also meet performance burdens. In a vacuum, the difference in pressure between the inside and outside of a spacesuit makes the suit rigid and difficult to move. This rigidity, while protective, renders normal manual activity even more difficult than the effect of the vacuum, because the hard fingertips of the gloves press against the wearer's fingertips, where the nerve endings and capillaries are most concentrated. After repeated impact, the capillaries shut down, causing numbness. These considerations make gloves the most difficult technological piece of spacesuit design because engineers must balance protection against tactile sensation.

The engineers at Hamilton Standard designed these gloves in 1968 to work with spacesuits for the Manned Orbiting Laboratory (MOL) program, developed by the United States Air Force.[1] Two prototypes in the Military Hamilton (MH) series, MH-7 and MH-8, were intended to provide greater mobility and dexterity than those of the Gemini and early Apollo suits. The present glove belongs to the MH-7 series.

Visible on the outside are the padding on the fingertips and palms and the steel tips that project over the fingernails, but these features tell only part of the story. Inside, a complex mechanism transmitted tactile information through the fingernails. The MH-series gloves came in standard sizes based on finger length and palm size, thus avoiding the need to custom-manufacture the gloves for every astronaut. To further refine the fit, internal laces allowed the finger lengths to be adjusted, to keep the wearer's fingertips in contact with the glove, even under pressure. A Y-shaped palm bar augmented grip strength, while enhancing movement between the thumb and little finger.

The distinctive external characteristics of the MOL gloves express its special features: the metal "fingernails" in the thumb and first two fingers pressed against the astronaut's own nail beds, providing direct sensory feedback. This design feature avoided the damage done by the pounding of more traditional soft-pressure glove fingers. The sharkskin grip pads on the thumb, first two fingers, and palm improved grip sensation and durability with less compression of the crew member's fingertip pads.

The Department of Defense canceled the air force space station in June 1969, when the cost of the Vietnam War and advancements in robotic satellite technology combined to make the MOL program a redundant expense. However, Apollo and subsequent astronauts complained about the discomfort in their hands and fingers resulting from their spacewalking-spacesuit gloves. The soft, blue silicone fingertips of the Apollo gloves became hard under pressure in a vacuum and frequently painful after hours of work. Although the designs for the early Space Shuttle and International Space Station spacewalking spacesuits initially emulated those for the Apollo suits, later glove designs have focused on eliminating pressure from the fingertip pads. The most recent generation of spacesuit design recalls features of the MOL glove, in particular, the translation of sensation through the fingertips and an improved grip. CL

---

[1] In 1963, the Kennedy administration tasked the air force with developing the MOL space station as a military analog of the popular and public National Aeronautics and Space Administration (NASA) human spaceflight program. The MOL effort was a "low-cost" space program that planned to use Gemini capsules and Titan III launch vehicles originally built for NASA flights that were later canceled.

HAWAIIANS DID NOT often trade, sell, or give away objects that were employed every day, such as poi pounders and other implements for preparing food. Even after such items became technologically obsolete, they were usually kept in families as heirlooms. The most important tool for everyday use was the pounder for preparing poi, a vegetable staple made from the steamed, pounded, and slightly fermented corm of the kalo plant. Poi, the staff of life, was eaten in large amounts each day, and its preparation required one or more stone food pounders, *pohaku ku'i poi*, and a large wooden pounding board. This knobbed style of pounder was designed to be grasped by the neck and is characteristic of the islands of O'ahu and Hawai'i. This large example weighs 4.3 kg (9 ½ lb.) and probably served for the first stage of beating to break down the whole tuber. AK

Stone Pestle
19th century

Polynesian (Hawai'i)
Carved stone
H x Diam: 24.1 x 15.9 cm (9½ x 6¼ in.)
Department of Anthropology
National Museum of Natural History
Smithsonian Institution
Washington, DC, E11043

THIS UNIQUE POUNDER is a mystery. Some Hawaiians believe it to be a pestle for the final stage of preparing poi. The handle of this finely polished black basalt pounder ends in a stylized head, identified by some as that of a *mo'o*, or lizard. Other Hawaiians hypothesize that this was a tool with which a *kahuna lapa'au*, a medical practitioner, would have pounded medicinal herbs. It weighs only 1.3 kg (2.8 lb.) and therefore seems more appropriate for pounding medicine than the very fibrous kalo. The tool was collected in Hawai'i during the United States Exploring Expedition of 1840, the first United States expedition to circumnavigate the globe. The objects gathered in the course of the voyage formed the founding collections of the Smithsonian Institution. AK

Pestle
Before 1842

Polynesian (Hawai'i)
Carved basalt
16.2 x 8.6 x 12.4 cm (6⅜ x 3⅜ x 4⅞ in.)
Collected by the United States Exploring Expedition, 1840
Department of Anthropology
National Museum of Natural History
Smithsonian Institution
Washington, DC, E3513

Making poi

Making poi, ca. 1890

THE MOUSE, A POINTING DEVICE that aids in performing operations on the computer screen, has become an integral tool in the digital age, acting as an extension of the user's hand. For years, the predominant design has consisted of a unit with one or more buttons and a wheel to control the cursor and other elements on the screen. With the advent of laptops and other mobile computers, portability and comfort have become increasingly desirable. The wireless Arc Touch mouse was designed with these criteria in mind. The lower portion of the body, which contains more than ninety parts, is jointed and flexible, allowing it to be stored flat in a bag or pocket for travel, then bent into a curve to fit the hand when in use. The minimal, ergonomic design includes large, flat buttons, and a simple flat metal touch strip that replaces the scroll wheel. The jointed section is covered in a skinlike silicone sleeve that makes the instrument comfortable and very easy to grip. The small transceiver that connects the Arc Touch to a computer can travel with it, magnetically held in place on the mouse's underside. CT

Computer Mouse with Transceiver: *Arc Touch*

Flexible Computer Mouse with Transceiver:
Arc Touch, 2010 and 2011
Designed by Microsoft Hardware User
Experience Design Team
(Redmond, Washington, USA)
Manufactured by Microsoft (China)
Polycarbonate, molded ABS plastic, silicone, metal
Mouse: 1.6 x 5.7 x 13 cm (⅝ x 2¼ x 5⅛ in.)
Transceiver: 0.5 x 1.3 x 1.9 cm (³⁄₁₆ x ½ x ¾ in.)
Cooper Hewitt, Smithsonian Design Museum
New York, Gift of Microsoft, 2011-60-1-a,b

WORK: HAND TOOLS

Controller of the Universe, Sketch 1

2007

Damián Ortega (Mexican, b. 1967)
Colored pencil and pen on paper and tracing paper
Courtesy of the Artist and Gladstone Gallery,
New York and Brussels, DO052

Controller of the Universe, Sketch 2

2007

Damián Ortega (Mexican, b. 1967)
Colored pencil and pen on paper and tracing paper
Courtesy of the Artist and Gladstone Gallery,
New York and Brussels, DO053

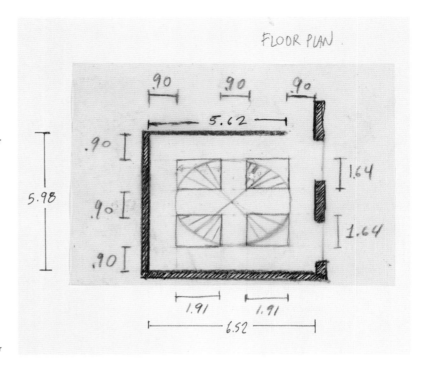

"What I wanted to show is the brutal technical control that is permanently available. The eye is at the center of the piece, and then you find a tool anywhere you look around you, and tools become an extension but also a frontier or filter. This is the same duality involved in any sort of human technology."[1]

DAMIÁN ORTEGA, on Controller of the Universe

DAMIÁN ORTEGA'S CONTROLLER OF THE UNIVERSE is a frozen explosion of hand tools, the very ones a visitor might expect in an exhibition about tools.[2] In their hovering and almost dreamlike state, the saws, planes, and axes are completely removed from their normal context. The suspended flotilla suggests alternative ways to look at tools, in the hope that the experience will transform the visitor's own ideas about what tools are and mean.

Tools can destroy as easily as they can help construct. They extend our body's ability to do things and at the same time come between us and our direct experience of the action. They are useful and completely human. Ortega explores such dualities in Controller of the Universe. The installation appears threatening to those standing at the perimeter but, by way of a cruciform path, the artist invites the visitor to experience the optimal viewpoint at the center. Here, balance and instability, construction and destruction, technological progress and human naiveté come together to reflect the human condition.

The placement of the piece in the exhibition—on axis with "live" images of a pulsating Sun that is part of a separate installation—underscores this perceived control of our universe, while the distant ball of fire reminds us so potently that this is far from the truth. We can tame it at times, use it to help us survive and endure and to enhance our lives in many ways, but we will never control it—even with a world of tools at our fingertips. MM

[1] Damián Ortega and Jessica Morgan, *Do it Yourself: Damián Ortega* (New York: Skira Rizzoli, 2009).

[2] The title of the work comes from a mural by Diego Rivera, commissioned for Rockefeller Center's Radio Corporation of American (RCA) building in 1932. The panel, painted in 1933 and initially titled *Man at the Crossroads Looking with Hope and High Vision to the Choosing of a New and Better Future*, featured two opposing views of society, capitalism, and socialism. A portrait of Vladimir Lenin represented the latter and, under pressure from critics, Nelson Rockefeller asked Rivera to remove the portrait. When Rivera refused, the building's management firm shrouded the mural and finally destroyed it, after failed attempts by Rockefeller and other individuals to save it. Later that same year, the Mexican government gave Rivera permission to paint a revised version of the mural—*Man, Controller of the Universe* (1934)—at the Palacio de Bellas Artes in Mexico City, where it remains today.

Controller of
the Universe

2007
→

Damián Ortega (Mexican, b. 1967)
Found tools, wire
2.85 x 4.06 x 4.55 m
(9 ft. 4 in. x 13 ft. 4 in. x 14 ft. 11 in.)
Collection Glenn and Amanda Fuhrman,
New York, Courtesy The FLAG Art Foundation
Shown installed at MoMA PS1, New York

IN THE JULY 1955 ISSUE of *Fortune* magazine, the American photographer Walker Evans celebrated iconic hand tools in a photographic essay, *Beauties of the Common Tool*. Referring to the hardware store as an "offbeat museum show," Evans praised the "undesigned" forms of classic tools and chided the "design-happy manufacturers" who dared to change the least detail. Tin snips, a bricklayer's trowel, chain-nose pliers, and a crate opener were, in Evans's eyes, standards of "elegance, candor, and purity." Ultimately, what Evans valued was the design, the construction that resulted from the maker's understanding of function, efficiency of form, and material. MM

Photograph: "T" Bevel
1955
Photograph by Walker Evans
(American, 1903–1975)
Gelatin silver print
Sheet: 24.4 x 19.4 cm (9 5/8 x 7 5/8 in.)
The J. Paul Getty Museum
Los Angeles, 84.XM.956.1066
Page 37

Photograph: The "Super-rench"—Two-Ended Wrench
1955
Photograph by Walker Evans
(American, 1903–1975)
Gelatin silver print
Sheet: 25 x 20.2 cm (9 7/8 x 7 15/16 in.)
The J. Paul Getty Museum
Los Angeles, 84.XM.956.1063
Page 38

Photograph: Tin Snips by J. Wiss & Sons Co., $1.85
1955
From *Beauties of the Common Tool*,
in *Fortune* magazine
Photograph by Walker Evans
(American, 1903–1975)
Gelatin silver print
Sheet: 25.2 x 20.3 cm (9 7/8 x 8 in.)
The J. Paul Getty Museum,
Los Angeles, 84.XP.453.1
Page 39

Photograph: Tape Reamer
1955
Photograph by Walker Evans
(American, 1903–1975)
Gelatin silver print
Sheet: 25.1 x 20.2 cm (9 7/8 x 7 15/16 in.)
The J. Paul Getty Museum,
Los Angeles, 84.XM.956.1053
Page 40

Photograph: Stahls Chain-nose Pliers (Over Actual Size), **from Eskilstuna, Sweden, $2.49**
1955
from *Beauties of The Common Tool*
in *Fortune Magazine*
Photograph by Walker Evans
(American, 1903–1975)
Gelatin silver print
Sheet: 24.9 x 19.9 cm
(9 13/16 x 7 7/8 in.)
The J. Paul Getty Museum,
Los Angeles, 84.XM.956.1057
Page 41

Photograph: Auger Drill Bit with a Flared Screwdriver End
1955
Photograph by Walker Evans
(American, 1903–1975)
Gelatin silver print
Sheet: 25 x 20 cm (9 7/8 x 7 7/8 in.)
The J. Paul Getty Museum,
Los Angeles, 84.XM.956.1059
Page 42

Photograph: Baby Terrier Crate Opener by Bridgeport Hardware Mfg. Corp., 69 cents
1955
from *Beauties of The Common Tool*
in *Fortune* magazine
Photograph by Walker Evans
(American, 1903–1975)
Gelatin silver print
Sheet: 25 x 20 cm (9 7/8 x 7 7/8 in.)
The J. Paul Getty Museum,
Los Angeles, 84.XM.956.1060
Page 43

Photograph: Bricklayer's Pointing Trowel by Marshall-town Trowel Co., $1.35
1955
From *Beauties of the Common Tool*,
in *Fortune* magazine
Photograph by Walker Evans
(American, 1903–1975)
Gelatin silver print
Sheet: 25.3 x 20.3 cm (10 x 8 in.)
The J. Paul Getty Museum,
Los Angeles, 84.XP.453.17
Page 44

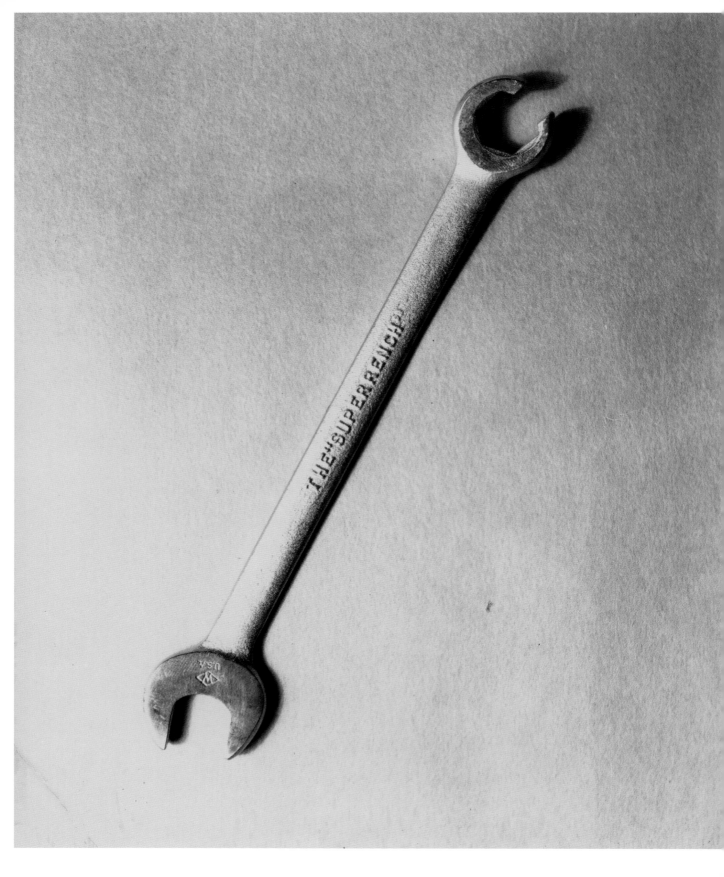

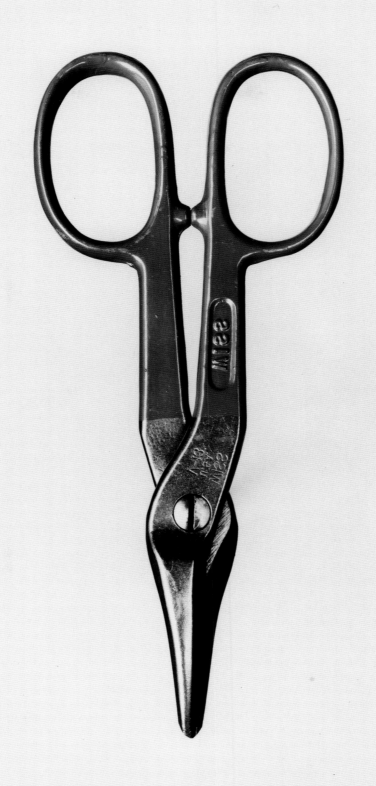

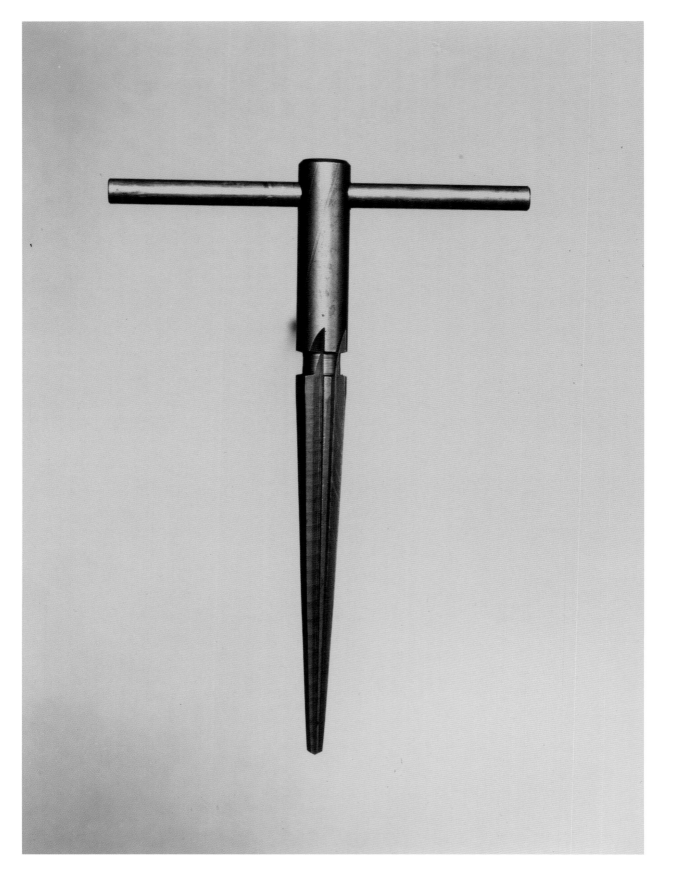

2 1/2 min. daylight sun 2 PM

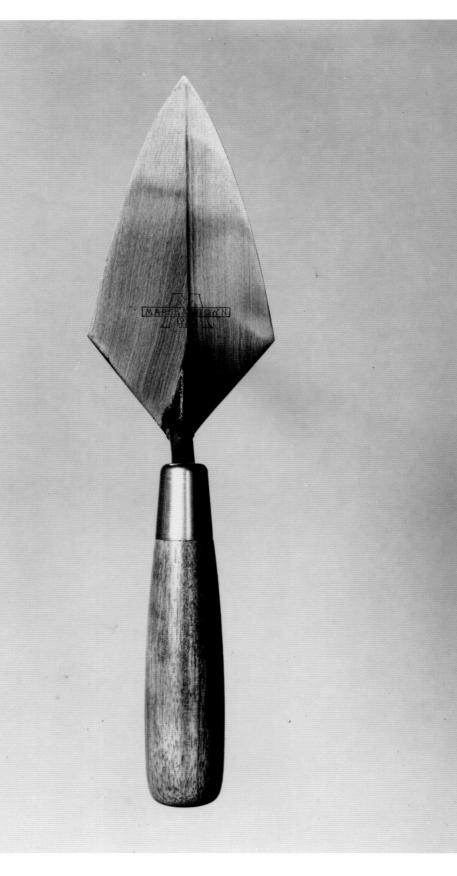

Bird Dart

Created before 1870s

Yup'ik
(Ungaliit, Norton Sound, Alaska, USA)
Carved cedar, carved ivory, sinew lashing
11.1 x 7.3 x 172.1 cm (4⅜ x 2⅞ x 67¾ in.)
Collection of Lucien M. Turner, 1876
Saint Michael, Alaska
Department of Anthropology
National Museum of Natural History
Smithsonian Institution
Washington, DC, E29847

YUP'IK MEN HUNTED geese and ducks at sea from kayaks using multi-pronged darts called *nuusaaq*. With the help of a throwing board they could hurl a *nuusaaq* long distances with great accuracy. This dart has a central point made of walrus ivory and three barbed side prongs designed to snag a bird by the neck or wing. It could be thrown overhand through the air or side-armed to skip it across the waves at floating birds. When launched into a flock, it might kill or snag several ducks at one time. Because darts are silent and don't frighten away other game in the area, these weapons were employed even after shotguns became available in the 1870s. AC

Handaxe #5

2011

↓

From the BC-AD, Contemporary
Flint Tool Design Series
Designed by Ami Drach
(Israeli, 1963–2012) and Dov
Ganchrow (Israeli, b. USA, 1970)
Flint, elastomer
13 x 8 x 6 cm (5⅛ x 3⅛ x 2⅜ in.)
Courtesy of Studio AmiDov

Blade #9

2011

↓

From the BC-AD, Contemporary
Flint Tool Design Series
Designed by Ami Drach
(Israeli, 1963–2012) and Dov
Ganchrow (Israeli, b. USA, 1970)
Flint, elastomer
4 x 4 x 1 cm (1⁹⁄₁₆ x 1⁹⁄₁₆ x ⅜ in.)
Courtesy of Studio AmiDov

Chef's Knife:
Primitive Knife
2013

→ ↓

Designed by Michele Daneluzzo
(Italian, b. 1988)
Manufactured by Del Ben (Maniago, Italy)
Hardened chrome-molybdenum-steel
Knife and base: 7.5 x 22.3 x 4.9 cm
(2¹⁵⁄₁₆ x 8¾ x 1¹⁵⁄₁₆ in.)
Courtesy of Michele Daneluzzo and Del Ben

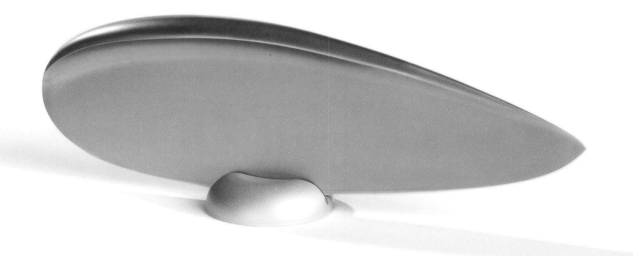

Halibut Hook
Created before 1881

↓ →

Tlingit (southeast Alaska, USA)
Carved wood, cord
14 x 30 x 5 cm (5½ x 11¹³⁄₁₆ x 1¹⁵⁄₁₆ in.)
Collection of John J. McLean, 1881
Baranof Island, Alaska
Department of Anthropology
National Museum of Natural History
Smithsonian Institution
Washington, DC, E45990

INDIGENOUS COMMUNITIES in Alaska were early practitioners of sustainable fishing and hunting for centuries. Partly because food was so difficult to acquire it was highly valued and treated with great respect. Rituals and prayers preceded the hunt and though the success of the immediate hunt was imperative, more vital still was the assurance on the part of the spirits that the animals would return next season in abundance.[3]

This ingenious and highly specialized fishhook suits exactly the behavior and anatomy of a halibut. The size of the *V*-shaped gap determined the size of the catch, making it impossible to hook a fish that was either too small or larger than a man could haul into his boat.

Halibut are bottom-feeding fish that can be caught in depths as great as 274.3 m (900 ft.). They can weigh up to 272.7 kg (600 lb.), but most are between 9 and 45.5 kg (20–100 lb.). Baited with octopus, the hook was anchored by stone sinkers and rose about 60 cm (2 ft.) off the sea floor. The more buoy-

[3] Cenami Up'nerkam Nallini, "On the Coast During Spring," in *Yuungnaqpiallerput/The Way We Genuinely Live: Masterworks of Yup'ik Science and Survival*, by Ann Pienup-Riordan (Seattle: University of Washington Press in assocation with Anchorage Museum Assocation and Calista Elders Council, 2007), 117.

ant upper section held the hook carved side up in the water. Sections of bull kelp, knotted together, provided flexible and nearly unbreakable lines up to 274.3 m (900 ft.) long. Bird-shaped floats were attached to the tops of the lines, and when a fish was hooked its weight pulled the bird float upright, signaling a catch. The fisherman then slowly drew the halibut to the surface and killed it with a blow from a club.[4]

The sensitive carving on this hook shows some type of land animal or hybrid, its protruding, ropelike tongue being swallowed by a fish. The tongue motif between two animals is present on many halibut hooks and represents a spirit exchange. The hook, as well as the club used to kill the fish, had to be made as beautiful as possible in order to please the spirit of the animal the fisherman was trying to catch. By not offending the halibut spirit, the Tlingit believed large numbers of fish would return to sustain the community.[5] In a region where fish constituted nearly 80 percent of the food supply, spiritual connections were vital to community survival. MM

---

[4] Jean-Loup Rousselot, William W. Fitzhugh, and Aron Crowell, "Maritime Economies of the North Pacific Rim," *Crossroads of Continents: Cultures of Siberia and Alaska*, by William W. Fitzhugh and Aron Crowell (Washington, DC: Smithsonian Institution, 1988), 154.

[5] William Fitzhugh in conversation with the author, November 8, 2013.

HAWAIIAN OCTOPUS LURES are tools of trickery, as a well-formed cowrie shell was said to attract an octopus like a beautiful woman arouses desire in a man. The lure, *leho he'e*, was used for fishing in water from 80 to 120 fathoms (146.4–219.6 m [480–720 ft.]) deep and were often used in pairs. It was shaken up and down, and this merry dancing attracted the octopus, which encircled the lure with its tentacles. Besides catching food, acquiring octopus in this manner was an aristocratic sport, and different kinds of cowrie shells were used during different parts of the day. This lure was collected by Nathaniel B. Emerson, who organized the Hawaiian section of the Alaska-Yukon-Pacific Exposition in Seattle in 1909. At the end of the Exposition, the collection was purchased by the US government and became part of the Smithsonian Institution collection. AK

Octopus Lure
Before 1909

↑

Polynesian (Hawai'i)
Cowrie shell, worked stone,
carved wood, cord, lashing
11.4 x 19.7 x 7.6 cm (4½ x 7¾ x 3 in.)
Collected by Dr. Nathaniel B. Emerson
exhibited at the Alaska-Yukon-Pacific
Exposition in Seattle, Washington, in 1909
Department of Anthropology, National
Museum of Natural History, Smithsonian
Institution, Washington, DC, E257827

KNOWN BY DIFFERENT NAMES in the languages of the Solomon Islands—
to'oheo in Sa'a and Ulawa and *toheo* in Uki/Ugi and Arosi[6]—this type of shell fishhook was
employed to catch mackerel, sardines, and other small oceangoing fish.[7] Today, indus-
trially manufactured metal hooks and lures have replaced them. This *V*-shaped hook
was cut from a shell with either metal or stone tools; four small roundels were etched
into the hook's sides and then darkened with a resin. On Uki/Ugi Island, the fruit of the
talo tree was burned and applied to the depressions. Once this was done, men attached
the finished hook to a line affixed to a length of bamboo. From a platform built over a
reef, the fishermen moved the hook up and down in the water to mimic the movements
of a small fish.[8] Making and using this hook required a great deal of virtuosity.

This hook was either collected directly by William M. Mann (1886–1960), who from
1915 to 1916 gathered insects throughout the Solomon Islands and Fiji, or it was given
to him by one of the many European government officials, traders, and missionaries
he encountered during his trip. He subsequently donated his material to the National
Museum of Natural History, Washington, DC. JB

Fishhook
Before 1917

Solomon Islands
Carved mother-of-pearl
1.1 x 2.9 x 0.3 cm (⁷⁄₁₆ x 1⅛ x ⅛ in.)
Department of Anthropology
National Museum of Natural History
Smithsonian Institution
Washington, DC, E399982

---

[6] For the term in Sa'a and Ulawa, see Ivens, *Melanesians*, 354; for Uki/Ugi, see Kaschko, "Archaeological Consideration,"
196; and for Arosi, see Fox, *Threshold*, 417.

[7] W.G. Ivens, *Melanesians of the South-east Solomon Islands* (London: Kegan Paul, 1927), 389.

[8] Michael Kaschko, "An Archaeological Consideration of the Ethnographic Fishhook Set on Uki Island, Southeast
Solomon Islands," ed. R.C. Green and M. Cresswell, *Southeast Solomon Islands Cultural History* Bulletin 11 (Wellington:
Royal Society of New Zealand, 1976), 195–6.

Fishhook

Before 1917

↓ →

Solomon Islands
Carved turtle shell, mother-of-pearl,
glass beads, fiber cord
2.5 x 1.4 x 8.3 cm (1 x ⁹⁄₁₆ x 3¼ in.)
Department of Anthropology
National Museum of Natural History
Smithsonian Institution
Washington, DC, E399972

THIS SOLOMON ISLANDS fishhook consists of a turtle-shell hook bound to a mother-of-pearl shank with a twisted fiber cord. At one end of the shank are two strings of bright blue European trade beads threaded on twisted fiber cord, which is further decorated with two tufts of red calico trade cloth. Fishhooks such as this one were made and used by men to catch ocean-dwelling bonito or skipjack tuna. Throughout the Solomons, the bonito was tradionally a sacred fish, belonging to a wider assemblage of relationships that included the smaller fish that bonito hunt in schools; the birds attracted to the chase; and ancestral beings that took the form of sharks. The first sighting of the bonito each season began a series of rituals during which young initiates were trained to catch these aggressive fish and thus learn about their place within the wider world.[9] In the southeastern Solomons, bonito hooks like this one were known as *pasa*.[10]

In the late nineteenth century, before metal tools became common, men cut the shank—made from marine shells, dugong bone, or both—with a piece of branching coral. The hook would have been obtained from a freshly killed turtle, whose shell was then heated and bent into shape.[11] The beads and the red calico decorating this hook were used throughout the Solomon Islands and the wider Pacific as payment for plantation labor and as trade items. These items of foreign manufacture were quickly adopted into the aesthetic systems of the Solomon Islands to enhance the objects' function and efficacy.

On Uki/Ugi Island, when a school of bonito was sighted, several men would board their canoe and paddle around the school. Those at the front of the canoe used one style of hook, while those in the back of the canoe ran a *pasa* attached by a line to a bamboo fishing pole. The shape of the shank imitates the body of a small fish, while in the water the beads move like the fish's tail. *Pasa* were employed without bait, the translucent shell shank and their colorful beaded tails acting as a lure for the bonito. Men typically possessed several of these hooks in the event one broke, and passed the hooks down as heirlooms.[12] In making and using these fishhooks, men were involved in a wider making and remaking of relationships with one another, with denizens of their environment, and with ancestral forces.

This hook was either collected directly by William M. Mann (1886–1960), who from 1915 to 1916 gathered insects throughout the Solomon Islands and Fiji, or the hook was given to him by one of the many European government officials, traders, and missionaries he encountered during his trip. He subsequently donated his material to the National Museum of Natural History, Washington, DC. JB

[9] Fox, *Threshold*; Ivens, *Melanesians*; Davenport, "Sculpture."

[10] Ivens, *Melanesians*, 134–5; Kaschko, "Archaeological Consideration," 193–5.

[11] Kaschko, "Archaeological Consideration," 193–5.

[12] Beasely, *Fish hooks*, 67–73; Woodford, "Fish-hooks," 130–2; Mead, *Material Culture*; Kaschko, "Archaeological Consideration," 193–5.

TOOLS

50

Fishhook

19th century

Polynesian (Hawai`i)
Whale tooth, cord
1 x 6.4 x 10.8 cm
(⅜ x 2½ x 4¼ in.)
Collected by Dr. Nathaniel B. Emerson
Exhibited at the Alaska-Yukon-Pacific
Exposition in Seattle, Washington, in 1909
Department of Anthropology
National Museum of Natural History
Smithsonian Institution
Washington, DC, E257801

IN HAWAI`I, FOOD was traditionally an important element in the interaction among people, the gods, and the environment. Fishing, agriculture, animal husbandry, and the harvesting, preparation, and eating of food were all carried out under the auspices of the gods: and were therefore surrounded by *kapu* (taboos). Certain foods were given as offerings to the gods; for example, the first fish caught was often left as an offering. *I`a*—fish, pig, dog, and fowl—was essentially a relish to be eaten with `ai, the staple vegetable foods, primarily poi (made from the kalo plant) and sweet potato. One took care not to offend Hāloa, the god of kalo. Mealtime was an occasion for pleasant conversation and joviality, not for discussions about business. Traditionally, men and women did not eat together, and certain foods were *kapu* to women. The practices relating to food and the tools for obtaining it, its preparation and consumption, and the utensils for serving it persist among many Hawaiians today.

Fishing was the most complex method of obtaining food and was related to the hierarchical Hawaiian status system. Chiefs required trusted servants to insure that their food and leftovers did not come into contact with sorcerers, who could pray over food touched by an individual to induce that person's sickness or death. Huge fishponds were constructed along the ocean front so that the waters were not overfished during spawning season and so there would be fish for the chiefs during seasons when fishing was *kapu*. The catching of fish is significant: in many parts of Polynesia it was the demigod Maui who fished up the islands from the sea with his magic fishhook.

In the absence of pottery in most of Polynesia, fishhooks in their myriad shapes, sizes, and changing styles have served to construct the major archaeological chronologies. Scholars have been able to establish important milestones in Hawai`i's prehistory on the basis of the more than five thousand fishhooks that have been excavated in the island chain. In addition, the fishhooks found at archaeological sites have suggested possible places from where the ancestors of the Hawaiians may have migrated. By contrast, there is often little information about the sources, histories, or individual biographies of many of the fishhooks in museum collections.

The Hawaiians' intimate knowledge of the sea included the wide range of fish and their habitats, as well as where and when to fish for the many types of fish found in Hawaiian waters. Fishing equipment and tools included spears, nets, nooses, traps, and fishhooks with their lines, as well as containers in which to carry the tools and the fish. The hooks were made from bird, pig, dog, or human bone; dog teeth; and pearl and turtle shell. Hawaiian fishhooks are of three main types. One-piece hooks have a straight or circular body with a knob for lashing and often inner or outer barbs, usually made of bone or shell. Two-piece hooks, often made of bone, have a shank and a point; these were tied together at the base. Large shark hooks are made of wood, with an inset bone or ivory point. Bonito hooks are composed of a pearl-shell-lure shank, a bone point, and a hackle of pig bristles. Large composite hooks, comprising a stone sinker, cowrie-shell lure, wood rod, and bone point were used to catch squid.

This one-piece whale-ivory hook was one of the objects in a collection exhibited at the Alaska-Yukon-Pacific Exposition, held in Seattle in 1909. At the end of the Exposition the collection, gathered by Nathaniel B. Emerson of Hawai'i, was purchased by the United States government and became part of the Smithsonian Institution. The collection includes many items of daily use, including several fishhooks. This example has an outer barb and is still lashed to its original line, made of *olonā* (*Touchardia latifolia*) and nearly 20 cm (8 in.) long.

The aesthetic aspect of traditional fishhooks is appreciated by contemporary artists, who today fashion them as pendants that are widely worn by Hawaiians as identity markers and by visitors. AK

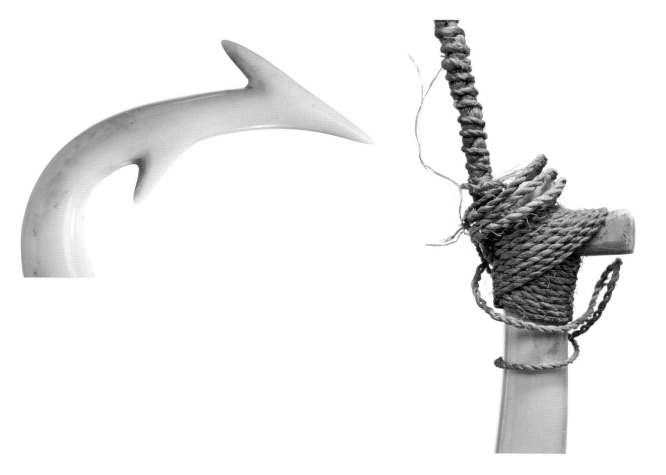

Fish Trap
Before 1929

Papuan (Papua New Guinea)
Plaited rattan, sago-palm ribs, cane
24.1 x 40 x 78.7 cm (9½ x 15¾ x 31 in.)
Transferred from the US Department
of Agriculture and Dr. E. W. Brandes
Department of Anthropology
National Museum of Natural History
Smithsonian Institution
Washington, DC, E344858

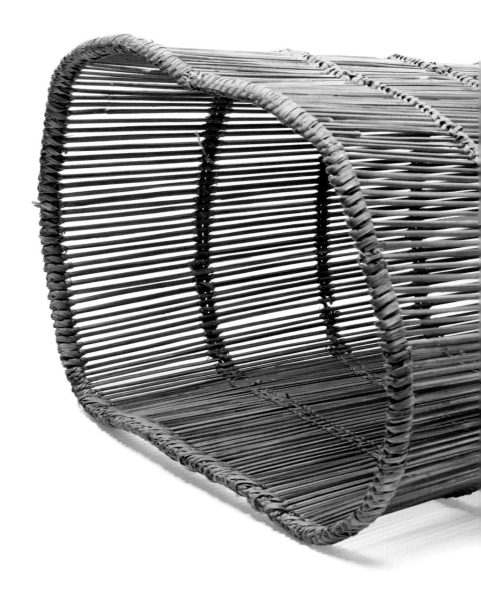

WOMEN OF THE AIRD HILL region of the Gulf of Papua in Papua New Guinea made this conical fish trap; it has never been used. The vertical frame of the fish trap is made of the midrib of a sago palm leaf. The stripped midribs were bound and spaced with fourteen bands of sugar cane cut in the forest, stripped, and braided into cordage. The cane was woven between the sago midribs and holds two lengths of unmodified cane around the outside of the trap. These strips of cane give the trap structural strength. The top, bound with tightly woven bands of stripped cane, forms the handle. The weaving technology and the knowledge of plants that are embodied by this fish trap underpin a range of objects, from houses to baskets and ritual objects.

A central feature of the region's fishing technology, traps such as this one are used as well as made by women.

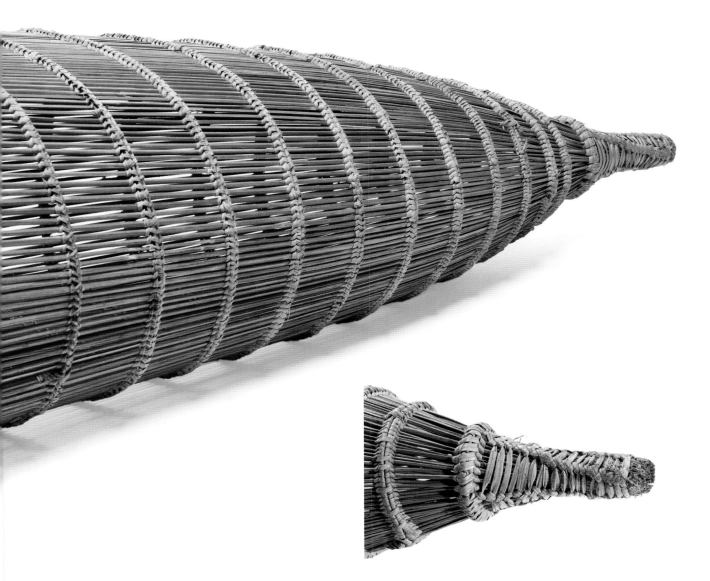

A woman typically possesses several and teaches her daughters how to craft them. Working in groups and deploying large weirs, women block one of the Gulf of Papua's many coastal streams and creeks at high tide. When the tide begins to recede, one group beats the water, while others move with their traps through the blocked waterway catching fish, turtles, and crustaceans. The fisherwomen take their catch back to the village in fiber baskets. This style of fish trap is still used throughout the Gulf of Papua today, alongside store-bought nylon fishing nets and hooks.

E. W. Brandes collected this fish trap and other objects during the United States Department of Agriculture's 1928 Sugarcane Expedition to New Guinea; this collection is now in the Smithsonian Institution's National Museum of Natural History, Washington, DC.[13] JB

[13] J. A. Bell, "The Sorcery of Sugar: Intersecting Agencies within Collections Made by the 1928 USDA Sugarcane Expedition to New Guinea," in *Reassembling the Collection: Indigenous Agency and Ethnographic Collections*, ed. Rodney Harrison, Anne Clark, and Sarah Byrne (Santa Fe: School of Advanced Research, 2013), 117–42.

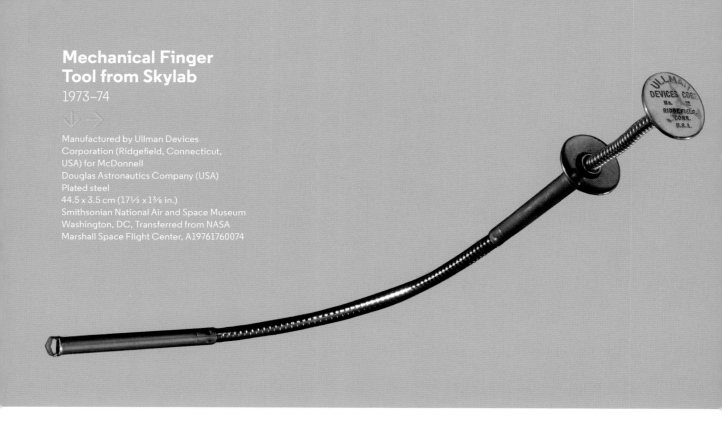

Mechanical Finger
Tool from Skylab
1973–74

↓ →

Manufactured by Ullman Devices
Corporation (Ridgefield, Connecticut,
USA) for McDonnell
Douglas Astronautics Company (USA)
Plated steel
44.5 x 3.5 cm (17½ x 1⅜ in.)
Smithsonian National Air and Space Museum
Washington, DC, Transferred from NASA
Marshall Space Flight Center, A19761760074

TOOLS ARE AS COMMON IN SPACEFLIGHT as they are in a handyman's garage or an auto-repair shop. Each space shuttle mission carried more than one hundred, and the International Space Station stocks even more. NASA's space-tools inventory numbers exceeded five thousand items, from the common to the custom-made. After all, the nearest hardware store is about 250 miles away—back on Earth.

Certain primary instruments are required for assembly and installation tasks, but astronaut crews must be prepared to deal with anything from a stuck bolt to a wiring problem, balky toilet, or torn solar panel. The challenge is to anticipate everything that could go wrong.

Tools for spaceflight are organized into two categories. One is in-flight maintenance (IFM), which includes mostly common hand tools purchased from hardware stores and applied to ordinary tasks inside the spacecraft. A wrench or a screwdriver works as well in space as it does on the ground, although the technicians typically attach a small strip of Velcro® to the handle of each tool so it can be secured to any of the Velcro®patches on the crews' clothing or on the interior of the vehicle to keep it handy.

IFM tools are often organized into kits by purpose, such as electrical or puncture repair. These are stowed in fabric pouches with little pockets for each device or in foam-padded trays with cutouts that hold each tool snugly in place in weightlessness. No one wants tools (or anything else) to float around the crew cabin and get lost. As in Earthbound workshops, equipment stowage and tool management are top priorities for efficiency in space.

Almost every item in these kits is familiar. There are Allen wrenches in a range of socket sizes, regular and Phillips-head screwdrivers, pliers, vise grips, a pry bar and hammer, scissors and other cutters, a hacksaw, and plenty of adhesive tape. Another practical instrument is a mechanical finger, a reach tool that enables the user to pick up something beyond arm's length or in too narrow a space for a hand to fit.

The mechanical finger featured here is from a kit assembled for Skylab, the US space station occupied from 1973 to 1974.

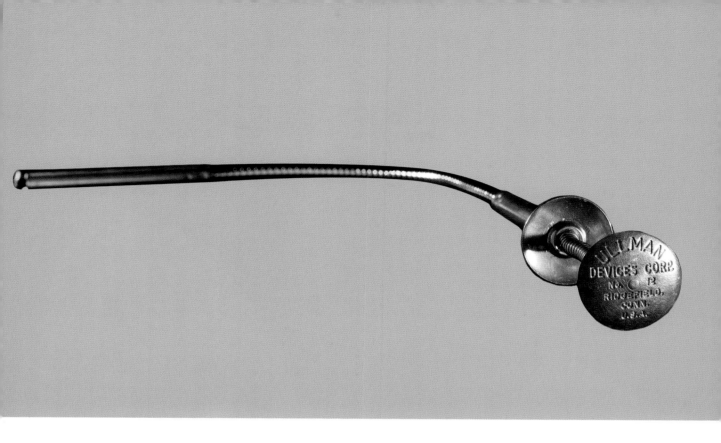

The inexpensive, low-tech tool can be bought in auto-supply and hardware stores. Made of chrome-plated carbon steel and aluminum, it has a flexible shaft and a plunger handle. Pushing the plunger with the thumb or palm extends the prongs at the other end to close around an object, which can then be pulled or lifted from its inaccessible position. It isn't rocket science, but it is adequate for the task.

The second category of tools comprises those for use on spacewalks. Extravehicular activity (EVA) instruments are more likely to be customized or custom-built than IFM implements. At the very least, an EVA tool must be equipped with a heavy-duty closed loop for a tether latch: to keep it from drifting away, each tool is leashed to the astronaut's wrist, to a caddy on the front of the spacesuit, or to a workstation on the remote manipulator arm.

EVA tools also tend to have larger handles and grips than similar tools on Earth, because astronauts wear pressurized gloves that are much larger and less flexible than their hands. Crew members have to be able to grip their tools without suffering discomfort or fatigue. A torque-wrench

handle might be at least twice as wide as its conventional counterpart, to provide a good, comfortable grip, or the wrench might have a palm wheel for fine turns. Battery-operated power tools are also featured in the EVA tool kit, to minimize the fatigue that can result from performing repetitive motions.

When unique tools are required for mission-specific tasks, engineers bring together design, human factors, materials, manufacturing, testing, and safety to invent and space-qualify new hardware.[14] In equipping astronauts with the tools they will or may need on the job, nothing is left to chance. Whether it is a humble screwdriver or a beautifully crafted precision tool for a unique purpose, they reflect the spaceflight work culture's insistence on practicality, preparation, and safety. VN

---

[14] NASA's Man-Systems Integration Standards document, in effect since the 1970s, is the master guide for everything affecting astronauts. Its chapter on EVA tools, connectors, fasteners, and other aids to crews combines common sense and lessons learned through hundreds of hours of tool handling in space and in training.

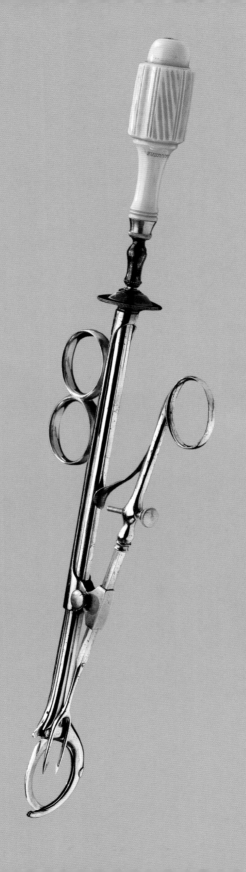

Tonsillotome
1855

Designed by Alfred-Armand-Louis-Marie
Velpeau (French, 1795–1867)
Made by Joseph-Frédéric-Benoît Charrière
(French, b. Switzerland, 1803–1876)
Brass, steel, ivory
8.5 x 2.8 x 27.8 cm (3⅜ x 1⅛ x 10¹⁵⁄₁₆ in.)
Smithsonian Institution
National Museum of American History
Washington, DC, Cat. 1978.0874.02

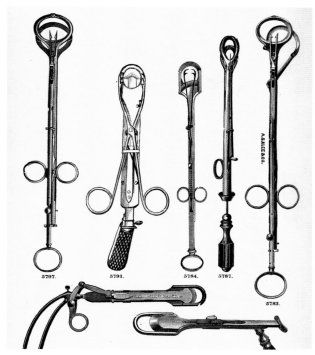

Designs for tonsillotomes in Surgical Instruments and Supplies, *1895, A.S. Aloe Co.*

SOMEONE RIFLING THROUGH a doctor's bag at the turn of the twentieth century would probably turn up a stethoscope, a percussion hammer, and a tonsillotome. The invention of the tonsillotome in 1828 greatly facilitated the process of removing tissue from deep in the throat of a squirming child or apprehensive adult. The contrivance, invented by an American physician, Phillip Syng Physick, presented a convenient way to remove pieces of a person's tonsils, transforming an extreme operation into a routine procedure. The instrument was a modification of the uvulatome, a similar-looking Dutch device for severing the uvula, the tissue that hangs from the back of the soft palate. Physick's original tonsillotome—also called a "tonsil guillotine"—used a razor blade to both compress the tonsil and cut it from front to back.

Starting in the 1740s, physicians were more inclined to prescribe tonsillotomies than tonsillectomies, that is, the partial rather than total removal of the tonsil, as the former avoided the lengthy recovery time and potentially dangerous consequences of the latter. By the early twentieth century, tonsillotomies were commonplace. From 1904 to 1907, the Department for the Diseases of the Nose and Throat at the Vanderbilt Clinic in Nashville, Tennessee, reported 2,820 operations, 1,114 of which were tonsillotomies. The widespread adoption of focal-infection theory in the early

1900s—the hypothesis that certain locations in the body serve as entry points for bacteria—led to increased support for various types of tonsil excision, since physicians believed that removing susceptible pieces of the tonsils eliminated such a portal.

The tonsillotome had several advantages over other tools for cutting tonsils. It required no expensive kit of other instruments and considerably less skill than a scalpel and forceps. A doctor could perform a tonsillotomy with one hand and no assistant. The instrument, as well as the blade, came in several different sizes to ensure that the correct portion of the tonsil was severed. The risk of cutting into the carotid artery, feared by Physick's bistoury-wielding contemporaries, was negligible. At the same time, although it maximized efficiency, the tonsillotome took some surgical glory away from the physician: doctors confident in their manual ability objected to this mediation and continued to use the bistoury. The pain ensuing from a tonsillotomy performed with the instrument was minimal, and most doctors worked without anesthetic. However, the removal of the second tonsil had to be performed as quickly as possible, before the patient began coughing up blood.

Practitioners customized and modified tonsillotomes to suit their individual needs and styles. In 1855, Alfred-Armand-Louis-Marie Velpeau designed this ornate example with an ivory handle and gold loops for the fingers; spears to hold the tonsil; and a sickle-shaped knife, rather than a blade, to sever it. Most doctors found his model impractical and awkward, and a number of variations by other practitioners followed.

Even after physicians accepted the importance of disinfection, sanitizing a tonsillotome was a challenge. The instrument, constructed from numerous minute parts, was not designed for easy disassembly. Tonsillotomes often caused postoperative infections, and pieces of tonsil left in the patient's throat produced complications. Unless the entire tonsil was removed, there was no guarantee that the tonsillitis and swelling would subside. The popularity of tonsillectomy procedures, and thus of tonsillotomes, declined rapidly by the mid-twentieth century. A study in 1963 on the benefits of tonsillectomy procedures concluded with the assertion that "tonsillectomy has no place in the relief of colds, coughs, influenzal disease, behavior upsets, or other non-respiratory illness."[15] SL

---

[15] W. J. E. McKee, "A Controlled Study of the Effects of Tonsillectomy and Adenoidectomy in Children,"*British Journal of Preventive and Social Medicine*, 17, no. 2 (1963): 49-69, http://www.jstor.org/stable/25565329 (accessed February 25, 2014).

Noyes Alligator Forceps

ca. 1950

→

Manufactured by Misdom-Frank
Corporation (Germany)
Stainless steel
11.4 x 14.3 x 0.3 cm (4½ x 5⅝ x ⅛ in.)
Smithsonian Institution
National Museum of American History
Washington, DC, Cat. M-09857

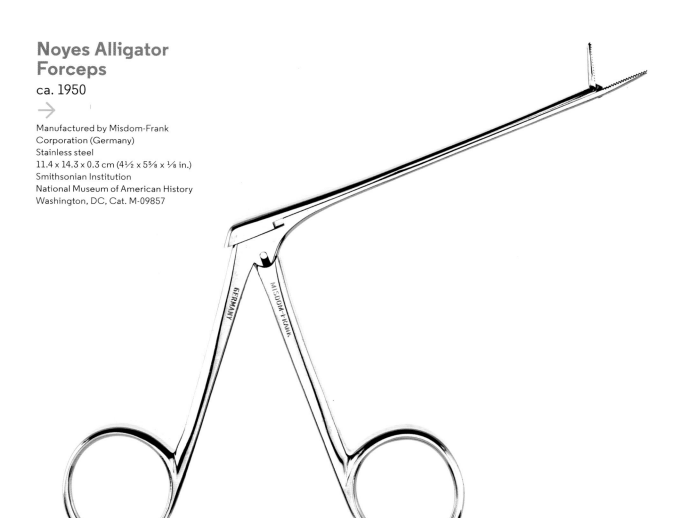

THE EARLIEST SURGICAL TOOLS were the healer's hands and fingers. Hands can pull back tissue, and probing fingers can grasp and pull out projectiles. Later, it was discovered that flint and obsidian could be fashioned into knives, hollow reeds and bamboo could serve to aspirate fluids, and sturdy twigs could be employed to hold back flesh.

With a few exceptions, the design of standard surgical tools has not changed radically for the past 150 years or so, nor have the basic gestures necessary to cut, explore, and close. What have changed are the understanding of diseases and the materials used to manufacture instruments. As the germ theory put forth by Louis Pasteur in the 1860s was accepted, all-metal instruments, which could be sterilized, slowly replaced hybrid instruments with wood, ivory, and stone handles, which could not. A succession of metals was introduced, including nickel in the 1890s; by around 1920, chromium-plated instruments were routinely found in hospitals and doctors' offices. Plating, however, has a tendency to peel away or wear through to the base metal after numerous sterilizations. Earlier in the twentieth century, researchers in Germany and the United States had experimented with formulas to produce a steel that was durable and more resistant to corrosion than other metals. The first stainless-steel instruments began to appear in catalogs around 1929.

As medicine separated into branches, instruments also became specialized, with manufacturers marketing numer-

Rake (Retractor)

ca. 1950

→

Manufactured by Klenk (USA)
Stainless steel, black oxide coating
21.9 x 3.2 x 1.3 cm (8⅝ x 1¼ x ½ in.)
Smithsonian Institution
National Museum of American History
Washington, DC, Cat. M-09850.01

ous versions, each with design features tailored to where and how the implement would be used—in the case of forceps and retractors, these might be the ear canal, within the abdomen, or on the surface of the skin, for example. The reputation of physician-inventors was often attached to their designs.

The forceps and retractor were handheld instruments designed for precision and strength. The Noyes alligator forceps is named for its inventor, Henry D. Noyes, a prominent professor of ophthalmology and otology at Bellevue Hospital in New York. His forceps first appeared in 1879, its alligator-shaped jaw a response to his particular need for an unobstructed view. And, indeed, because of the forceps's slender arms, it can be used with a speculum.

Also known as a "rake," the Volkmann retractor, named for a nineteenth-century German surgeon, Richard von Volkmann, comes with either blunt or sharp prongs. This retractor dates from about 1950 and was manufactured by Klenk. It has a black oxide coating over stainless steel, and though its nonreflective surface is an advantage, it tends to scratch easily. This retractor comes in a variety of sizes, from one to four prongs, and can be used for general procedures or specialized operations such as plastic surgery.

Both instruments were part of the armamentarium of Dr. Julius Lempert, an otologist (a doctor who specializes in the structure and function of the ear). In 1961, Dr. Lempert donated them, with other instruments, to the Smithsonian's Division of Medicine and Science. JC

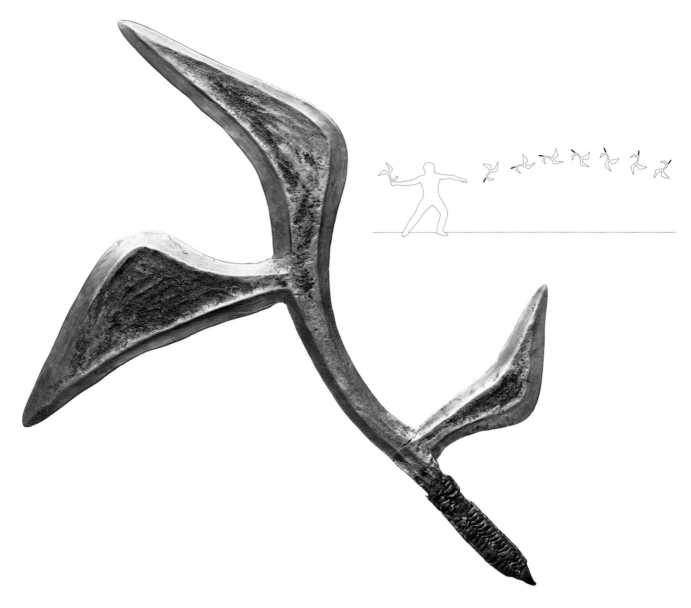

THESE EXAMPLES ARE TWO of sixty throwing knives collected by Herbert Ward in the Congo Free State, now the Democratic Republic of the Congo, between 1884 and 1889. Weapons like the *Y*-shaped example (above) were used primarily in central Africa, where they served in warfare and for hunting. To be aerodynamically effective, a throwing knife requires a particular height–width ratio and a standardized weight, and its handle is covered with a tight-fitting material, like the braided fiber on this example, in order to maintain the instrument's balance. When thrown, the knife rotates around its center of gravity; the dark color applied to the middle of the blade draws the eye to the sharp edges that reflect the sunlight as the weapon spins toward its target. The two most common ways to throw are underhand horizontally from the hip or vertically over the shoulder, like a spear or javelin. While these multi-

Throwing Knife
Created before 1889
↑

Yangere people
(Democratic Republic of the Congo/
Central African Republic)
Iron, handle covered in braided fiber
1.3 x 24.1 x 38.4 cm (½ x 9½ x 15⅛ in.)
Herbert Ward Collection
Department of Anthropology
National Museum of Natural History
Smithsonian Institution
Washington, DC, E322652-6

bladed weapons could inflict serious wounds, most groups' arsenals in the past also included bows, arrows, and spears. Made of local iron, knives were fashioned by professional blacksmiths. Smiths were not only masters of the technical skills required to forge and shape iron, but they were steeped in the ritual aspects of their work. A smith's tools included an anvil on which to pound out the iron, several types of hammers and chisel-like tools, and materials and instruments to sharpen the blades and prepare the surface of the knife. While engineered to be thrown, these multibladed knives had other practical uses; for example, they could be employed as daggers in hand-to-hand combat, as axes, and as blades to cut a path through the brush. Because iron was such a valuable material, these knives were prestige items and could be used as currency. MJA

(above right and opposite right) *Illustrations based on throwing diagrams, from Mark Leo Felix, Kipinga: Throwing Blades of Central Africa*

Throwing Knife
Created before 1889
↑

Ngbaka people
(Democratic Republic of the Congo)
Iron, handle covered in bark cloth
and tied with braided fiber
1.9 x 33.7 x 35.9 cm (¾ x 13¼ x 14⅛ in.)
Herbert Ward Collection, Department
of Anthropology, National Museum of
Natural History, Smithsonian Institution
Washington, DC, E322652-11

WORK: HAND TOOLS

Spade Blade
Before 1855

Japanese
Cast iron
3.8 x 12.1 x 24.8 cm (1½ x 4¾ x 9¾ in.)
Collected by Commodore Matthew C. Perry
in 1853–54, Department of Anthropology
National Museum of Natural History
Smithsonian Institution, Washington, DC, E378

Plowshare Blade
Before 1855

Japanese
Iron
3.8 x 16.5 x 22.9 cm (1½ x 6½ x 9 in.)
Collected by Commodore Matthew C. Perry
in 1853–54, Department of Anthropology
National Museum of Natural History
Smithsonian Institution, Washington, DC, E380

Sickle Blade

Before 1855

Japanese
Iron
4.8 x 20.3 x 23.2 cm (1⅞ x 8 x 9⅛ in.)
Collected by Commodore Matthew C. Perry
in 1853–54, Department of Anthropology
National Museum of Natural History
Smithsonian Institution, Washington, DC, E385

Hoe Blade

Before 1855

↑

Japanese
Cast iron
1.6 x 10.8 x 26 cm (⅝ x 4¼ x 10¼ in.)
Collected by Commodore Matthew C. Perry
in 1853–54, Department of Anthropology
National Museum of Natural History
Smithsonian Institution, Washington, DC, E376

These four tools are selected from the objects acquired during Commodore Matthew C. Perry's historic voyages to Japan from 1853 to 1854. The expedition not only initiated trade and diplomatic relations between the US and Japan, but it also led to the first collection of Japanese artifacts at the then-new Smithsonian Institution (originally given catalog numbers 1, 2, and so on, within the anthropology department). Although the Perry collection is made up largely of reciprocal gifts from the ruling shōgun, approximately one-third of the artifacts were bought by the expedition.[16] Because these purchases included ethnographic and agricultural items, it may be inferred that the hoe and spade blades, plough share, and hand sickle shown here were almost certainly from this group, rather than gifts.[17]

Traditionally, the relationship between Japanese tool users and their implements is an intimate one, because the latter are believed to contain a crucial spiritual element. In the words of the Japanese artisan and teacher Ōdate Toshio, "Utility and appearance must be enhanced by a tool's 'presence,' that is, its refinement and dignity. Presence is what the toolmaker—the blacksmith—imbues his creation with as a result of his commitment to his craft; it is the spirit of the tool that records the blacksmith's ability through the years to face the uncertainties of life, to overcome them, and master the art of living."[18] It is because of this sentiment that tools, especially those hand-crafted by specialized artisans, are accorded particular respect.

One manifestation of this respect is that six forged-blade or tool-making practices are included among the 201

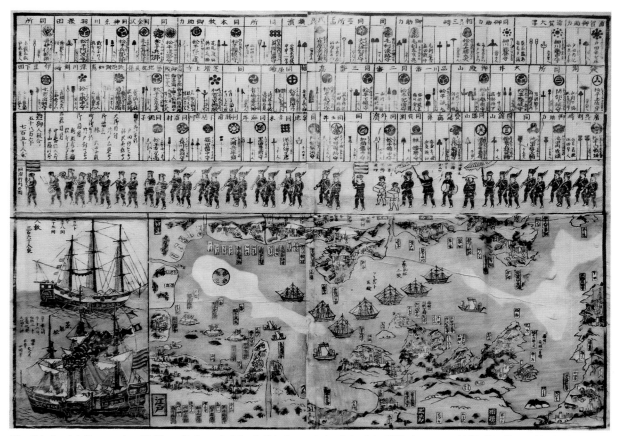

Woodblock print, Commodore Matthew C. Perry Arriving in Edo (present-day Tokyo), in 1853, Japan, ca. 1853; 48 x 69 cm (18 ⅞ x 27 ⅝ in.); National Anthropological Archives, National Museum of Natural History, Smithsonian Institution, Washington, DC, NMNH-NAA MS7145

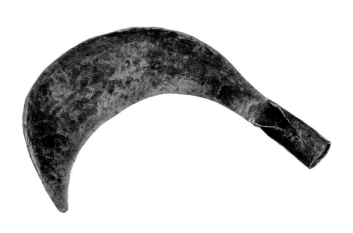

Sickle blade

The workshop of Ishiguro Akio, designated a traditional silversmith of the Tokyo region, 2009

that were designated as traditional crafts of Japan by the Ministry of Economy, Trade, and Industry in 2009. These include *echizen uchihamano*, the forged blades made in Echizen Province during the Edo period (1603–1868). In this region, now part of Fukui Prefecture, communities of metal workers began to specialize in sickles much like the one shown above as early as the fourteenth century. Subsequent generations of artisans have continued this practice, using virtually identical tools and materials. As in the past, most of today's traditional Japanese metal workers and tool makers work seated cross-legged on the floor in the middle of their small workshop, with most of the instruments required for their craft hanging on the walls in easy reach. The number of tool makers trained in traditional methods has been declining for several decades, so today many practitioners work alone or with one or two apprentices.

In a transmission model that can be traced to the Edo period, masters were notoriously secretive about their knowledge, even with their own apprentices, who generally had to learn by *nusumi keiko*, "stealing the master's secrets."[19] Furthermore, given the proprietary nature of craft knowledge, apprentices were often forbidden from even setting foot inside artisan households to which they

did not belong. By contrast, apprentices today often have opportunities to observe the methods, tools, and materials of practitioners to whom they are not directly apprenticed and who may not have apprentices themselves. This can occur in training sessions organized by specific craft guilds or during demonstrations and informal discussions with visiting apprentices in the workshops of individual *shokunin* (artisans).

Today, craft masters and the wider communities of artisans are increasingly open about sharing their expertise, in order to ensure that the masters' knowledge will be passed on. Then as now, in tool making as in other areas, Japanese artisans have proven adept at recasting inherited traditions in ways that harmonize with the ideals that underpin them. **PMT & RP**

[16] At the time of the expedition, it was mistakenly believed that these gifts were from the emperor (Houchins, *Artifacts of Diplomacy*, 5). However, the gifts in fact originated from either Tokugawa Ieyoshi (shōgun from 1837 until his death on July 27, 1853) or his successor, Shōgun Tokugawa Iesada, who ruled until 1858.

[17] Chang-Su Houchins, *Artifacts of Diplomacy: Smithsonian Collections from Commodore Matthew Perry's Japan Expedition (1853–1854)* (Washington, DC: Smithsonian Institution Press, 1995), 1, 5, 122.

[18] Toshio Ōdate, *Japanese Woodworking Tools: Their Tradition, Spirit, and Use* (Newton, CT: The Taunton Press, Inc., 1984), 179.

[19] Horishi Irie, "Apprenticeship Training in Tokugawa Japan," *Acta Asiatica*, 54 (Tokyo: Tōhō Gakkai, 1988), 1–23.

Crew inspecting tunnel chamber

Clovis Point
ca. 11,000 BCE

Eastern North America
Chert from north central Ohio
12.4 x 3.2 x 1 cm (4⅞ x 1¼ x ⅜ in.)
Department of Anthropology
National Museum of Natural History
Smithsonian Institution
Washington, DC, A581650

Fluted Point
ca. 11,000 BCE

Found near the New Mexico–Texas border
Chert (from Edwards chert formation
located north of Austin, Texas, USA)
6 x 2.5 x 0.6 cm (2⅜ in. x 1 in. x ¼ in.)
Department of Anthropology
National Museum of Natural History
Smithsonian Institution
Washington, DC, A581651

THESE SPEAR POINTS, dating to between 13,200 and 12,900 years ago, represent one of the first widespread cultural and technological traditions in North America. The distinctive shape of the points and the characteristic flute, or channel, driven up from the base characterize a style that was followed by artisans across what is today North America. The fact that these design traits persisted across great distances is evidence of close social interactions and provides an example of how a material object can express cultural identity.

The smaller of the two is from the New Mexico–Texas border, the other is from eastern North America.[20] Projectile points like these have been found near mammoth kills across North America, revealing that dispatching large animals was part of early subsistence practices. Clovis points, however, were undoubtedly used as tools for other functions as well, including hunting smaller game, rituals, and cutting. JAMG

[20] The term "Clovis" refers to the location, Clovis, New Mexico, where they were first described.

Obsidian Scalpel No. 10110–03

2013

Made by Fine Science Tools
(California, USA)
Obsidian blade, bamboo
12.3 × 0.5 × 0.5 cm (4³⁄₁₆ × ³⁄₁₆ × ³⁄₁₆ in.)
Courtesy of Fine Science Tools

Chopper

1.85 million years old

Oldowan, Early Stone Age
(Olduvai Gorge, Tanzania)
Volcanic rock (nephelinite)
7.6 x 8 x 6 cm (3 x 3⅛ x 2⅜ in.)
Department of Anthropology
National Museum of Natural History
Smithsonian Institution, Washington, DC
Control No. 2065648, Field No. I-EgMK

TOOLS CRAFTED AND USED BY OUR human ancestors appear in the prehistoric record dating back at least 2.6 million years; the earliest tools were made of stone. The three objects shown here are some of the oldest human-made tools in the Smithsonian's collections.

The simply altered stone, called a "chopper," from the famed archaeological site at Olduvai Gorge, Tanzania, is around 1.85 million years old. The discovery of such artifacts at Olduvai Gorge gave the name to the world's oldest Stone Age technology, the Oldowan. Choppers were made using a hammerstone to knap (repeatedly strike off) sharp useful flakes along an edge. The stone is a volcanic rock called nephelinite, from a lava flow south of Olduvai. This basic technology, which produced tools for cutting, pounding, and crushing, enabled humans to obtain new foods and increase the amount of meat, tubers, and roots in their diet.

The classic handaxe is a teardrop-shaped stone tool knapped on both sides; for this reason, it is sometimes called a "biface." The example on the following page, also from Olduvai Gorge, is around 1.4 million years old. It is made of trachyte, a type of volcanic rock obtained east of Olduvai Gorge. This tool illustrates the period of technological innovation known as the Acheulean, which followed the Oldowan and would predominate between 1.76 million and 150,000 years ago in Africa, parts of Asia, and Europe. No one is entirely sure about all the ways in which handaxes were employed; they probably served multiple functions, including cutting, chopping, and whittling wood; digging for tubers and roots; breaking open animal bones to access marrow; and as the cores from which the sharp flakes were struck that were used to butcher the meat from animal carcasses. While the earlier Oldowan technology included only small, minimally altered tools, the larger handaxes made by Acheulean tool makers were sharpened all the way around the perimeter, providing a more effective way of continually knapping sharp flakes

Illustration of the process of using a rounded hammerstone to knock sharp flakes off a more angular core

while collecting food on the go. Over time, handaxes would become smaller, more portable, and often very refined. The second handaxe (overleaf, right-hand page) is from the celebrated Paleolithic site of Saint-Acheul, in northern France, which gave its name to the Acheulean technology. The tool is around 300,000 years old, and it was collected for the Smithsonian between 1883 and 1890 by a curator, Thomas Wilson. The handaxes discovered at Saint-Acheul in the 1850s were among the first Stone Age implements to be found. They demonstrated the existence of early human species that preceded our own and illustrated their tool-making techniques.

While handaxes varied in size, symmetry, and the type of stone employed, the basic shape remained consistent over the Acheulean's long time span. The Saint-Acheul handaxe is made of flint, which occurs throughout the Somme Valley, in northern France. The basic process of striking flakes from a stone core with a rounded hammerstone is often called "flint knapping," as many of the oldest archaeological artifacts found in Europe are made of flint. In time, groups of early humans from different regions of the world began to produce more distinctly styled handaxes and other stone tools. **BP & RPotts**

Handaxe

1.4 million years old

Acheulean, Early Stone Age
(Olduvai Gorge, Tanzania)
Volcanic rock (trachyte)
17.8 x 10.2 x 6 cm (7 x 4 x 2⅜ in.)
Department of Anthropology
National Museum of Natural History
Smithsonian Institution, Washington, DC
Control No. 2065648, Field No. Loc. 77-IIV

Handaxe
300,000 years old

←

Acheulean, Early Stone Age
(Saint-Acheul, France)
Flint
11 x 7 x 4.7 cm (4⁵⁄₁₆ x 2¾ x 1⅞ in.)
Department of Anthropology
National Museum of Natural History
Smithsonian Institution
Washington, DC, A146025

Pocket Knife/ Multitool: *Victorinox@work*

2011

Designed and manufactured
by Victorinox (Switzerland)
Stainless steel, aluminum oxide (alox),
cellulose acetate-butyrate, (Cellidor®)
USB flash drive
7 x 1.9 x 1.3 cm (2¾ x ¾ x ½ in.)
Cooper Hewitt,
Smithsonian Design Museum
New York, Gift of Victorinox, 2013-56-2

DESCENDED FROM A UTILITARIAN, multi-bladed pocket tool designed for soldiers in the field, the lightweight Victorinox@work multitool knife is an implement for the digital age. It contains not only traditional instruments—blade, combination nail file and screwdriver, scissors, key ring, tweezers, and retractable pen—but a detachable 4/8/16/32 GB USB (Universal Serial Bus) flash drive for use with computers and other electronic devices. This model indicates the ways in which daily tasks and the associated tools have changed the 122-year-old tool for the twenty-first-century user.

The Swiss Army knife, as its name suggests, began as a practical tool for the Swiss military. First produced in the late 1880s by a German manufacturer, the archetypical multipurpose device was developed by a Swiss cutler, Karl Elsener, in 1891. Elsener's 1891 knife contained a steel blade, a reamer, a can opener, and a screwdriver in a metal and wood housing. Dissatisfied with the weight and limited functions of this first version, by 1896 Elsener had succeeded in attaching tools on both sides of the handle using an innovative spring mechanism that also held the instruments in place when opened. This model was slightly more compact and easier to hold, had a more elegant outline, and required only two springs for six tools. The 1896 version, which can be considered the template for today's multitool design, was well received by the Swiss Army and later by the public. By 1897 the knife was sporting the now-familiar red housing and, by 1908, the Swiss federal cross in a shield was embossed on its side. Only knives produced by Victorinox and one other manufacturer, Wenger, are permitted to display the emblem. Stories of use by the military, explorers, and even astronauts have made the Swiss Army knife synonymous with dependability and quality in function and design. Both the form and the emblem seem to inspire the confidence of contemporary consumers, whether the knife serves as a convenient multitool for daily activities or a compact emergency tool kit. CT

iPhone (First Generation)

2007

Designed by Jonathan Ive
(British, b. 1967) and Apple Industrial
Design Team
Manufactured by Apple Computer, Inc.
(Cupertino, California, USA)
Glass, aluminum, plastic
11.4 x 6.1 x 1.2 cm (4½ x 2⅜ x ⁷⁄₁₆ in.)
Cooper Hewitt,
Smithsonian Design Museum
New York, Gift of Roland L. Trope
2009-29-1

When the iPhone was launched in 2007, it was promoted as a camera, phone, and iPod. Today it is...

notes	drawing pad	email	reservations
strobe light	schedule planner	reviews	alarm clock
tides	exercise tracking	weather	cloud storage
maps	eye chart	keyboard	messages
spellcheck	find iPhone	camcorder	santa tracker
social networking	news	star chart	world geography
calculator	font maker	share documents	data storage
photo album	mirror	calendar	sky map
health tracking	time management	library	first-aid assist
banking	food ordering	qr code scanner	stopwatch
police siren	architecture finder	magazines	thermometer
gps	blood pressure monitor	e-reader	national park locator
fitness calculator	guitar tuner	scanner	time zones
stereo	barcode scanner	mars globe	planet guide
pedometer	timer	mass times	tip calculator
television	meditation	sketchpad	shopping
microphone	nautical codes	event tickets	how-to/diy
flashlight	wedding planner	metronome	journal
cab finder	ticketing	sign language	check-in (ticket)
knot guide	music identifier	preparedness	anatomy guide
clock	hotel locator	speedometer	transit guide
moon phases	museum locator	musical instruments	music streaming
wikipedia	speaker phone	survival guide	trip planner
radio	wi-fi finder	bike-share finder	books
movies	track expenses	payments	doctor locator
recorder	internet	track invitations	world clock
white noise	video calls	digital	mail
ruler	transportation	podcasts	menstrual tracker
language translator	spirit level	address book	slide rule
closet organizer	moon globe	converter	etc...
dictionary	translator	reminders	
pet	recipes	voice memos	
directions	key	stock ticker	

WE ARE SOCIAL CREATURES, and our fundamental need to connect with one another and to record and disseminate knowledge has been the impetus behind the development of many tools of communication. These implements not only create community, but amplify ideas and information into forms that people can understand, transmit, and remember.

Adornment communicates status and can project power—consider the business suit. An elaborately carved canoe prow from the Maori of New Zealand is a prestige tool, charged with meaning. Its intricate carvings are meant to dazzle and convey its owner's wealth and position, giving him a critical advantage in trade negotiations and in sustaining the social order.

Communication tools register or convert data into recognizable symbols that inform us in a variety of ways. The knotted time ball made by a woman of the Klikitat people of British Columbia was a memory aid for important events in her life, in much the same way that embroidered samplers of nineteenth-century America listed a family's birth, marriage, and death dates. The Flame's winter count illustrated pivotal events for several generations of Lakota people, helping them to remember and record their nation's past. As information accumulated, these mnemonic devices acted as physical and virtual scrapbooks—prosthetics for the brain.

Symbols and codes have been part of cultures throughout time, and manifest our innate desire to grasp concepts and information by simplifying patterns into basic units. The quipu, a knotted recording system from a nonliterate society, was used most notably by the Inca. The postal barcode, one of the most important tools of our modern mail system, standardizes and distills information to a series of parallel lines that, when decrypted by electronic scanners, results in a letter delivered right to your door. While not visible, the underpinning of our digital tools is a binary code that transforms all information into 1s and 0s, giving us results beyond the capacity of our minds.

Networks evolve from using tools. Denis Diderot's *Encyclopédie* is an example of how printing and the mass production of books can document and spread information. Communication tools continue to be invented and designed to accelerate the speed at which we connect with others—how we disseminate and receive information. In today's itinerant world, where the telephone and email allow us to be in at least two places at once, tools that are portable and provide access to information are highly valued. With them, we can travel lighter, carrying our entire library or thousands of hours of our favorite music or movies in our pocket, while forming new communities and global conversations via the Internet.

(opposite) *Quipu (detail), made between 1400 and 1532, Inca*

COMMUNICATE

Quipu

Made between 1400 and 1532

→

Inca (Pachacamac, Peru)
Knotted and twisted cotton fibers
Primary cord length: 2.4 m (7 ft. 10½ in.)
Pendants: about 40 cm long (15¾ in.)
Department of Anthropology
National Museum of Natural History
Smithsonian Institution, Washington, DC
A365240

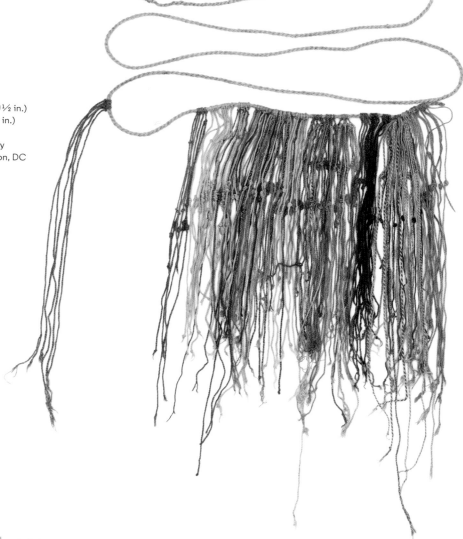

LONG ASSOCIATED WITH THE INCA, the quipu came to play an integral role in the expansion and administration of their empire during the mid-fifteenth century. Consisting of a main cord and attached strings with knots, quipus were used as recording and communication devices. They could vary in size from main cords only 30 cm (1 ft.) long, with a few strings, to examples more than 1 m (1 yd.) long, with hundreds of strings. The knots at intervals on the subsidiary strings represent decimal units; these recorded census information linked to the collection of taxes from local communities. Such taxes were imposed in the form of labor on public works, military duty, or service to administrators. Cords of different colors were common, with the various pigments helping the quipu keeper to recall the significance of the recorded numbers. Quipus were also used as memory aids by official historians and gene-alogists. Several hundred quipus are known in collections worldwide. This example is from Pachacamac, near Lima, on the Pacific coast. JK

(above left) *Chief accountant and treasurer, Tawantin Suyu khipuq kuraka, authority in charge of the knotted strings, or quipu, of the Inca kingdom, in* El primer nueva corónica y buen gobierno; *1615; Guaman Poma*

USB Flash Drives

2009

↓

Designed by Vincent Baranger (French, n.d.)
Jean Sébastien Blanc (French, n.d.),
Anthony Lebossé (French, n.d.),
Claire Renard (French, n.d.)
5.5 Designers
Manufactured by LaCie (China)
Aluminum, integrated circuit
iamaKey: 5.7 x 2.5 x 0.5 cm (2¼ x 1 x ³⁄₁₆ in.)
CooKey: 5.7 x 2.5 x 0.5 cm (2¾ x 1 x ³⁄₁₆ in.)
itsaKey: 7.9 x 3.3 x 0.5 cm (3⅛ x ¹⁵⁄₁₆ x ³⁄₁₆ in.)
Cooper Hewitt, Smithsonian Design Museum
New York, 2012-32-1, 2012-32-2, 2012-32-3

AMONG THE MOST convenient tools for storing, transporting, and retrieving data is the USB (Universal Serial Bus) flash drive, also known as a thumb drive or memory stick. Buried within each is a microprocessor the size of a fingernail that can be disguised in virtually anything—a twig, plastic sushi, jewelry, a plastic bar bearing a company's logo, or, as in these examples, a beautifully made aluminum key.

Keys come in all shapes and sizes. A familiar shape, kept on a ring, something we are not likely to forget. It is also a metaphor for unlocking knowledge. But what appears perfectly mundane also has the power to store huge amounts of information. Rather than customize the key with the traditional serrated edge, it can be personalized with whatever data the user chooses to store on it. The equivalent of thousands of photographs fits on the chip concealed within each of these 64 GB key-shaped flash drives. We marvel at the attributes of these miniature storage devices, but precisely because they are so small and portable, flash drives can also be devastating clandestine weapons. Like mysterious suitcases, they can discreetly smuggle secrets, including classified documents. Flash drives are now tools of cyberespionage and cyberwarfare, a prime means of infecting others' computers with their own onboard software. CM

Casts. Inscription: be-el-šu-nu/ARAD d.IM/ù d.ša-la (Belshunu, servant of [the gods] Adad and Shala)

Cylinder Seal and Two Casts

2nd millennium BCE

↑ →

Old Babylonian (Hillah, Iraq)
Seal: worked slate
Casts: plaster
Seal: H x Diam: 2.5 x 1.3 cm (1 x ½ in.)
Casts: H x W: 3.8 x 7 cm (1½ x 2¾ in.)
Department of Anthropology
National Museum of Natural History
Smithsonian Institution
Washington, DC, A207910

THROUGHOUT THE ANCIENT Near East, cylinder seals, made of stone, metal, or glass, were tools for marking property. In some cases, their impressions on clay or wax even served to lock doors. Generally, the cylinder was rolled over damp or semi-hardened clay or wax, leaving a legible inscription; the piece of clay or wax was affixed to an object or sealed a door. The design on the seal was carved in recess with a flint point sharpened with metal tools; different local contexts and eras produced carvings of varying artistic quality. According to contemporary written sources, every citizen of Babylon possessed at least one seal, which was worn as a pendant; both women and men seem to have owned them. The Old Babylonian cuneiform inscription on this example identifies the original owner of the seal as a certain Belshunu. Flanking the inscription are two figures on either side, a nude female and a horned, turban-wearing warrior god, the deities Shala and Adad, as well as two flanking figures on each side, in long robes with horizontal stripes, probably worshippers of their cults. AN

Three views of cylinder seal

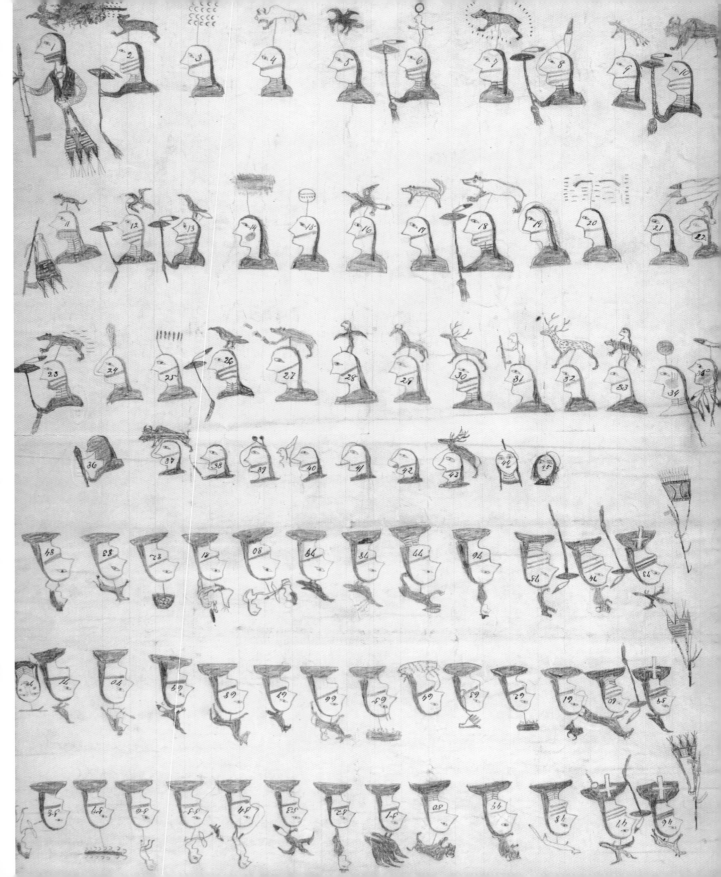

Big Road
Census
1881 or 1882

Big Road (Lakota people, USA)
Colored pencil, graphite,
and watercolor on paper
Sheet: 41 x 34 cm (16⅛ x 13⅜ in.)
National Anthropological Archives
Smithsonian Institution
Washington, DC, NAA MS 2372
(INV 08631100)

THE OGLALA LAKOTA chief Big Road produced this pictorial roster in 1881 or 1882, after his band was assigned to the Standing Rock Indian Agency, in parts of what are today North and South Dakota, and the agent there demanded a list of his followers. Each man is identified by a small image suggesting his name, such as Bear Looking Back (top row, second from the left) and Low Dog (second row, first image). The leaders of family bands are shown holding a pipe and pipe bag, while men who have led war expeditions brandish a war club. This sheet of paper has served many purposes. To the government agent, this census was an instrument of control, while to Big Road it was an assertion of chiefly authority. When the document passed to the Smithsonian scholar Garrick Mallery, he published it as a piece of evidence in the new study of cultural development.[1] A century later, the Lakota artist Arthur Amiotte used scraps of images from it in one of his signature collages, Amiotte's work combines visual traces from a personal, tribal, and national past to construct a wry commentary on Lakota history.[2] CG

[1] Garrick Mallery, "Pictographs of the North American Indians: A Preliminary Paper," in Fourth *Annual Report of the Bureau of American Ethnology to the Secretary of the Smithsonian Institution 1882–'83*, ed. J. W. Powell (Washington, DC: Government Printing Office, 1886).
[2] Arthur Amiotte and Janet Catherine Berlo, *Arthur Amiotte: Collages, 1988–2006* (Santa Fe, NM: Wheelwright Museum of the American Indian, 2006).

FEEDBACK SYSTEMS EMPLOYED in computation today take note of many of our actions, our habits, our shopping preferences. Pedometers, thermometers, scales, devices for checking blood sugar or blood pressure are all single-purpose tools for self-monitoring. However, a contemporary obsession with data, metrics, and being fit has spawned a new variety of wearable "smart" devices that up the ante, not only for tracking, but for managing—even optimizing—our physical performance. The Jawbone UP24 wristband is one such personal feedback system. Conveniently worn 24/7, the data-collecting bracelet records the wearer's level of physical activity, as well as the quality of sleep and eating habits, and communicates an instant summary. Available in a range of colors, the Jawbone UP24's flexible spring-steel inner core adjusts to any wrist size and contour. Wearable monitors are in the nascent stages, but the possibilities for tools that get to know the wearer and their habits and also encourage individuals to track and regulate their behavior, and connect to others, including their doctors, can be very empowering. CM

Wristband:
Jawbone UP24
2013

Designed by Yves Béhar
(Swiss, b. 1967) of fuseproject (USA)
Manufactured by Jawbone (USA)
Hypoallergenic TPU rubber,
nickel-plated TR-90 nylon,
electronic components
1.7 x 7.4 x 5.5 cm
(1¹⁄₁₆ x 2¹⁵⁄₁₆ x 2³⁄₁₆ in.)
Courtesy of Yves Béhar
and fuseproject

Camera: *SX-70*

1972

Designed by Henry Dreyfuss (American, 1904–1972) and James M. Conner (American, b. 1922)
Manufactured by Polaroid Corporation (USA)
Metal, plastic, leather
Open: 12.5 x 10.5 x 17.7 cm (4¹⁄₁₆ x 4⅛ x 6¹⁵⁄₁₆ in.)
Cooper Hewitt, Smithsonian Design Museum, New York, Museum purchase through gift of Neil Sellin, 1999-2-2-a

INSTANT PHOTOS AND IMMEDIATE gratification are expected now more than ever as evidenced by Instagram, today's global photo-sharing bulletin board. Although a few minutes slower than smartphones in delivering results, the SX-70 was the first camera to achieve one-step photography. Introduced in 1972 by Edwin H. Land, the co-founder of the Polaroid Corporation, the SX-70 is a single-lens reflex camera that revolutionized instant photography. Polaroid manufactured cameras as early as 1947, but the SX-70 is a complex system that embodied major innovations in both form and function. Unlike previous cameras, the electronic SX-70 required the photographer to merely point, focus, and click—then pull the snapshot that emerged from the camera and wait for it to develop in just three minutes. The immediacy of the experience engaged the photographers, transforming them into active participants. The first to employ an instant film pack that included a built-in battery, the camera ejected pictures automatically, without the chemical residues required by previous models. Sleek and compact when folded flat, the SX-70 is encased in a brushed-chrome shell accented with protective leather that enhanced its appeal as a stylish portable accessory. It was used by photographers such as Ansel Adams, Walker Evans, and Andy Warhol. JP

Time Ball (Mnemonic Device)

Created before 1920

Klikitat (Nicola Valley,
Southern British Columbia, Canada)
Knotted cordage of *Apocynum canabinum* (Indian hemp)
8.5 x 9.8 cm (3⅜ x 3⅞ in.)
National Museum of the American
Indian, Smithsonian Institution
Washington, DC, 10/297

"Time is a relationship between events,

Kept fresh in memory by selected objects on knotted hemp.

Connection is as vital as Separation.

The strand is begun by a woman at her marriage.

By the time she is a grandmother,

The unity of life is wrapped and remembered in a Time Ball."[3]

THE TIME BALL is a mnemonic device, or memory aid, unique to the Klikitat and Yakama people of the Columbia Plateau, a geographical region that includes parts of present-day Washington, Oregon, Idaho, and southern British Columbia. Women from these cultures were the creators and keepers of time balls, which used knots and special markers to create diaries or personal records of their lives. Both the Klikitat and Yakama people are part of the broader Columbia Plateau culture that lived in northwestern North America and included more than thirty different groups.[4] Surrounded on the east side by the Rocky Mountains and on the west by the Cascades, the Plateau consists of elevated plains crossed by several river systems, including the Columbia and the Fraser. The Fraser's Great Bend forms roughly the northern border, while the Blue Mountains define the southern edge.[5] The Klikitat and Yakama people, who live in the northwest Plateau, belong to a common language group known as Sahaptin.[6] Despite the existence of other Native language families and many regional dialects, Plateau people are connected by strong cultural ties—the most important being the seasonal movements for food, especially salmon, the region's principal food source.[7] The Plateau people recognized their cultural similarities, and members from different groups formed close and lasting ties through trade, marriage, material culture, and religious beliefs and ceremonies.[8]

Unlike the knots of the quipu, which recorded decimal units related to Incan recordkeeping, the knots of the time ball, or *ititamat*, registered significant life events. *Ititamat* loosely translates as "a counting-the-days ball." When a young woman was considered ready for marriage, she started her first time ball, using the fibers of the *Apocynum canabinum* plant, commonly known as Indian hemp or dogbane, a much-valued material used in Plateau baskets, bags, and nets. Meaningful occasions, such as marriage, the birth of a child, or the death of family members were highlighted with special markers, such as a glass bead, a shell, human hair, or a fragment of cloth. The markers stood out from the simple knots that recorded the passage of individual days. Women undoubtedly noted events of broader interest to their group, marking days of bounty, hardship, or even conflict.

As a woman grew older, her time ball contained the history of her family and the extended community. If the *ititamat* became too large to handle, she started a new one.[9] Maintaining her time ball was so essential to a woman's identity that she was buried with it.

J. D. Leechman wrote that in 1911 he found a deerskin pouch hanging from the corner post of a fence surrounding an Indian grave in a cemetery in Nicola Valley, British Columbia; it contained two time balls, three additional lengths of knotted cordage, a brass button, and four dentalium shells attached to sinew (see previous page).[10] Dentalium shell, exchanged in trade with Northwest Coast people for thousands of years, was a prized decorative material that served as a form of currency and denoted status and wealth.[11]

The largest time ball, when extended, is about 55 m (180 ft.) long, with more than 6,600 knots.[12] Most are in groups of 6 or 7, possibly reflecting days of the week. Some scholars have speculated that the knots in some cases recorded lunar cycles. What is clear is that these were highly personal items, and a variety of time and recordkeeping styles must have existed. While some examples mark notable events with glass beads or shells, this particular time ball has knots with human hair, fragments of cotton and woolen cloth in different colors, dried sinew, deerskin, a piece of braided cord, and grocer's string. It is likely that the hair and the clothing fragments served as potent reminders of individuals of consequence, while sinew and deerskin could recall an especially bountiful hunting season. Conversely, skin and sinew could serve as markers for scarcity, as scraps of animal hide and salmon skin were cooked over a fire and eaten during times when food supplies dwindled.[13]

Life on the Plateau was organized around the seasonal movements relating to food gathering. Men and women had distinct but equally important roles in securing food for their group. In springtime, able-bodied members left the winter village so women could gather wild plants, especially the camas root, a food staple. In late spring and early summer, the group moved to the rivers, where men fished for salmon, while women cleaned and dried the fish. In late summer and fall, movement shifted to the uplands, where women picked huckleberries. In early fall, men hunted for deer and elk or late-running salmon, while the women dried the meat and prepared animal skins for clothing. In winter, the ceremonial season began, and the group retreated to their winter villages. It was a period marked by winter dances, storytelling, and socializing. Families and friends from neighboring villages came together to reestablish the close ties lost during the food–gathering time.[14] Because their activities contributed more than half of the annual food supply, women enjoyed great status and influence in their village.[15]

A woman's time ball must have served as an impressive tool for storytelling, as she unwound it to relay the physical and spiritual experiences of her family and tribe to the younger generation. KR

Reading a time ball

[3] Morris L. Uebelacker and Jeffrey S. Wilson, *Time Ball: A Story of the Yakima People and the Land* (Yakima, WA: Yakima Nation, 1984), 189.

[4] Larry Cebula, *Plateau Indians and Quest for Spiritual Power, 1700–1850* (Lincoln: University of Nebraska Press, 2003), 8.

[5] Lillian A. Ackerman, *A Necessary Balance: Gender and Power Among Indians of the Columbia Plateau* (Norman: University of Oklahoma Press, 2003), 7.

[6] Vivian M. Adams, "In a Spiritual Way: A Portrait of Plateau Spirituality," in *Native Arts of the Columbia Plateau: the Doris Swayze Bounds Collection* (Seattle: University of Washington Press, 1998), 35.

[7] Richard G. Conn, "The Plateau Culture Area and Its Art," in *Native Arts of the Columbia Plateau: the Doris Swayze Bounds Collection* (Seattle: University of Washington Press, 1998), 42.

[8] Cebula, *Plateau Indians and Quest for Spiritual Power*, 9. [9] Alex Saluskin, "Old Days and the Present," in *Treaty Centennial, 1855–1955, the Yakimas* (Yakima, WA: The Republic Press, 1955), 57.

[10] John Douglas Leechman and M.R. Harrington, *String Records of the Northwest* (New York: Museum of the American Indian, Heye Foundation, 1921), 9-10.

[11] Vivian M. Adams, "In a Spiritual Way," 35.

[12] Leechman, *String Records of the Northwest*, 9.

[13] Cebula, *Plateau Indians*, 25.

[14] Uebelacker and Wilson, *Time Ball*, 189.

[15] Andrew Fisher, *Shadow Tribe: The Making of Columbia River Indian Identity* (Seattle: University of Washington Press, 2010), 18–19.

Cuneiform Clay Tablet

ca. 2000–1595 BCE

Mesopotamia; Clay/mud
4.1 x 3.5 x 1.3 cm (1⅝ x 1⅜ x ½ in.)
Department of Anthropology
National Museum of Natural History
Smithsonian Institution
Washington, DC, A315235

WITHOUT A WRITTEN LANGUAGE, how does a community visually express quantities, inventories, contracts that can be mutually understood and agreed upon? Cuneiform is not a language, but a writing system—one of the world's oldest—that employs code symbols like the letters and syllables we use today. Everyday cuneiform (from the Latin word for wedge-shaped) was invented in what is modern-day Iraq around 3200 BCE and was in use until around 300 CE. With a stiff reed or stylus, probably made of wood, people inscribed the characters on semihardened clay, an ideal surface for taking impressions. Cuneiform tablets served for business documents and inventories, in schools, and to register events and write poetry—virtually everything we use writing for today. The script, which is broken at the top, is Old Babylonian. Although the purpose of this specific tablet cannot be confirmed, it contains the personal name of Ili-bani and the place names Babylon and Isin. This suggests the wording of a typical contract, in which a person from one city might sell barley to someone from another city. Babylon, one of the most important cities in Mesopotamia, is mentioned in the Bible and is known mainly through the stele of King Hammurabi, one of the earliest law codes in cuneiform.[16] More than half a million ancient cuneiform tablets are preserved today. AN

---

[16] Department of Oriental Antiquities, Musée du Louvre, Paris, Sb 8.

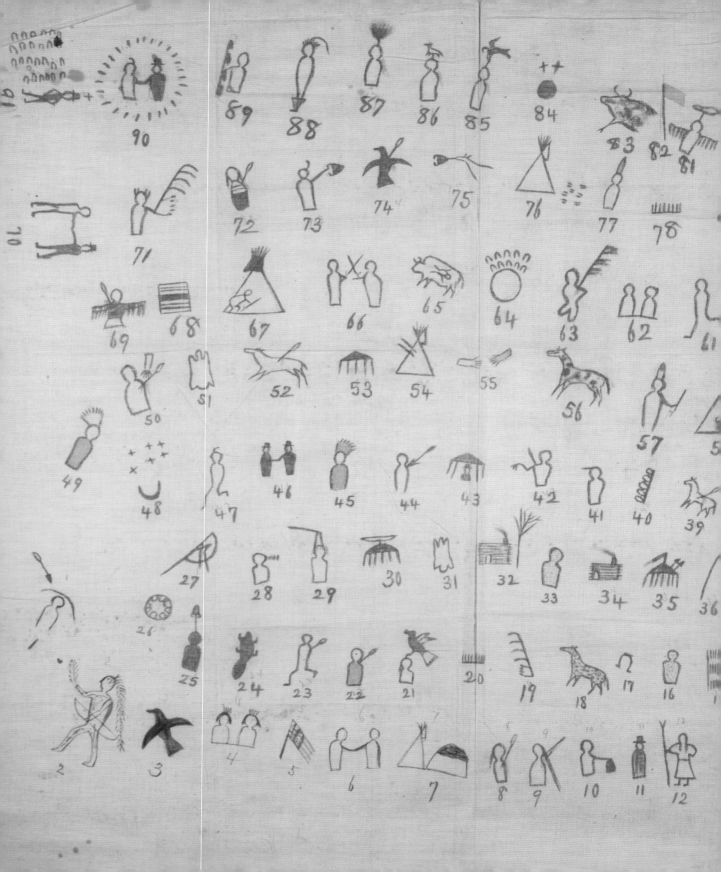

The Flame Winter Count (Copy)
Covers 1786–1876

Copied by Lt. Hugh T. Reed
(American, n.d.) in 1887 from original
by Boíde (The Flame)
(Lakota people, USA)
Ink on muslin
89 x 90 cm (35¹⁄₁₆ x 35⁷⁄₁₆ in.)
Gift of Lt. H. T. Reed
National Anthropological Archives
Smithsonian Institution, Washington, DC, 08633800

THIS MUSLIN CHART replicates a "winter count" kept by Boíde, a Lakota man whose name translates as The Flame. The Lakota, the western branch of the Sioux, marked the past by giving a name to each year, numbered by winters. Winter-count keepers—the men responsible for remembering the years in order—often made pictorial charts for personal reference. Each picture served as a memory aid for a particular year name, helping to keep them in the correct sequence. This image, covering the period from 1786 until 1876, reads in serpentine fashion from top to bottom. Multiyear names were part of a shared historical system, such as number 48, which represents a dramatic meteor shower in the winter of 1833/34.

Winter counts were copied over and over, each version valued for the information it contained. To ensure that his knowledge would be preserved, in 1877 The Flame worked with an army officer and an interpreter to produce this copy, along with a text explaining each entry.[17] CG

[17] For an interpretation of each entry on this count and information on other Lakota winter counts, visit http://wintercounts.si.edu or see *The Year the Stars Fell: Lakota Winter Counts at the Smithsonian*, eds. Candace Greene and Russell Thornton (Lincoln, NE: University of Nebraska Press, 2007).

Man painting figures on a buffalo skin winter count.

Photograph, Ernst Herzfeld and team making impressions of Great Terrace Inscription, Persepolis, Iran, probably between 1923 and 1934; Modern print from archival negative; Matted: 29.6 x 100.5 cm (11 ⅝ x 39 ⁹⁄₁₆ in.); The Ernst Herzfeld papers, Freer Gallery of Art and the Arthur M. Sackler Gallery, Film negative 4071

THE EARLY WESTERN travelers to the ruins in Egypt, Greece, and the Middle East often took talented draftsmen with them to make drawings of the ancient monuments and sculptures. The eighteenth century, however, witnessed the introduction of a new method of recording the reliefs and inscriptions found on these venerable traces. The practice of molding paper "squeezes" from ancient monuments heralded a new age of scientific documentation. Today, the Smithsonian's Museums, including the National Museum of Natural History and the Freer|Sackler Galleries, hold some five hundred paper squeezes taken from monuments in Egypt, Iraq, and Iran, many of them documenting early cuneiform inscriptions.

A squeeze is essentially a molded negative impression of a carved surface. Today, scholars have a number of early accounts about the practice at Persepolis. In 1826, for instance, Ephraim Gerrish Stannus "made several long shallow boxes of wood, in which he put quick lime, applied them to the sculptures, and allowed them to remain until thoroughly dry."[18] In 1844, Victor Lottin de Laval sponged a set of reliefs and inscriptions with water, then applied thin papers onto the stone to form the negative impressions.[19] A photograph, taken probably in 1923, and notes preserved in the Freer|Sackler archives illustrate the method the archaeologist Ernst Herzfeld and his team used to take impressions of the great inscription of Darius on the south wall of Takht-e Jamshid at Persepolis: "I did them all with cigarette paper, folded three times. The result is good," noted Herzfeld.[20] The photographer Hans von Busse, assisting Herzfeld during his excavations at Persepolis wrote in a letter to his father on September 23, 1933: " . . . One takes enough large sheets of extremely thin cigarette paper that is carefully hammered on with a hard brush, while damp. When it is well molded to the form, new layers are progressively overlaid. . . . Once it is dry

one can lift off the paper layers, which are now firmly stuck together, and one has an exact reproduction of the original."[21] Fifty-seven of such squeezes made by Herzfeld at Persepolis, including parts of Old Persian, Elamite, and Babylonian inscriptions, are preserved.

Herzfeld produced the Freer|Sackler squeezes between 1923 and 1933, some at the excavations he led at Persepolis—ancient Parsa—in southwestern Iran between 1931 and 1934. Persepolis was the impressive capital of the Achaemenid Empire between the late sixth century BCE and around 330 BCE.[22] The inscriptions on the monuments preserve information about their construction, and the squeezes aided Western scholars in deciphering and reconstructing the texts. In addition, the texts made possible the instruction and training of new generations of philologists, just as casts of sculptures were employed to teach students of art and history.[23]

Indeed, these impressions not only preserved the inscriptions, but they also became (unintentionally) the receptacles for pigments that must have been embedded in the carved cuneiform characters and stripped off in the squeeze-making process.[24] It is surprising that pigments survived the papier-mâché squeezing, and Herzfeld never commented on the pigments in the inscriptions.

From a conservation standpoint, squeezes have done irreversible harm to monuments.[25] As the eminent conservation scientist Alfred Lucas, who worked for the Egyptian Antiquities Service between 1923 and 1932, wrote: "Stone objects [that] bear inscriptions must on no account be wetted until the painted surface has been protected from the action of water, or the paint will probably be destroyed. The necessary protection may be given by spraying or otherwise treating the surface of the stone with some material that is insoluble in, and unacted upon by, water."[26]

The history of squeeze making on ancient monuments highlights questions about priorities and one of the ongoing tensions in contemporary archaeology, between obtaining information and preserving an object's physical integrity. **AN**

[18] Alex Saluskin, "Old Days and the Present," in *Treaty Centennial, 1855–1955, the Yakimas: Dedicated to the Treaty Chiefs and Yakimas yet Unborn*, by Click Relander and Confederated Tribes and Bands of the Yakama Nation, Washington (Yakima, WA: Republic Press, 1955), 57.

[19] Nicole Zapata-Aubé, ed., *Lottin de Laval: archéologue et peintre orientaliste, 1810–1903* (Bernay: Éditions de l'Association pour la promotion de la culture, 1997).

[20] Note by Ernst Herzfeld, N-84, November 22, 1923, page 18, Ernst Herzfeld Papers, Freer Sackler Archives.

[21] Correspondence by Ernst Herzfeld, September 23, 1933, page 4, Ernst Herzfeld Papers, Freer Sackler Archives.

[22] Alexander Nagel, "Ernst Herzfeld," in *Tehran 50: ein halbes Jahrhundert deutsche Archäologen in Iran: eine Ausstellung des Deutschen Archäologischen Instituts in Zusammenarbeit mit dem Museum für Islamische Kunst, Staatliche Museen Berlin. . . . .*, ed. Barbara Helwing et al. (Mainz, Germany: von Zabern, 2011), 42–65.

[23] See, for example, Nagel, *Persepolis*.

[24] Nagel, *Persepolis*; Nagel, "Colouring the Dead."

[25] Alison Richmond and Alison Lee Bracker, eds., *Conservation: Principles, Dilemmas and Uncomfortable Truths* (Oxford: Butterworth-Heinemann, 2009).

[26] Alfred Lucas, Antiques, Their Restoration and Preservation (London: Arnold, 1924), 25.

Squeeze of Foundation Inscription of Darius I at Persepolis (detail)
Made between 1923 and 1934

Made under the direction of Ernst Herzfeld
(German, 1879–1948)
Southern Terrace Wall, Persepolis, Iran
Paper
Sheet: 88.9 x 96.5 cm (35 x 38 in.)
The Ernst Herzfeld Papers, Freer Gallery of Art
and the Arthur M. Sackler Gallery
Washington, DC, FSA A.6 06.C061

Flight Data Recorder F1000 ("Black Box")

1995

↓

Manufactured by Loral Data
Systems (USA)
Epoxy-glass circuit cards,
integrated-circuit chips, integrated
connectors, stainless-steel housing
20.3 x 55.9 x 12.2 cm (8 x 22 x 4¹³⁄₁₆ in.)
Smithsonian National Air and Space Museum
Washington, DC, Gift of Loral Data Systems
A19950036000

INVESTIGATORS REQUIRE ACCURATE flight data to determine
the causes of aircraft accidents. The now-obsolete F1000 Solid State Flight Data
Recorder (SSFDR) could register between six and twenty data parameters over
twenty-five hours, while surviving impacts of 100 G, temperatures of 1,000 °C
(1,832 °F), and immersion in seawater for up to thirty days. The minimum data
it recorded included altitude, airspeed, heading, vertical acceleration, time, and
the duration of radio transmission. The F1000 was usually paired with a unit that
recorded cockpit voice communications.

Flight data recorders are often called "black boxes," because older aircraft
electronic equipment was painted black to radiate excess heat. Today, they are
painted orange to make them easier to find in the wreckage of a crash site. A radio
beacon also helps investigators locate the recorder. The F1000, the first certified
SSFDR, substituted semiconductors and integrated circuits for less reliable and
less durable magnetic tape.

Today's FDRs are far more crashworthy and can record hundreds of parameters;
in addition, the flight-data and cockpit voice recorders are now sometimes
combined into a single unit. RC

International
Safety Symbols

Developed by the International
Organization for Standardization

PROHIBITION
Red ring, diagonal bar with black symbol, white background

SAFE CONDITION
Green square with white symbol

MANDATORY ACTION
Blue circle with white symbol

WARNING
Yellow triangle with black border and black symbol

GRAPHICS CAN BE TOOLS. They convey a message. In the world of public communication, symbols are designed both to attract attention to hazardous situations and to advertise places offering joyous experiences. Thus, one sign on a mountain road informs a driver of the danger of ice, while another announces a turnout where one may stop and safely appreciate a panoramic view. Good graphic design, which uses color and form rather than words, can increase international understanding by avoiding a local language while promoting effective visual tools, both elements of a worldwide acceptance of what the anthropologist Margaret Mead called "glyphs."[27] The search for a shared social experience has counterparts in the spheres of personal communication and of brands, exemplified, for example, by the Christian cross, the Nike "swoosh," the Ferrari horse, and the Lacoste alligator. The selection of nine International Safety Symbols shown here is based on a civic use of "universal" symbols comprising geometric shapes that are color coded as part of a global project to standardize warnings and actions required concerning safety, risk, and hazardous environments. The design challenge for safety symbols—which can mean the difference between life and death—is that they must be immediately recognizable regardless of one's language. There is no room for ambiguity. The edges are often outlined, underscoring the message like an exclamation mark. One of the most common, a prohibition sign, is a red ring punctuated with a diagonal bar against a white background. **CM**

[27] Gyorgy Kepes, *Sign, Image, Symbol* (New York: George Braziller, 1966), 113.

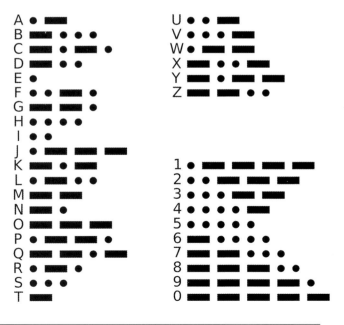

Sent from the lower depot at Baltimore to Washington Saturday May 25.th 1844. Saml. F. B...

W h a t h a t h G ...

FOR CENTURIES WE COMMUNICATED with words, sounds, and pictures, then books and newspapers, but how to transmit information quickly and reliably over long distances? Drums, smoke signals, and carrier pigeons were solutions for finite expanses, but a global industrial world required more. In the mid-nineteenth century, the telegraph, an electrical system, revolutionized communication, negating time and distance, and Samuel F. B. Morse's code was created to be its "language." Morse, an artist turned inventor, translated numbers and the Latin alphabet into combinations of dots and dashes. These were transmitted instantly across wires via electrical impulses conveyed in series of long and short "clicks," with skilled operators just as speedily interpreting the coded messages. Five years after the first long-distance Morse-Vail telegraph was successfully launched on May 24, 1844, there were 12,000 miles of telegraph lines in the United States and, by 1868, underwater cables linked America and Europe.[28] Akin to Morse's electrical messaging feat, today's digital technology converts all data—letters, numbers, and images—into a binary code also composed of two symbols: 1s and 0s. CM

International Morse Code

1. The length of a dot is one unit.
2. A dash is three units.
3. The space between parts of the same letter is one unit.
4. The space between letters is three units.
5. The space between words is seven units.

TOOLS

28 Harold Evans, with Gail Buckland and David Lefer, *They Made America: From the Steam Engine to the Search Engine: Two Centuries of Innovators* (New York: Little Brown and Company, 2004), 75

Superintendent of Elec. Mag. Telegraphs.

D h r o u g h t.

Telegraph Message:
"What hath GOD wrought"
May 24, 1844

↑ ↓

Transmitted from Washington, DC
to Baltimore, Maryland, via Morse code
Invented by Samuel F. B. Morse (American, 1791–1872)
and Alfred L. Vail (American, 1807–1859)
Ink on paper
3.8 x 70.5 cm (1½ x 27¾ in.)
Smithsonian Institution
National Museum of American History
Washington, DC

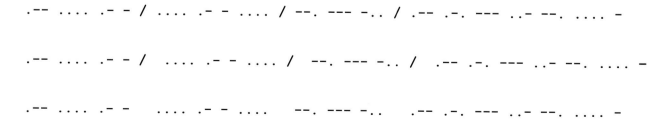

(above) *"What hath GOD wrought" in Morse code, using three different online translators*

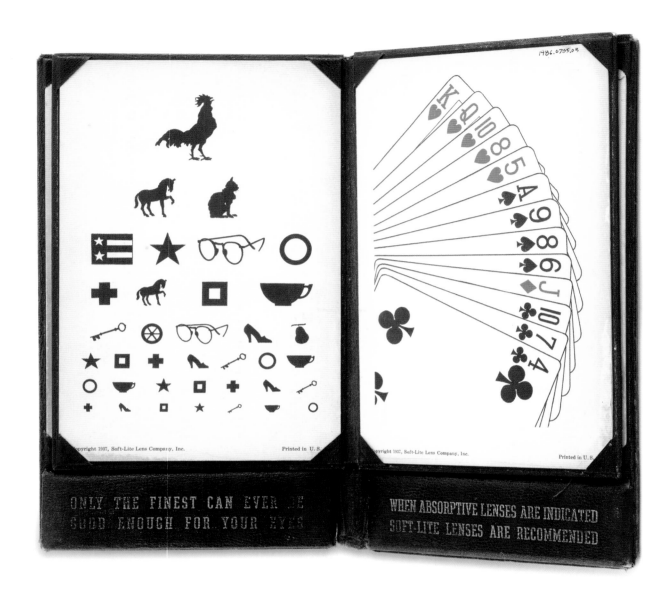

ONLY THE FINEST CAN EVER BE
GOOD ENOUGH FOR YOUR EYES

WHEN ABSORPTIVE LENSES ARE INDICATED
SOFT-LITE LENSES ARE RECOMMENDED

Visual Aids
for Eye Testing
ca. 1937

Manufactured by Soft-Lite Lens
Company, Inc. (USA)
Paper, cardboard, laminated canvas
Open: 20.5 x 24 x 1.5 cm (8¹⁄₁₆ x 9⁷⁄₁₆ x ⁹⁄₁₆ in.)
Smithsonian Institution
National Museum of American History
Washington, DC, Cat. 1986.0705.03

WE TAKE TESTS EVERYDAY—for a driver's license, for cholesterol,
to confirm a password change. Tests are so much a part of life that we seldom
notice the mass of information embedded in them. This booklet of simple eye tests
from the 1930s captures a host of assumptions about people and their cultural com-
petencies, from card-playing and singing to understanding train schedules and
shorthand. The first standardized eye chart is believed to have been developed
by a Dutch ophthalmologist, Herman Snellen, in 1862. Snellen's test of visual acuity
set a standardized distance from patient to chart of 20 feet in the United States
and 6 meters in Europe. His chart has eleven lines of optotypes, that is, symbols,

ONLY THE FINEST CAN EVER BE
GOOD ENOUGH FOR YOUR EYES

WHEN ABSORPTIVE LENSES ARE INDICATED
SOFT-LITE LENSES ARE RECOMMENDED

from a single large letter at the top to the smallest letters at the bottom. The letters are carefully shaped so as to balance the amount of white to black space of the optotypes. The chart is inexpensive and portable. Other charts followed, such as the Lea chart designed in Finland in 1976 that uses objects, like a house or a ring, to cater to children and others who are preliterate. In the late nineteenth century, a Swiss eye specialist, Edmund Landolt, devised a chart with the letter C oriented in different directions and, in 1923, two Russian opthalmologists, Sergei Golovin and D. A. Sivtsev, invented a chart consisting of two parts, one the Landolt C and the other made up of Cyrillic letters as optotypes. CM

KENNETH KOLB & COMPANY
ADVERTISING & PUBLIC RELATIONS

6123 Loyola Avenue
New Orleans, Louisiana 70118-6209

NEW ORLEANS LA 701

03 APR 2006 PM 4 L

NATIONAL PHILATELIC COLLECTION
SMITHSONIAN NATIONAL POSTAL MUSEUM
MR 570   PO BOX 37012
WASHINGTON DC
20013- 7012

This envelope was mailed on April 3, 2006, the first day normal mail-processing operations resumed for first-class mail in New Orleans, following Hurricane Katrina. The ZIP code, rendered as a barcode, is at the bottom of the envelope.

FOR MORE THAN two hundred years, mail in the American colonies and then the Unites States moved from sender to receiver by the simple act of someone reading and interpreting the destination. Before 1863, processing mail meant sending it to the right town, where individuals picked it up from the local post office. When the Post Office Department began delivering mail to homes and businesses during the Civil War, the system naturally became more complex.

Until the mid-twentieth century, there were enough postal workers for the growing volumes of mail, but the post–World War II explosion in population and number of businesses threatened to overwhelm the nation's post offices. Between 1945 and 1960 the number of pieces handled each year jumped by more than 40 percent, from 37.9 billion to 63.7 billion; the best clerks could move 600 envelopes an hour by hand. Machines were designed to process mail using a numerical system: in 1963 Americans were asked to add five numbers to each mailing address—the ZIP (Zone Improvement Plan) codes.[29]

ZIP codes were now integral to every aspect of mail handling, including machinery design and processing methodology. Even decisions about where to locate post offices were based on the five-digit numbering system. Meanwhile, the volume of mail kept climbing, reaching 106.3 billion pieces in 1980. Six hundred envelopes per hour per employee were no

longer enough to keep up with demand. Advances in technology made possible the next leap—the barcode reading system. Computerized machines interpreted each address, compared it to a master database, and sprayed a barcode representing that address onto the envelope or other packaging. Machines down the line also used these barcodes to pass the mail through the system. By the mid-1980s, mail was whizzing through address-scanning machines at the rate of 24,000 pieces an hour. At first these machines read only printed addresses, but as handwriting-recognition capabilities steadily improved, more handwritten mail traveled through the new systems, and ever-newer, more sophisticated machines processed that mail. At the turn of the twenty-first century, barcoded letters were speeding through machines at almost 35,000 letters per hour.

The most advanced postal barcode, in use as of 2013, is the Intelligent Mail barcode (IMb), each of which tucks thirty-one digits, or units, of information into sixty-five bars. The IMb holds a wealth of messages, including ZIP codes, data that reveal how the piece was presorted, whether it is first-class

[29] Each five-digit ZIP code represents a group of addresses; they might be homes or businesses, schools or apartment houses. One five-digit number might encompass ten thousand delivery points, which would be spread out over many square miles in a rural area or concentrated within a few city blocks. The first digit represents a region of the country. The next two digits stand for a central post-office facility in the region. The last two digits represent a specific post office or postal zone.

mail or a periodical, the business sending it, automatic address-forwarding information, the destination address, and item-tracking content. So much information can be included in one such barcode that mailers could post a billion pieces at one time and receive a unique identification code for each one. Businesses placing an IMb before mailing receive a substantial discount on rates and other benefits: when a business's preaddressed reply envelope is returned, the firm can forecast its arrival date. That makes their business more predictable and profitable.

Even though the volume of mail has declined dramatically in recent years, 40 percent of the world's correspondence transits through the United States Postal Service each year. The IMb is a critical tool in keeping operating costs down—and the mail moving. NP

Intelligent Mail Barcode or Postal Code
2013

Designed by two private companies, postal engineers, and State University of New York staff

Please forward to the appropriate individual in your organization. Thank you.

Gaylord Bros Inc PO Box 4901 Syracuse, NY 13221-4901

PRSRT STD
US Postage PAID
Gaylord Bros Inc

NATIONAL POSTAL MUSEUM
PO BOX 37012
WASHINGTON DC 20013-7012

0002
T132
02285
05

A catalog mailed to the National Postal Museum in 2013 shows an example of the Intelligent Mail barcode.

THIS ORNATE CANOE PROW, *tauihu,* is a power object. Most likely from a war or fishing canoe, it is laden with symbolism that communicates its significance as a social force meant to impress onlookers and embolden users. Canoes, *waka,* were some of the most important possessions of the Maori chiefs, who were concerned with their lineage and their ancestors' original migrations from central Polynesia. This prow belonged to Chief KiwiKiwi from the Bay of Islands, on New Zealand's North Island.

Canoe prows feature a stylized carved head projecting forward on a long neck with tattooed designs on the face and a protruding tongue. The aggressive figure at the front of the prow was believed to forcefully part the seas, the domain of the god Tangaroa. The figures and spirals, part of the complex symbolism of the Maori, are found across a variety of their wood carvings. Traditionally, wood was worked with stone tools and a mallet of wood or whalebone and was carried out under ritual restrictions. AK

Canoe Prow
Created before 1840

Maori (New Zealand)
Carved wood, red ocher
42 x 44.5 x 110 cm
(16⁹⁄₁₆ x 17½ x 43⁵⁄₁₆ in.)
Department of Anthropology
National Museum of Natural History
Smithsonian Institution
Washington, DC, E3790

BRIDGES ARE TOOLS to get people across divides, deliver them from one place to another, and assist in completing tasks. They are often engineering feats of great beauty and complexity, supported by large numbers of people and resources. Communication devices are bridges between people. The Tellatouch Braillewriter, designed for users who are deaf-blind, closes the distance between people who rely upon sight and sound and fingertips to connect. The device employs neither batteries, electrical signals, memory chips, nor paper. The case is always pleasantly cool to the touch. Its brown, smooth plastic was intended to look like a leather attaché case.

Braille is a tactile language developed in France by Louis Braille, a teacher of the blind, in the 1820s. Standardized in 1932, the language contended for primacy among several competing tactile codes; in addition, there are several types of Braillewriters, slate-styluses, refreshable Braille displays, talking computers and books, and other inventions to generate and enhance communication. The Tellatouch is very much a product

Tellatouch Braillewriter
Designed ca. 1945 and Manufactured ca. 1952

By the American Foundation for the Blind (USA)
Plastic, metal, leather
Open: 9.5 x 25 x 27.3 cm
(3 ¾ x 9 ¹⁵⁄₁₆ x 10 ¾ in.)
Smithsonian Institution
National Museum of American History, Washington, DC
Cat. 306619.11

of mid-twentieth-century design: its postwar styling quotes briefcases, pocket flasks, and automobile seats. Compared to a large, heavy iron Braille-writing typewriter from 1900, the Tellatouch conveys fashion and corporate office as much as words.

The keyboard resembles that of a conventional typewriter, but each key lifts a Braille letter one at a time on the opposite side of the console, where a person reads the six-point cells that composes the letters. Since the device strings letters and words together, constantly refreshing itself, it feels like having a conversation.

The machine was developed by the American Foundation for the Blind in the 1940s in New York. The AFB was founded by a philanthropist who wanted to provide support and resources for troops returning from World War I with permanent vision loss—Helen Keller was AFB's celebrity advocate for many years. Since then, the organization has continued to assist and advocate for vision-impaired people; the Tellatouch's design extends its utility to hearing-impaired individuals as well.

The Tellatouch made its debut before the flood of computer-based options that require more training to be effective. It is, in a sense, an example of "stone-age" technology—mechanical, not electronic—but it works when more advanced tools lose power or break down. KO

The six-point cells with which Braille letters and numerals are composed.

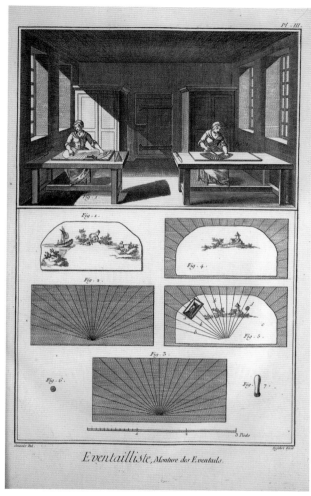

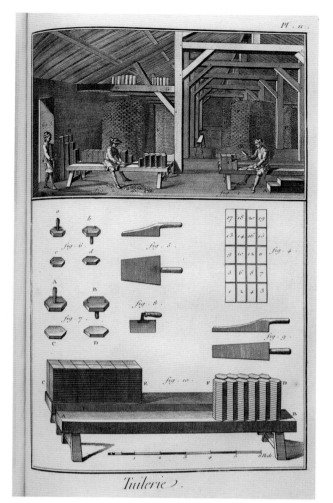

Fan making: workers attach paper to strips of wood

Tile manufacture: interior of a tile warehouse with equipment shown below

Encyclopédie, ou, Dictionnaire raisonné des sciences, des arts et des métiers (Encyclopaedia, or a Systematic Dictionary of the Sciences, Arts, and Crafts) 1751–65

↑ →

Co-edited by Denis Diderot (French, 1713–1784)
and Jean le Rond d'Alembert (French, 1717–1783)
Published by Chez Briasson, David, Le Breton,
and Durand (Paris, France)
Leather-bound paper boards, paper
Open: 40.1 × 53.5 × 13.2 cm (15¹³⁄₁₆ × 21¹⁄₁₆ × 5³⁄₁₆ in.)
Courtesy of Smithsonian Libraries, Washington, DC
Gift of Marian Hague, f AE25 .E53X 1751

WITH THE *ENCYCLOPÉDIE*, the French philosopher Denis Diderot's ambition was to gather all human knowledge into a single work. While not quite that vast in scope, the *Encyclopédie* was, and remains, a remarkable tool. The original project was inspired by the two-volume *Cyclopaedia* published by Ephraim Chambers in London in 1728, which was initially planned to be translated into French by an Englishman, John Mills. However, Diderot, who desired to create a much more comprehensive compendium of world knowledge, considered both the translation and scope of the two volumes and rejected them. With his collaborator for the first volumes, Jean Le Rond d'Alembert, Diderot ultimately published seventeen volumes of text between 1751 and 1765 and eleven volumes of plates between 1762 and 1772.

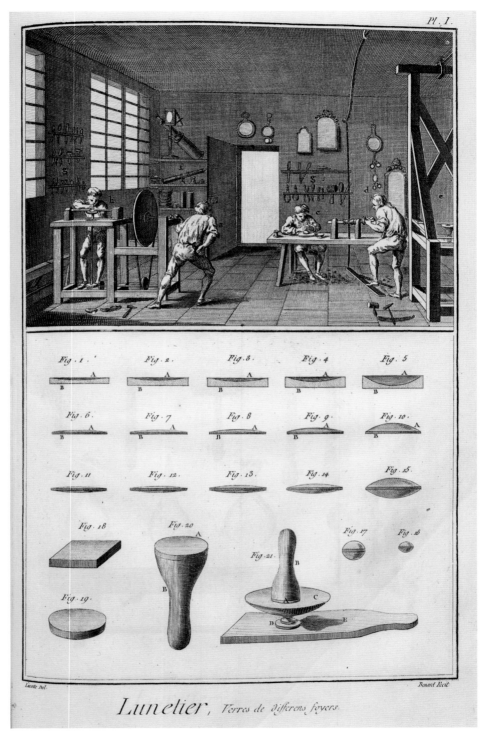

Pl. I.

Fig. 1   Fig. 2   Fig. 3   Fig. 4   Fig. 5

Fig. 6   Fig. 7   Fig. 8   Fig. 9   Fig. 10

Fig. 11   Fig. 12   Fig. 13   Fig. 14   Fig. 15

Fig. 18   Fig. 20   Fig. 21   Fig. 17   Fig. 16

Fig. 19

Lacotte Del.   Bourat Fecit.

Lunelier, Verres de differens foyers.

(above) *Optician's workshop and types of lenses; (opposite) Glove-making tools*

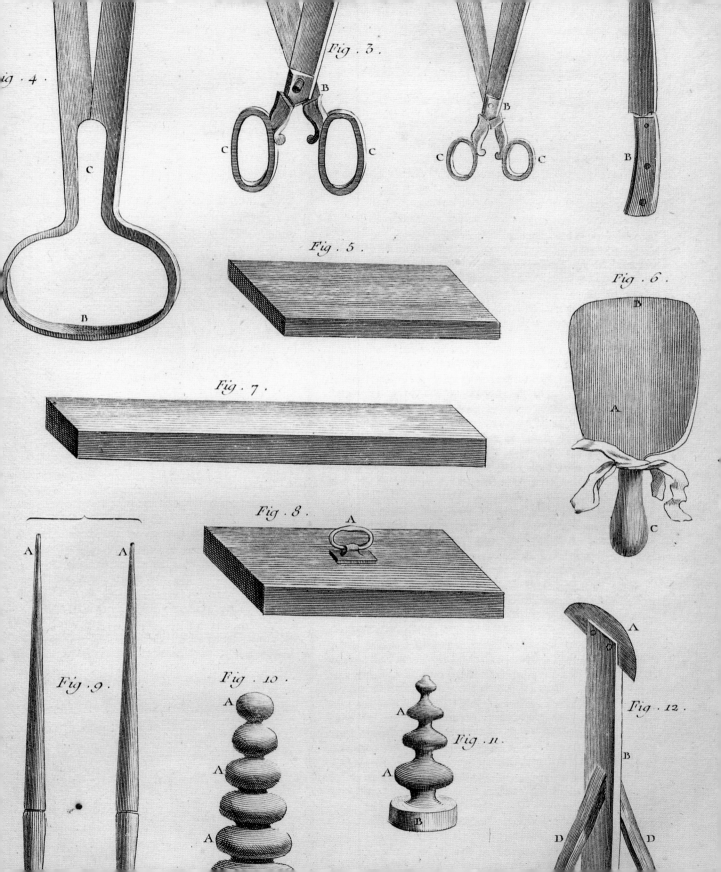

The *Encyclopédie* is a product of its time, the Age of Enlightenment. Diderot brought together more than one hundred men of letters, physicians, scientists, artisans, and scholars such as Montesquieu, Rousseau, and Voltaire as contributors. The overarching purpose was not only to expose people to new ideas on such subjects as the rights of individuals, but also to document and illustrate craft materials and processes. By 1789, after the publication of several editions, more than 25,000 copies were distributed, listing among the subscribers Thomas Jefferson, James Madison, and James Monroe.

In the first edition of the *Encyclopédie*, Rousseau, Voltaire, and Diderot promoted enlightenment principles, notably the ideas that knowledge was a product of human reason rather than divine intervention or nature, and that less state control of the economy and trade was desirable. Such writings caused Diderot's license to publish to be revoked in 1759 by the French government, since they challenged the authoritarian power of both the monarchy, under Louis XV, and the Roman Catholic Church.

This first edition was published secretly. Subsequent printings were widely supported by literate members of the French middle and upper classes, who were eager for access to the information and progressive theories found in the *Encyclopédie*. Its popularity attests to the fervor of an emerging enlightened society seeking change, which a decade or so later would manifest in the French Revolution.

A central focus of the *Encyclopédie* was the mechanical arts (later to be called "technology"), so that this information would reach a wide audience, urge experimentation and innovation in production methods, and reveal the secrets of contemporary manufacturing and handicraft practices. This was both new and controversial: for the first time, "common" trades such as cork cutting and knife grinding were systematically described in detail, including the raw materials and the machines or tools required in the manufacturing process. The more than 2,900 plates not only illustrate the manufacturing process step by step, but also detail simple tools, as well as more intricate machinery.

This aspect of the *Encyclopédie*, too, aroused controversy, as artisans felt that exposing their manufacturing secrets would hamper the monopoly they held on their trades. The making of goods to be exported—a major source of revenue for the French government—would be compromised if these processes were accessible internationally.

Diderot, however, believed that access to information about trade processes would stimulate competition among manufacturers and encourage improvements in production. He devised a framework to integrate knowledge by creating a common language for each trade that would be supported by images and arranged alphabetically. Contributors who observed the artisans at work compiled information that included: raw materials (origins, variant qualities, how to prepare and process), products made from these materials, analyses of the necessary tools and machinery (their component parts and their assembly), illustrated text on the main tasks and workmanship, and the definition of terms associated with the art or trade. The article on glass making, for example, begins with text on rare materials, followed by an explanation of the manufacturing process in the shop environment, a detailed analysis of tools and equipment, step-by-step tasks, final products, and glass-making terms.

The comprehensiveness and quality of the essays vary, depending on the writer's ability to access and understand the working of the craft shop and the intricate methods familiar to the artisans. Many entries report standard procedures, rather than, as Diderot had hoped, experiments or theoretical ideas on new and improved production methods.

The *Encyclopédie*, however, was a landmark publication. For the first time, information on the processes of the mechanical arts was accessible to a very wide audience of emerging industries and technical schools, thereby breaking the monopoly on trade secrets held by the craft guilds. The compendium documents the state of the traditional arts and the tools and machinery available to eighteenth-century manufacturers on the threshold of the Industrial Revolution. The *Encyclopédie* is a valuable research tool that documents Enlightenment ideals, as well as the materials and manufacture of handcrafted objects that we study today. **SVD**

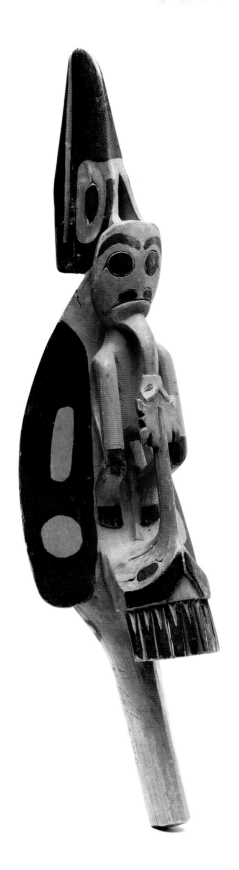

Raven Rattle
Created before 1910s

Tlingit, Haida, or Tsimshian (southeast Alaska, USA)
Carved and painted wood
32.1 x 7.6 x 8.9 cm (12⅝ x 3 x 3½ in.)
Collected by Rev. Sheldon Jackson, 1877–94
Department of Anthropology
National Museum of Natural History
Smithsonian Institution, Washington, DC, E316756

FLIGHT AS A MEANS of communing with the divine is a concept many cultures have expressed through symbolic iconography often drawn from nature. Among peoples of the Northwest Coast of the United States, clan leaders, dancers, and shamans were traditionally responsible for connecting events in daily life to the remote, but powerful realm of the spirits. The function of these intermediaries was to ward off evil and danger and to harness the spirits' healing powers. Raven rattles like this one were important artifacts in this sphere, tools of negotiation, and conduits to the supernatural domain. These dialogues were facilitated by Raven, who the community viewed as a mythical creator, while the bird, frog, tongue, and reclining figure also incorporated into the carving relate to specific legends. In particular, when the rattle was used in curing ceremonies, the bird and animal tongues were believed to enable healing and clairvoyant powers.[32] These rattles were used during dances by clan leaders and other high-status people, the wealthy hosts of memorial feasts, in the Tlingit culture, or in spirit-possession ceremonies, among the Haida and Tsimshian. Rattles were carved in one piece, split and hollowed, filled with seeds or stones, and bound back together. When shaken, the sound helped summon the supernatural world. CM

[32] Although shamans more commonly used globular or puffin-beak rattles during healing ceremonies, John Reed Swanton (*Contributions to the Ethnology of the Haida*, fig. 2) illustrates a carving of a shaman dancing with a raven rattle. In the story, "He Who Got Supernatural Power from His Little Finger," a shaman detects a witch with the aid of her bird-shaped rattle (Swanton, *Haida Texts*, 238–51).

WHOLE EARTH CATALOG

access to tools

Fall 1968

$5

Whole Earth Catalog: access to tools
Fall 1968

Compiled and edited by Stewart Brand
(American, b. 1938)
Published by Portola Institute, Inc.
(Menlo Park, California, USA)
Paper
36 x 28 cm (14³⁄₁₆ x 11 in.)
Courtesy of Kentucky Historical Society
(Pamphlet Fall 1968; 051 W628)

OVER TIME, TOOLS for extending communication networks and opening access to information have fostered the democratization of learning and the empowerment of people. In 1968, the writer and maverick Stewart Brand launched his offbeat paperback journal, the *Whole Earth Catalog*. The unspoken goal was to encourage its readers towards greater self-sufficiency and a shared sense of community. In particular, the publication was inspired by the counterculture movement of the mid-1960s and early 1970s, which sought new models of social order espousing individual freedom, egalitarianism, and limited economic dependence upon the wider society. The inaugural fall 1968 edition showed 133 selected objects; by 1971, the *Catalog* had expanded to include more than 1,000 entries and had sold more than a million copies, with issues published sporadically after 1972 until 1998. The 1968 cover featured one of the first satellite images of Earth as seen from space. Above the iconic image, dramatically silhouetted against the black background of limitless space, are the words WHOLE EARTH CATALOG and, below them, the subtitle, *access to tools*. Oversize and graphically powerful, with no borders depicting countries on planet Earth, the cover conveyed a compelling message that we are all connected, and the publication achieved cult status.

Each edition contains a statement of purpose: an item was listed if it was deemed "1. Useful as a tool. . . ." In the preface of every edition, Brand wrote:

> We are as gods and might as well get good at it. So far, remotely done power and glory—as via government, big business, formal education, church—has succeeded to the point where gross defects obscure

actual gains. In response to this dilemma and to these gains a realm of intimate, personal power is developing—power of the individual to conduct his own education, find his own inspiration, shape his own environment, and share his adventure with whoever is interested. Tools that aid this process are sought and promoted by the WHOLE EARTH CATALOG.

The 133 entries in the *Catalog*'s first edition were grouped under seven themes: Understanding Whole Systems, Shelter and Land Use, Industry and Craft, Communications, Community, Nomadics, and Learning. The intellectual sources were, among others, Norbert Wiener, Marshall McLuhan, Buckminster Fuller, and Gregory Bateson. The "tools" ranged from periodicals, meditation guides, and machines to potters' wheels, mail-order catalogs, camping gear, and self-help tips. In other words, useful tools to invent and shape your life. The *Catalog* was printed on newsprint with multiple typefaces and mixtures of photographs, bits of text, and readers' comments.

The impact of this array went beyond the objects shown: it also brought people together in an exercise that was as educative as it was communal. The publication created for its audience a sense of purposefulness and control. In the words of one reader, "Walking to the bathhouse today, holding my new twenty-ounce hammer, I suddenly understood the *Whole Earth Catalog* meaning of 'tool.' I always thought tools were objects, things: screw drivers, wrenches, axes, hoes. Now I realize that tools are a process: using the right-sized object in the most efficient way to get a job done."[30]

This precomputer compendium was a user-generated database of disparate tools from varied sources and cultures that celebrated small-scale technologies as a way for individuals to improve their lives. Steve Jobs famously referred to it as "one of the Bibles of my generation," likening it to Google.[31] It was a precursor of today's global information-distribution system, the World Wide Web. CM

30 Fred Turner, *From Counterculture to Cyberculture: Stewart Brand, the Whole Earth Network, and the Rise of Digital Utopianism* (Chicago: University of Chicago Press, 2006).
31 Steve Jobs (commencement address at Stanford University, Stanford, California, June 12, 2005).

THE FIRST HUMAN TOOLS expanded the diet of our early ancestors and protected them. Nature was the greatest provider of materials for creating these tools, which people fashioned for hunting, foraging, and protecting themselves from inhospitable environments and other dangers. The exquisitely carved ivory snow goggles of the Iñupiaq people of Alaska not only safeguarded the eyes from blinding reflections off snow-covered landscapes, but also enhanced the wearer's distance vision like a pinhole camera. A water- and windproof parka meant the difference between life and death for Yup'ik fishermen of Alaska, which made it imperative for seamstresses to follow the complex stages of turning sea-mammal intestine into an impermeable fabric. The success of these "second skins" relied on the assuredness of the maker's skills and her understanding of performance needs in a garment. Similarly, an astronaut's spacesuit is an indispensable life-support system for withstanding extreme conditions; the suit's designers and engineers must overcome many challenges to achieve flexibility and mobility in zero gravity.

The pursuit of longevity has contributed to advancements in medicine that would have been unimaginable even a generation ago. Prosthetics for the heart and limbs have prolonged life and increased its quality, while redesigned delivery systems for anesthesia and for smallpox vaccination have made drugs more effective and safer to use. A maskette from the Mau people of West Africa also combats negative forces and protects in a time of crisis.

The desire to detect diseases before they become life-threatening has led to the current phenomenon of the "lab-on-a-chip," which picks up important health information and sends it to handheld devices. The Gene-RADAR® and the Kernel of Life can immediately diagnose various disease strains by testing a drop of blood or saliva in the field. The Vscan™ is a portable ultrasound unit that displays images of organs in real time and transmits them to medical professionals anywhere in the world, truly an application of effective global health care. While not all survival design is about life and death, the innovations in this section show how the will to endure continues to inspire and drive us toward smarter solutions.

SURVIVE

(opposite) *Ballistic Face Mask, 2013*

Parka
Before 1925

↓

Yup'ik (Yup'ik Eskimo)
Doyon Limited
Kuskokwim region (Alaska, USA)
Beluga whale gut, sinew, grass twine
136 x 109 cm (53 9/16 x 42 15/16 in.)
National Museum of the American
Indian, Smithsonian Institution
Washington, DC, 22/7435

FEATHER-LIGHT, GOSSAMER-THIN, and shaped with elegant simplicity, the gut parkas created by the Arctic sea hunters of Alaska and coastal Canada provided protection from wind, rain, and stormy seas. Constructed from the intestines of sea mammals, including seals, beluga whales, walrus, and sea lions, they are cleaned, inflated, dried, and split into long ribbons of gut. According to Yup'ik elders, this parka is made of beluga-whale gut, identifiable by the width of the strips.

The intestine, which is composed of many layers of collagen and muscle, allows nutrients to be absorbed by the body, while preventing substances from traveling back through the gut wall. It is a dense material that is pierced by capillaries in the living animal, but these close upon the animal's death, making the "skin" impermeable and resistant to decay. The membrane is extremely tough, a trait necessary to perform its biological function of contraction and withstand great pressure.

The practical properties of gut were exploited by Alaska Native people to make a highly functional performance fabric, which women skilfully sew into beautiful and extremely practical parkas. This Yup'ik example was sewn with sinew (animal tendon). The watertight seams were created with a two-thread combination, in this case sinew and twine—grass is a common sewing material—secured in place with a running stitch.

The final test of impermeability consisted of tying the sleeves at the wrists and filling the entire garment with water, checking carefully to make sure that not a drop leaked through. Parkas with extra wide skirts enabled a kayak hunter in rough weather, to tie the bottom edge of the parka securely around his kayak's cockpit to keep water from swamping his craft. Even waves breaking over the bow could not penetrate the parka's watertight construction. The wide skirt also allowed it to function as a sleeping bag. When the sleeper's knees were drawn up to the chin, the whole body was snugly encased in a garment that was unfailingly warm and dry on the bitterest of winter nights. As Paul John, a Yup'ik elder reported, "We put parkas on as insulation inside our cotton parka covers when it's cold and windy and our body feels suddenly insulated and warm. Like a shield, wind will not enter and the heat will stay inside."[1]

While gut parkas were extremely practical, they had spiritual purposes as well. For example, Native doctors wore one or more when practicing curing ceremonies, and traditional belief held that the dry rustling of a gut parka as the wearer moved signified the presence of helping spirits. The garments were also worn in some ceremonies as a means of purification.

Neva Rivers, a Yup'ik parka maker, described the long process of turning raw intestines into a finished product. She concluded, "It ends with gratitude when it's finished. And now it has become a useful item after it was a useless intestine. How smart!"[2] MJL & KM

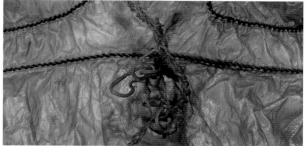
Detail of stitching

Francis Usugan holding dried seal gut, Toksook Bay, 1980.

Outdoor portrait of Uliggaq (Ella Pavil), dressed in a seal-gut parka and standing next to a dipnet full of tomcod, on the Calista Native Corp. in Kwigillingok Alaska, USA.

[1] Cenami Up'nerkam Nallini, "On the Coast During Spring," in *Yuungnaqpiallerput/ The Way We Genuinely Live: Masterworks of Yup'ik Science and Survival*, Ann Fienup-Riordan et al. (Seattle: University of Washington Press, 2007), 155.

[2] Ibid., 152.

Mark V Pressure Suit (Developmental)
1968

Manufactured by B. F. Goodrich Co. (USA)
Nylon, rubber/neoprene, brass, aluminum,
neoprene-coated nylon, steel, PVC,
cotton-canvas, leather
160 x 76.2 x 26.7 cm (63 x 30 x 10½ in.)
Smithsonian National Air and Space Museum
Washington, DC, Transferred from NASA
1980-0041-000

Mark V: Modified Shoulder

Mark IV flexibility demonstration, B.F. Goodrich, 1960s

THIS OLIVE GREEN GARMENT is a demonstration model of B. F. Goodrich's (BFG) Mark V pressure suit. The suit's right arm, with a large convoluted shoulder and elbow hinges, shows particular design developments and features that were being tested at the time. The torso has a diagonal zipper for flexibilty in the torso and hips, two pressure gauges, and one opening; there is a pressure gauge on the suit's left arm and another on its left leg.

BFG originally designed the Mark V spacesuit for the Apollo Program of the early 1960s. The oversize shoulder joint provided greater mobility than previous models, but its size would not allow all three Apollo astronauts to sit side by side in a spacecraft the width of a small car's front seat. Although it was not used for the mission, the suit provides a window into one company's history and the way in which specialists talk about technologies and adapt them.

What at first glance looks like a Frankenstein contraption reflects one corporation's efforts to translate its aviation successes to the space age. The Mercury spacesuits that BFG also built for NASA were modified versions of the Mark IV pressure suits that US Navy pilots wore in the 1950s. BFG had won the Navy contract because of the company's long experience with making flight suits, dating back to its work with the American racing pilot, Wiley Post. During the 1930s, BFG and Post together created the first aviation pressure suit, which allowed Post to fly higher—and therefore faster—inside his unpressurized cockpit. At the time, pressure suits had to provide the pilot with a continuous supply of oxygen for the duration of his flight. In the age of pressurized cockpits, the flight suit became what pilots referred to as a "get-me-down" suit: its life-preserving features would only be needed if the aircraft systems failed or the pilot ejected.

The Mercury spacesuits operated like aircraft pressure suits. They were not designed to function in a vacuum (zero and microgravity), but only as a backup for the spacecraft's primary systems. If they were to work outside the spacecraft, additional technological challenges would have to be overcome. In a vacuum, wearing a spacesuit could feel like being inside a highly pressurized balloon; the astronauts would find it impossible to bend their joints; their hands and arms would extend uselessly out to the sides, unable to flex. Engineers had to design restraint and joint systems that could withstand the internal pressures of the suit and still allow the astronaut to bend and flex in order to do meaningful work.

BFG submitted the suit to NASA in 1968 for an Apollo mission. The radical redesign of the right arm contrasts with the more traditional left arm, which has a rigid outer ball-bearing race in the shoulder; the ball bearings, which assured flexibility, are visible upon close inspection. The green cover layer is whipstitched into lacing cord that is attached to the bearing, allowing free movement and no snagging. The innovative right side displays a large, exposed device that both guides a restraint cable and serves to maintain the suit's internal oxygen pressure. A shock-absorption system allows the astronaut to flex by loading the springs with each movement.

The Mark V demonstration pressure suit, a 1960s artifact of conversations among engineers, astronauts, and spacecraft designers, remains a tool for continuing research on how to facilitate human movement inside a spacesuit in a vacuum. CL

Maskette
Late 19th–early 20th century

Mau people (Guinea, Côte d'Ivoire)
Wood, copper alloy, encrustation
29.1 x 8 x 6 cm (11⁷⁄₁₆ x 3⅛ x 2⅜ in.)
Gift of Lawrence Gussman
in memory of Dr. Albert Schweitzer
98-15-11, National Museum of African Art
Smithsonian Institution
Washington, DC

Facial Armor: *Ballistic Face Mask*

2013

Manufactured by International
Armor Corporation (USA)
Kevlar®
28.3 x 21.7 x 9.2 cm
(11⅛ x 8⁹⁄₁₆ x 3⅝ in.)
Museum purchase

WHETHER DESIGNED TO PROTECT against the elements, diseases, malevolent spirits, or other people, masks attest to some of the fundamentals of human existence: the perils and hostility of the surrounding world. Modern industrial masks, like this terrifying bullet-resistant headgear, are portraits of our technological society. They speak directly and powerfully of the dangers of the age. This shield extends the body's capability to engage with life-threatening situations and has one overriding purpose: to keep the wearer alive. Made of Kevlar®, it is part of the armor worn by law-enforcement officers during raids or when apprehending snipers. Its design is a visual expression of its purpose: with the individual totally effaced, its sinister appearance ups the ante of confrontation and intimidation. Concealing all but the eyes, it gives the wearer an immediate advantage, serving to unnerve and frighten the suspect into compliance. **CM**

Snow Goggles
Created before 1916
↓

Iñupiaq (Alaskan Iñupiat Eskimo)
Point Barrow, Arctic Slope Native
Corp. (Alaska, USA)
Carved mammoth–fossil ivory
2.7 x 11.2 x 2 cm (1 1/16 x 4 7/16 x 13/16 in.)
National Museum of the American Indian
Smithsonian Institution, Washington, DC
5/4349

SNOW GOGGLES, which reduce the amount of light entering the eyes, are the surest protection against snow blindness—an extremely debilitating condition caused by excessive ultraviolet radiation reflected off snow-covered landscapes. Conditions are especially hazardous in springtime, when the sun is brighter.

These hand-carved, finely contoured ivory goggles made by the northwest Alaskan Iñupiat is one of a number of styles, all of which fit comfortably over the eyes. Some examples from the region incorporate visors, and some are made of wood, but they all feature either slits, as here, or small holes. These piercings allowed the wearers to see without squinting, but they also enhanced the user's vision, like a pinhole camera. This was particularly useful when hunting seal or white foxes in the spring. Although occasionally referred to as "snow glasses," they had an advantage over goggles with glass lenses, because they never fogged up. MM

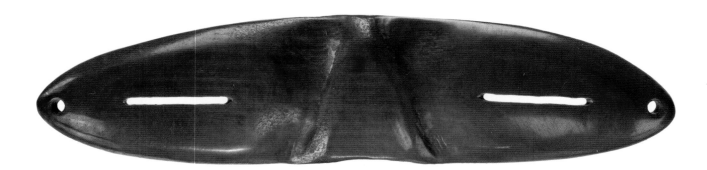

(opposite) *Anavik, a Kilusiktogmiut man, wearing bone snow goggles. Banks Peninsula, Bathurst Inlet, N.W.T. (Nunavut).*

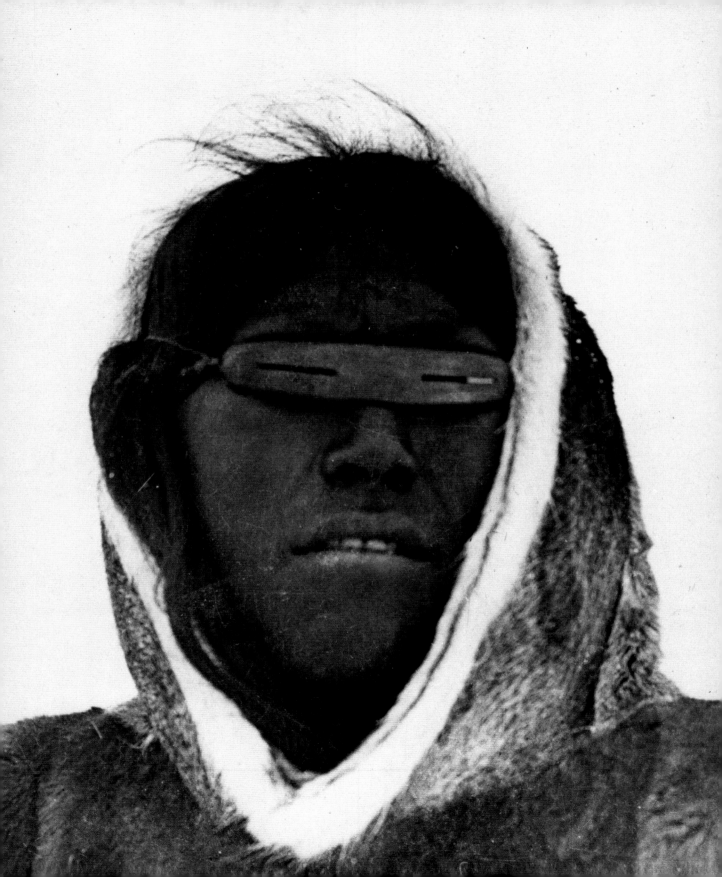

Running blade
Flex-Foot
Cheetah® Xtend

Before 2000, revised 2012

Designed by Van Phillips (American, b. 1954),
updated by Christophe Lecomte (French, b. 1979)
engineered by Hilary Pouchak (American, b. 1958)
Manufactured by Össur (Aliso Viejo, California, USA)
Molded plain-woven carbon fiber,
unidirectional carbon fiber epoxy resin
51 x 7 x 31.7 cm (20 ¹⁄₁₆ x 2¾ x 12½ in.)
Cooper Hewitt, Smithsonian Design Museum
New York, Gift of Össur

THE FLEX-FOOT CHEETAH® XTEND is a J-shaped, custom-built, high-performance prosthetic human foot designed primarily for sports activities. Van Phillips, later a medical engineer and the inventor of the prosthetic, lost his leg below the knee at the age of twenty-one and was dissatisfied with the prosthetics available to him. He began to investigate lightweight, flexible, and strong carbon-fiber composites, traditionally used in the aerospace industry, as the primary material. The form of the prosthetic was inspired by the rear leg of a cheetah, the fastest animal on Earth. Woven carbon fiber is molded into a shape that acts as a springboard. Unlike traditional prosthetics, the inclined midsection directs the ground contact toward the front two inches of the "toe." A C-shaped segment stores energy, compressing and springing back, propelling the runner forward. JG

April Holmes of the United States competes in the Women's 100-meter at the London 2012 Paralympic Games at Olympic Stadium.

Jarvik-7 Total Artificial Heart
1985

Designed by Robert Jarvik
(American, b. 1946)
Manufactured by Symbion, Inc.
(Salt Lake City, Utah, USA)
Polyurethane, Dacron®, polycarbonate, Silastic®,
Velcro®, titanium, pyrolytic–carbon
24.8 x 14 x 14.3 cm (9¾ x 5½ x 5⅝ in.)
Smithsonian Institution
National Museum of American History
Washington, DC, Cat. 1987.0474.01

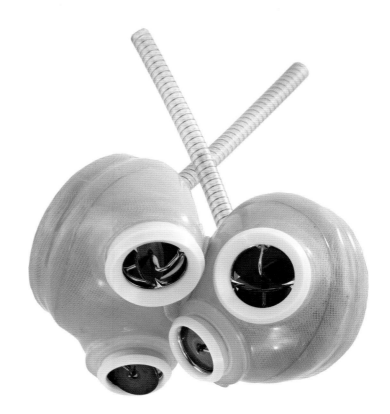

IN 1985, THIS JARVIK-7 Total Artificial Heart replaced the diseased organ of twenty-five-year-old Michael Drummond, who lived with the pump inside his chest for nine days before undergoing a heart transplant. The Jarvik-7 artificial heart consists of two ventricles made of Silastic®, a soft silicone-rubber plastic developed in 1948 by Dow Corning Corporation. The ventricles are held in place by an oval piece of Velcro® an innovation first manufactured commercially in the early 1960s. The use of Velcro to keep the two pieces connected permits further fine-tuning of the heart's placement within the chest, or, if required, the removal of a ventricle. Each ventricle has two titanium and pyrolytic-carbon Medtronic Hall® tilting-disk artificial heart valves, replacing the Bjork-Shiley valves originally employed in the first Jarvik-7 artificial hearts. The interior diaphragm is made of four thin layers of Biomer, a polyurethane that provides the pump with greater strength and durability. A pneumatically operated driver regulates the flow of blood into and out of the heart, as well as the number of heartbeats per minute.

Scientists, doctors, and engineers labored for more than twenty-five years to develop an artificial heart. The signifi-cant challenges included finding suitable blood-interface materials to prevent the formation of clots, propelling blood through the device without damage to the blood, and finding a power source that could ensure reliability.

At the University of Utah, Dr. Willem Kolff, inventor of the first workable artificial-kidney machine, directed a research pro-gram that successfully addressed many of these obstacles. A researcher at the university, Robert Jarvik, MD, made several key design changes to an earlier Utah heart model, applying a new material, a Biomer polyurethane blood surface, and alter-ing the device's shape from spherical to elliptical, allowing it to fit more easily into the chest cavity.

Initially, the Jarvik-7 was intended exclusively to be a per-manent replacement for heart-failure patients who were ineligible for a human-heart transplant. In 1982, Dr. William DeVries implanted the artificial heart into Barney Clark, a sixty-two-year-old dentist, who lived 112 days with it. The procedure of removing a patient's heart and replacing it with a mechanical pump received international attention. Today, more than 1,200 Jarvik-7-type artificial hearts have been implanted as an initial stage of the transplant process. JC

Ether Inhaler

ca. 1846

Designed by William T. G. Morton
(American, 1819–1868)
Glass, horn, metal, textile wrapping,
wooden base (not original to object)
27.9 x 31.8 x 30.5 cm (11 x 12½ x 12 in.)
Smithsonian Institution, National Museum
of American History, Washington, DC
Cat. M-09244

BY THE MID-NINETEENTH CENTURY, the Industrial Revolution was in full swing across New England, as machines gradually replaced hands in shoe making, textile manufacturing, and armories. Medicine, however, was slow and uneven in its transition to more complex tools. Tools are agents of social change. Inherently conservative fields, such as those that deal with life and death, move with caution. In the 1840s, surgeons still relied upon their own strength and agility for successful patient outcomes, and patients relied upon whiskey, laudanum, something to bite on, and a burly surgical assistant to restrain them. Surgery was a dramatic performance with equally dramatic consequences. Doctors cut into the body as a last resort, usually on a sunny day near large windows. Survival depended upon rapid execution: because of the extreme pain and the severity of the patient's reaction to it, only the stout of heart survived. Consequently, there was an urgent need for safe and effective sedation.

In the 1790s, a group of chemistry students, including Humphrey Davy, had used nitrous oxide, also known as "laughing gas," to produce insensitivity. But it was a Massachusetts dentist, Horace Wells, who introduced anesthesia into operations. In 1845, he saw a traveling showman demonstrate laughing gas and realized its potential for his dental work. Wells tried it on himself and pulled his own tooth. The following year, he convinced John Collins Warren, a surgeon at Massachusetts General Hospital, to let him demonstrate how to pull a tooth with the assistance of nitrous oxide. Unfortunately, Wells did not give his patient enough gas, and the patient loudly expressed his pain. Wells gave up dentistry after that. In 1848, his mind destroyed by repeated experiments and despondency, he took his own life.

As luck and the close-knit Boston medical community would have it, Wells's fellow dentist, William T. G. Morton, saw Wells's demonstration and continued experimenting with chemical anodynes. Ether and chloroform were new and promising sedatives at the time, despite their drawbacks. Ether smelled very pungent and foul. It was also highly flammable, making it potentially dangerous when additional lighting was needed. Physicians preferred chloroform over ether because it was more pleasant and less was required. Chloroform also allowed for quicker recovery, but its major disadvantage was that it could cause sudden death. Nonetheless, Morton persevered and succeeded in pulling teeth

painlessly from a patient under ether sedation. In 1846, he convinced Warren to use ether during the removal of a neck tumor. This time it was a success. The report "Insensibility during Surgical Operations Produced by Inhalation," in the *Boston Medical and Surgical Journal*, put anesthesia on the map.[3] Within a year, this "anaesthestic"—the word was coined by the physician Oliver Wendell Holmes—was employed in nearly every surgery where it was available. Some years earlier, in 1842, Crawford Long, a doctor in the small Georgia town of Jefferson, successfully delivered nitrous oxide during the removal of a tumor. Long has an equal claim to the first use of anesthesia and would have been famous for it, had he published his results.

Although this simple two-necked glass tool solved general technical questions related to management of the gases, the fumes tended to leak, and the volatile gases were hard to contain and deliver to a specific point. Later designs would limit administration of the gas to the patient and not to others in the room as well. But the problem of how to quiet a writhing human was solved—patients were limp and then awoke with no memory of what had transpired. To diminish vomiting from the foulness of ether, physicians mixed it with chloroform, which helped somewhat. The field of anesthesia eventually became a specialty of its own. In modern practice, physicians distinguish four types of drugs: tranquilizers, which cause drowsiness; narcotics, which control pain; general anesthesia, which induces loss of consciousness; and muscle relaxants, which release tension in the tissue.

The device for administering the anesthesia consisted of a glass vessel containing a sponge soaked with the evaporating chemical; the patient inhaled the resulting gas through a tube. In 1922, Morton's son donated this inhaler, used in the first operation in 1846.

The impact of anesthesia on patients' comfort was immediate; its effect on operations and related tools took a little longer. Surgical instruments became lighter and finer, because the surgeon no longer had to rush and forcefully cut. With less haste in the operating theater, outcomes improved greatly. KO

---

[3] Henry Jacob Bigelow, "Insensibility During Surgical Operations Produced by Inhalation," *Boston Medical and Surgical Journal* 35, no. 16 (1846): 309–17.

Smallpox Vaccination Needles

1970s

Manufactured by Wyeth Laboratories
(Pennsylvania, USA)
Metal
6.5 x 0.1 cm (2⁹⁄₁₆ x ¹⁄₁₆ in.)
Smithsonian Institution,
National Museum of American History,
Washington, DC
Cat. 1985.3109.100.1–3

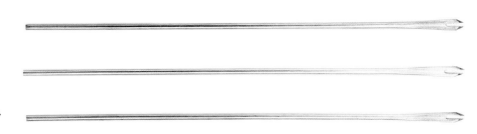

THE SIMPLICITY AND BEAUTY of these smallpox vaccination needles are the result of economics, accumulated knowledge, and observation of the human body. Before the bifurcated-needle design, vaccinators used many, remarkably similar devices for the task. And, long before anyone understood why the procedure was effective, workers performed a guileless sequence of actions for getting inoculate—the virus in the form of pus or scab or, in the twentieth century, droplets—into the percutaneous (outer) layers of the skin, just deep enough for the body to react. This basic task did not change over time, from the first attempts in ancient India, around 1,000 BCE, then in Europe in the eighteenth century, until the last person was vaccinated in 1979. Most tools for this activity were small and pointed, dull enough not to break the skin, yet sharp enough to penetrate easily and shallowly. The smallpox vaccine, unlike other vaccinations, did not have to be injected into the blood or muscle. Skin is an ideal location to provoke an immune reaction because it contains antigen cells from the immune system.

Inventors patented vaccination hand tools with variations on spring-action, lancet, and syringe designs. The drops of vaccine were always pressed into a small patch of skin, usually on the arm, with five to fifteen pushes. Vaccinators used disposable bone or glass points, resembling collar stays; the federal Food and Drug Administration outlawed bone and ivory points in the early 1900s. Following World War II, the armed forces, ever mindful of cost because of the large number of troops, used hydraulic-powered guns instead of needles to propel pressurized liquid into the skin.

The jet-injector, a boon to mass vaccination, was employed on hundreds of thousands of recruits. Since jet-injectors were acceptable to those who were averse to any kind of needle and because they penetrated intradermally, or between the layers of skin, physicians used this delivery system for a range of immunizations and drugs. The device, sometimes called the "peace gun" because it was painless, had two shortcomings: it had many parts, making it vulnerable to breakage; and the vaccinator had to be trained.

In 1967, the World Health Organization enlisted governments and health agencies around the world to join forces and eradicate smallpox from the entire human population. Efficiencies of scale were necessary to achieve that goal—the manufacturing of thousands of vaccination points, the training of workers worldwide, and the production and distribution of millions of doses. The points with which the vaccine was delivered were imprecise and wasteful, especially if the vaccinator did not press hard enough. This was true of the most common technique, which was to press two drops into the arm with the spatula end of a lancet. Nor was the popular, high-technology jet-injector a good match for the effort.

Introduced in 1968, the bifurcated needle was a small innovation that dramatically assisted the global eradication effort. The simple tine design was the brainchild of a microbiologist, Benjamin Rubin, of Wyeth Laboratories, in collaboration with an engineer, Gus Chakros, of the Reading Textile Machine Company. It occurred to Rubin that a sewing-machine needle might be adapted for vaccination.

The two men worked out how to grind the needle into a double-pronged fork shape. As luck would have it, capillary action held liquid within the tiny split in an amount sufficient for successive jabs and effective inoculation.

The bifurcated needle decreased the waste of inoculate by as much as 50 percent. It provided accurate, consistent dosage and puncture efficiency and met technical standards for delivery. Vaccinators did not require extensive training, nor were complicated field techniques necessary to measure and deliver the vaccine—the tines of the slim steel needles held the exact dose in drop form. Batch-cleaned and sterilized, the needles could be used over and over again. The design of the bifurcated "Pronged Vaccinating and Testing Needle" (US Patent 3,194,237) remained remarkably close to the early bone points and their purpose, despite the hundreds of years of intervening history. **KO**

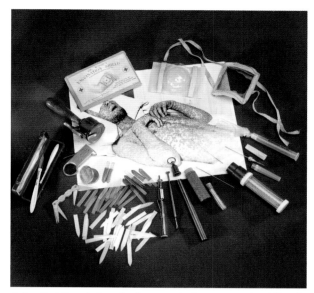

Before the bifurcated needle, these vaccinators were used to deliver the smallpox vaccine.

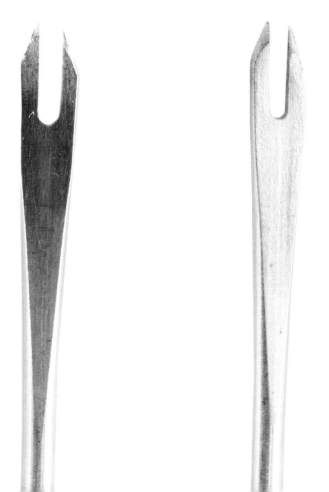

Penicillin
Culture Vessel

1940–41

↓

Designed by Norman G. Heatley
(British, 1911–2004)
Manufactured by James
MacIntyre & Company (UK)
Ceramic, slip cast
(glazed interior, unglazed exterior)
Overall: 9 x 23.2 x 34.5 cm (3½ x 9 x 13½ in.)
Smithsonian Institution, National Museum
of American History, Washington, DC
Cat. M-06669

Stacked vessels at the Sir William Dunn School of Pathology (University of Oxford Medical Sciences) growing the mold from which penicillin was extracted, early 1940s.

IN 1928, A SCOTTISH BACTERIOLOGIST, Alexander Fleming, discovered the bacteria-killing properties of a mold growing on one of his *Staphylococcus* cultures. Fleming published his discovery in 1929, naming the "mold juice" penicillin after the *Penicillium* mold that produced it. In the late 1930s, Howard Florey, Ernst Chain, Norman Heatley, and their colleagues at the Sir William Dunn School of Pathology at the University of Oxford isolated, refined, and purified penicillin for use as an effective antibiotic.

One of the challenges faced by the Oxford team was to produce enough penicillin to allow testing on humans. The mold grew only on the surface of a nutrient broth, and the broth yielded a minuscule amount of penicillin. In 1940, Heatley designed a shallow, rectangular culture vessel for optimal growth and efficient harvesting. His design was inspired by the hospital bedpans then used for culturing.

Although transparent glass was the preferred material, with the country at war, British manufacturers could not provide such vessels. Fortunately, a Staffordshire pottery, James MacIntyre & Company, produced a slip-cast ceramic model quickly and inexpensively. The flat-sided containers could be efficiently stacked—upright for sterilization and horizontally during incubation; the unglazed exterior prevented slippage during handling and thus further reduced costs. Production began in late December with 174 of the vessels and, by February 1941, the Oxford team had enough penicillin to test the drug on humans. This was one of the first drugs to successfully treat bacterial infections, including syphilis and wound infections. It saved thousands of lives during World War II and is still widely used today. JG & DW

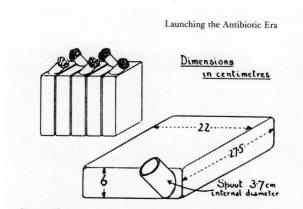

Launching the Antibiotic Era

Dimensions in centimetres

22

27.5

6

Spout 3.7 cm internal diameter

Figure 7. The ceramic culture vessels specially made by James Macintyre & Co. Ltd., Burslem.

Diagram of a culture vessel shown flat and stacking vertically.

DETECT

Ultrasound Machine: *Vscan*™

2012

↓

Designed and manufactured
by GE Healthcare
(Little Chalfont, Buckinghamshire, UK)
Internal: ultrasound transmitters and receivers,
signal processor, computer-on-chip
External: magnesium and plastic covers
Device unit: 13.5 x 7.3 x 2.8 cm
(5⁵⁄₁₆ x 2⁷⁄₈ x 1⅛ in.)
Probe: 12 x 3.3 x 2.6 cm (4¾ x ¹⁵⁄₁₆ x 1 in.)
Courtesy of GE Healthcare

IMMEDIACY IS THE KEY characteristic of today's mobile technology. This ability to obtain and analyze information instantaneously can also have life-altering repercussions. The Vscan™, a pocket-size ultrasound device slightly larger than a smartphone, is a diagnostic tool that can take a quick look inside the human body. The Vscan™ ultrasound technology allows a clinician to directly capture an image and interpret it at the patient's bedside. The clamshell device automatically goes into scanning mode when opened. The clinician glides the probe over the surface of the patient's skin. The probe's circuitry sends sound waves that are converted into images of organs or real-time blood flow, which are displayed on the handheld screen. Images can be transferred to a computer and emailed remotely.

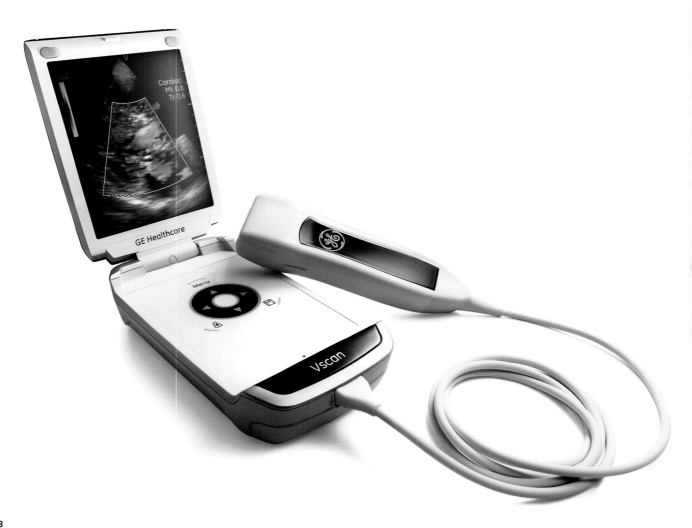

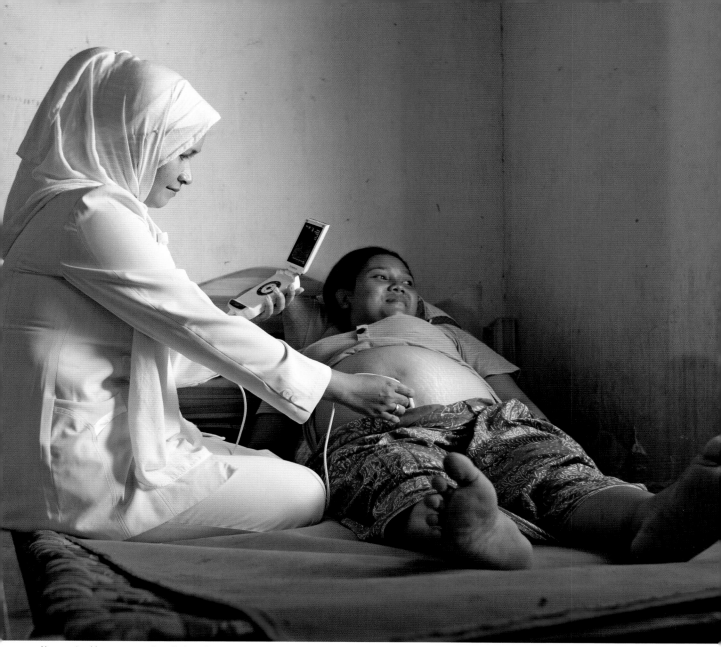

Nurse using Vscan™ on patient, Indonesia

This innovative device can be used worldwide in many clinical settings and has the potential to impact the way health care is delivered. For example, due to its portability and ease of use, clinicians in rural and underserved areas of the world can potentially identify and triage high-risk patients, evaluate pregnancy-related issues, and determine the next step in the care process. The impact of more information and time-saving diagnoses using mobile technology like Vscan™ could ultimately translate into reduced cost of care, increased access to health care, and increased quality of care. MM

Gene-RADAR®
2005

Invented by Dr. Anita Goel
(American, b. 1973)
Designed by Nanobiosym:
Team leader: Dr. Anita Goel
Team members: Dan Triggs, Lisa Goel
(Cambridge, Massachusetts, USA)
Plastic, nanochips, wireless data
transmission, integration
microelectronic circuits
3.8 x 27.9 x 20.3 cm (1½ x 11 x 8 in.)
Courtesy of Nanobiosym

THE "LAB-ON-A-CHIP" is a worldwide phenomenon in health care. It is driving advances in technology so that new forms of chemical, optical, biological, and genomic sensing and analysis can be available anytime, anywhere. With an assortment of handheld devices and specialized software, companies make it possible for individuals to efficiently and inexpensively access information about their physical condition and improve their health and well-being.

The grand-prize winner of the X PRIZE Foundation's 2013 Nokia Sensing XCHALLENGE competition, established to accelerate the development of this technology, was Nanobiosym's Gene-RADAR®. The user places a drop of blood or saliva on a nanochip and inserts it into the device. Gene-RADAR® can detect the presence and even quantify the DNA/RNA biomarker (or fingerprint) of the disease in real time. HIV, malaria, and tuberculosis are just some of the global health threats that it can diagnose.

Gene-RADAR® requires neither constant electricity nor running water and can be operated with minimal training by health-care providers and consumers. By decentralizing the infrastructure needed to diagnose and manage disease, devices such as Gene-RADAR® help to make health-care access available on a global scale. MM

MoboSens: *Smartphone Liquid Sensor* (Prototype)

2011

Designed by Logan Liu (American, b. 1978)
Manufactured by MoboSense LLC (Illinois, USA)
Smartphone plug-in electrochemical
sensor, microfluidic chip, microelectronic
integrated circuits
2 × 5 × 3 cm (¾ x 2 x 1⅛ in.)
Courtesy of the University of Illinois
at Urbana-Champaign

THE MOBOSENS IS A SENSOR that allows anyone with a smartphone to detect contaminated water and analyze biofluids. The sensor plugs into a cell phone through the audio jack; the phone app controls the sensor and shows the nature and precise amounts of contaminants in a single drop of water on the sensor—nitrate, arsenic, chromium, and pathogenic bacteria, among others. An on-line map permits the results to be communicated in real time, so users can monitor and share local environmental data.

Representing another innovative solution from the X PRIZE Foundation's 2013 Nokia Sensing XCHALLENGE, the MoboSens can also identify contaminants or illnesses in the user's body by analyzing blood, urine, and saliva. By combining technologies—mobile devices, social media, sensors, and geographical information systems—the MoboSens delivers an affordable product that could revolutionize digital health care. MM

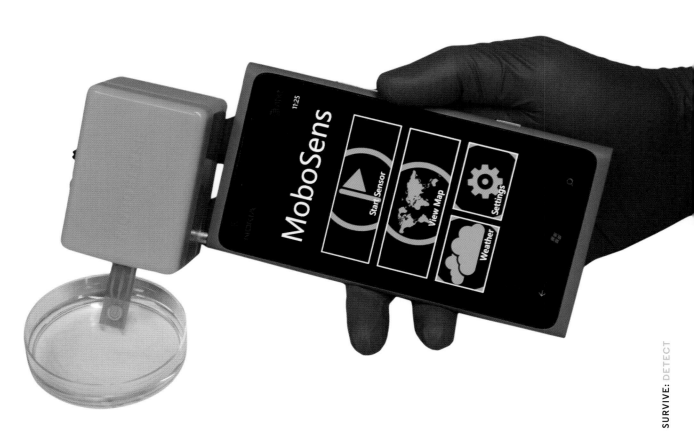

Diagnostic Health-care Device: *Kernel of Life* (Prototype)

October 2013

Designed by Yves Béhar (Swiss, b. 1967),
Noah Murphy-Reinertz (American, b. 1978)
and Arthur Kenzo (French, b. 1985)
Manufactured by fuseproject (USA)
Computer-machined ABS plastic,
leather, aluminum, paint
5.4 x 5.4 x 0.9 cm
(2⅛ x 2⅛ x ⅜ in.)
Courtesy of Gates Foundation
and *WIRED* magazine

IN THE DEVELOPING WORLD, the nearest doctor can be days away, making the diagnosis and treatment of chronic illnesses like malaria complicated. One possible solution to this challenge is the Kernel of Life, a medical "amulet" that tests blood, saliva, urine, and breath, and transmits the results by Bluetooth to a mobile app, allowing patients to be monitored continuously and remotely via the cloud.

The superslim, 5 cm (2 in.) disk slides open to reveal a microperforated pad divided into a rainbow of quadrants: red for blood, blue for saliva, yellow for urine, and green for breath. The pad separates the biofluids, parses them, and then transmits the data. The app can work with a range of smartphones and standard handsets.

A major problem for designers has been how to transform biological material, which has traditionally relied on more complex paper-based testing, into data. With the Kernel, digital analysis simplifies the process and embeds it in a reusable device. The Kernel has a self-sterilizing mechanism that activates when it is closed; the pad only needs to be replaced periodically; there are no moving parts; and, the device has to be recharged only every two weeks. Most importantly, its users can monitor themselves and also receive reminders about medication and treatment. With the need to reduce health-care costs while expanding health coverage to underserved populations around the world, innovative technology such as the Kernel can begin to close the gap, making medical care cost-effective through good design. MM

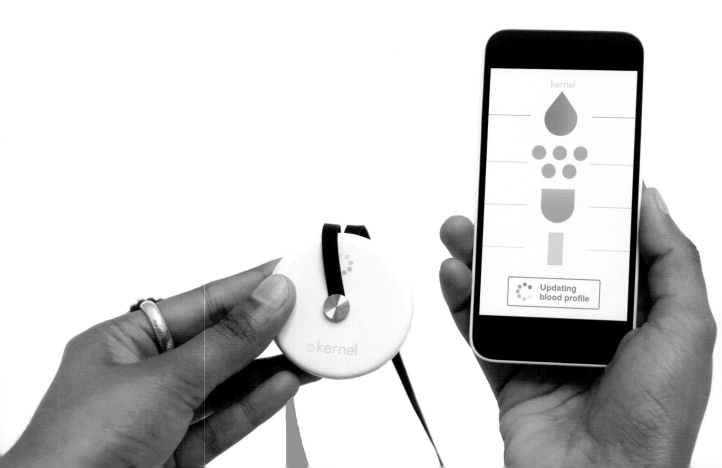

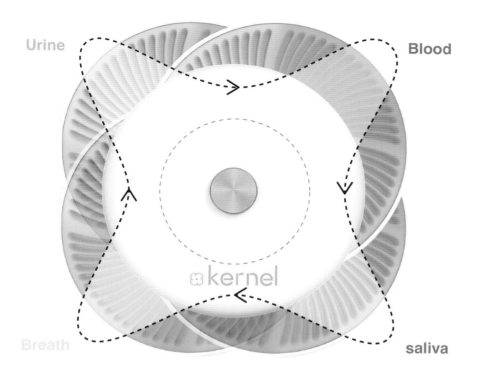

Urine

Blood

Breath

saliva

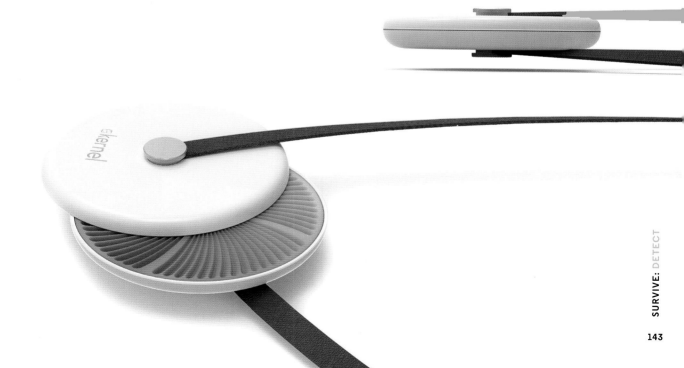

WHERE AM I? is a question we ask ourselves when ascending from the subway to a strange neighborhood or driving on unfamiliar roads at night. Sometimes this question is answered on a map by the bold red words YOU ARE HERE or by the pulsing blue dot on our smartphone. Whatever the format, good wayfinding results from observing the world around us and understanding how we relate to it.

To determine latitude, a fifteenth-century mariner would hold up an astrolabe to measure the Sun or a star's angle above the horizon then consult an astronomical table. Starting in the mid-eighteenth century, navigators used a sextant to determine their position at sea by measuring the lunar angle between the moon and the Sun or a star. Both these instruments allowed for real-time calculations, as does our current Global Positioning System (GPS) or, in the next generation of navigational systems, the Time and Inertial Measurement Unit (T-IMU), which can measure position even if GPS is unavailable.

Maps and charts visualize the data obtained from these instruments or from the accumulation of geographical knowledge over generations. A stick navigation chart from the Marshall Islands, for instance, maps ocean swells and currents as well as the relative distances between islands. These carefully constructed devices, memorized by sailors before an ocean voyage, incorporated the same kind of information and visual language of straight and curved lines found in World War II escape maps, which illustrated ocean currents and prevailing winds to assist downed airmen in enemy territory.

Driven by scientific inquiry and the increased need for accuracy, measuring tools have proliferated and become more standardized and precise. The invention of the clock permitted more accurate navigation when coupled with angle-finding instruments such as the sextant. Although an abacus and a calculator may be equal in accuracy, the calculator is more universal. Both answer the question HOW MUCH?, and the tactility of the material and the articulation of the beads and buttons make them equally pleasing to hold and to use.

Today, so much data is available to quantify and analyze, that designers, like mapmakers, must distill this information into comprehensible and accessible formats. Planetary, a software application, enables the user to quantify a music collection as images of celestial bodies. Similarly, a 3D laser scanner is a high-definition surveying tool that maps and visualizes sites and surfaces in such rich detail that we are able to replicate a building's interior to within a 0.635 cm (¼ in.).

With such diverse cultures, materials, and technologies featured in the measuring tools on the following pages, it is both reassuring and profound that they all can lead us to our destination or answer.

MEASURE

(opposite) *Diagram, Computer-generated print of a Microsized Timing and Inertial Measurement Unit (T-IMU), 2014, MicroSystems Laboratory of the University of California, Irvine.*

Microsized Timing and Inertial Measurement Unit (T-IMU)

April 20, 2014

→

Designed by students at the UC Irvine
MicroSystems Laboratory
Made by UC Irvine MicroSystems Laboratory
(Irvine, California, USA)
Single-crystal silicon, polyimide, gold, copper
Micro-Electro-Mechanical Systems (MEMS)
Lithography-based microfabrication utilizing Deep
Reactive Ion Etching (DRIE), wet chemical etching,
Low-Pressure Chemical Vapor Deposition (LPCVD),
metal electroplating
Folded T-IMU pyramid: 5.4 x 4.5 x 4.06 mm
($\frac{7}{32}$ x $\frac{3}{16}$ x $\frac{5}{32}$ in.)
MicroSystems Laboratory of
the University of California, Irvine
with students and post-docs (2004–14)
The research is sponsored by the MicroSystems
Technology Office of the Defense Advanced
Research Projects Agency (DARPA)

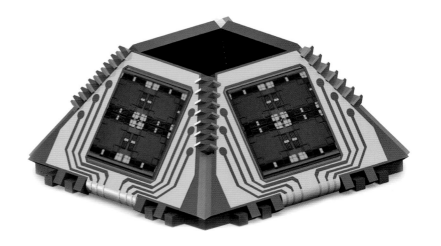

THE TIME AND INERTIAL MEASUREMENT UNIT (T-IMU) is a microscale navigation system that can measure position with high precision, even if GPS is not available. It provides a powerful example of how tools can be designed for a wide range of applications in a very small package. An experimental device to provide fully integrated positioning and navigation, the T-IMU was developed as part of a project of the Defense Advanced Research Projects Agency.

The T-IMU is an example of a Micro-Electro-Mechanical System (MEMS), which includes structures so small that a microscope is required to see them. The ability to manufacture MEMS makes it possible to embed new tools within portable devices. The "time" part of the T-IMU refers to its time reference. All navigation systems must include time measurement. This was true centuries ago, when mariners used sextants and chronometers to determine position. It's still true today, with systems such as GPS, which works by utilizing precise atomic clocks on orbiting satellites and measuring the arrival times of signals moving at the speed of light. GPS time must be exact to billionths of a second for global navigation systems to operate correctly.

In the T-IMU, time measurements provide references for the inertial sensors and also act as backup if GPS is temporarily unavailable. The accuracy of the T-IMU's time reference over short periods is on a par with that of some atomic clocks: it will not drift more than one billionth of a second over a couple minutes, but its stability decreases over longer periods. Therefore, the T-IMU cannot completely replace time distributed from GPS or atomic frequency standards, but it can be used briefly when it is out of range of those data sources.

The "inertial" part of the T-IMU refers to sensors, such as gyroscopes and accelerometers, that detect movement. Gyroscopes in the T-IMU have vibrating masses that react when the T-IMU is rotated or moved. Accelerometers detect movement by means of a microscopic weight that shifts slightly every time the unit moves.

Inertial navigation systems have long been used on aircraft and ships. Civil aircraft employ inertial navigation to cross continents and oceans. Navigation systems developed for naval surface vessels and submarines included equipment to detect movements and record their latitude and longitude.

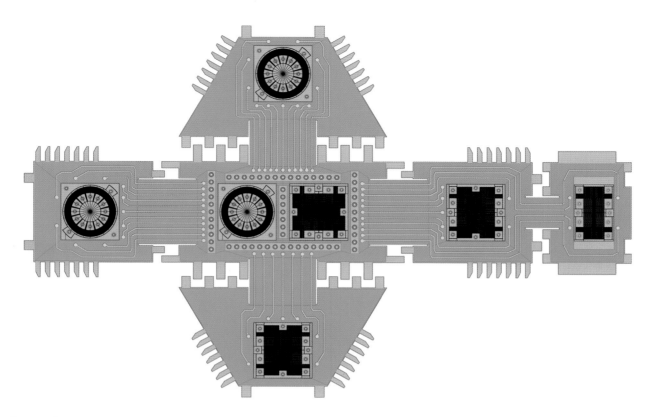

Diagram, Computer-generated print of a Microsized T-IMU (detail), 2014, MicroSystems Laboratory of the University of California, Irvine

The navigation equipment for a large ship often occupied an entire room, in contrast to the microscopic size of the T-IMU.

For inertial navigation to work, rotation in roll, pitch, and yaw must be measured, along with the linear movement in three dimensions. A fully integrated positioning and navigation system must therefore include at least three gyroscopes to detect rotation and at least three accelerometers to detect linear motion.

Three versions of the T-IMU have been designed at different sizes. The smaller ones can be placed within minuscule devices, but larger units can measure movement with greater sensitivity. A group of T-IMUs can be produced on a single silicon wafer. Each unit is then folded into its final configuration. The T-IMU's pyramidal shape was designed to provide structural integrity and to hold sensors in multiple orientations to detect motion in different directions. Each face of the T-IMU holds a gyroscope or accelerometer sensor. An additional sensor keeps track of time. The T-IMU's time and movement sensors were designed to be integrated on a single chip, making it smaller and more resistant to vibra-

tions and thermal changes. Some types of atomic clocks are becoming small enough to fit into mobile devices, but the T-IMU consumes much less power than these "chip-scale" atomic-frequency timepieces.

Developed to advance the technology of positioning and navigation for aircraft and missiles, among other platforms, the T-IMU also shows how future tools could become integrated into handheld devices. Today's mobile phones and gaming consoles include three-axis gyroscopes and accelerometers for measuring movement. The T-IMU's gyro and accelerometer package is more than three hundred thousand times more sensitive and stable than similar components in common mobile phones. Its timing reference, when integrated with the radio signals used by mobile phones and other digital devices, could potentially lead to the development of new timing and positioning applications. These new tools could provide navigation assistance when satellite systems are not available and meet needs for indoor navigation, such as delivering goods to specific store shelves and supporting emergency response. AJ

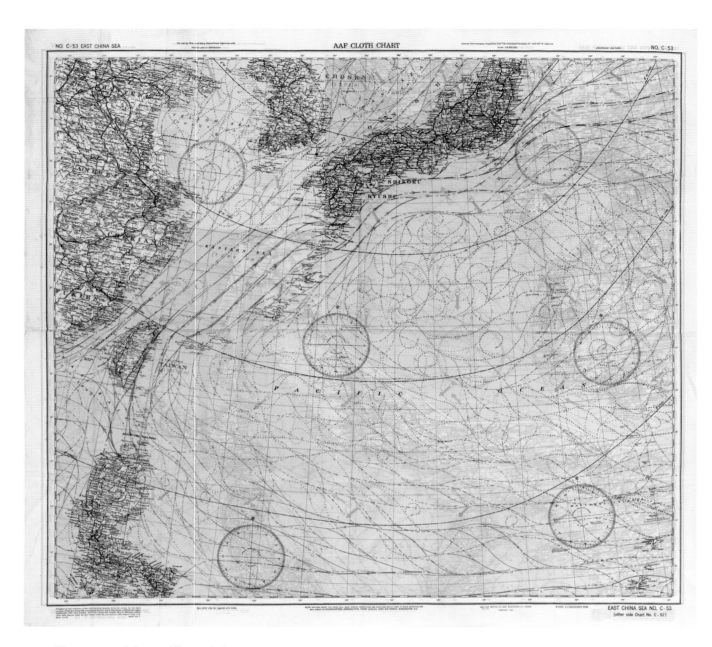

Escape Map (Double-sided): C-52 Japan and South China Seas and C-53 East China Sea

1945

↑ →

Manufactured by the Army Air Forces (USA)
Printed on plain-weave acetate rayon
79 x 86 cm (31⅛ x 33 ⅞ in.)
Cooper Hewitt, Smithsonian Design Museum
New York, Gift of Richard N. Fried, 1992-140-1

TOOLS

DURING WORLD WAR II, air power was a critical to military strategy. To assist airmen shot down behind enemy lines in avoiding capture, they were provided with cloth "Escape and Evasion" maps. In the Pacific theater, crews flying over vast bodies of open water were also provided with similar maps. Known as "drift" maps, they illustrated known ocean currents and prevailing winds to assist in navigation if airmen found themselves isolated in a life raft.

These cloth maps were initially made of silk, but obtaining the textile became difficult because the major supply sources in Asia were under the control of the Japanese. For a suitable substitute, the American military turned to DuPont and their synthetic-fiber fabric, rayon. The cloth maps had many advantages over paper maps. They were easily hidden inside the lining of flight clothing, could endure harsh weather and combat conditions, would not disintegrate in water, and could be opened and closed quietly. However, applying traditional paper-printing techniques to cloth posed certain problems, such as ink smearing during printing and running when exposed to water. The Army Map Service turned to the board-game industry for assistance. Companies such as

Milton Bradley typically printed game boards on linen, which was then mounted to a cardboard backing. These printing techniques were highly transferable to military needs. By the end of the war, more than 3.5 million maps were printed by game companies, textile firms, and the Government Printing Office under contract for the United States military.

This map, at a scale of 1:4,000,000, was printed for the Army Map Service in February 1945. Examples like this one would have been issued to both Army Air Forces and navy air crewmen. On the obverse is map C-53 showing the East China Sea; on the reverse, map C-52 depicts Japan and the South China Seas. Characteristic of a Pacific region map, the predominant features are the wind- and water-current lines. The green lines represent the direction of currents from May through September, the red lines, from November through March. During the transition months of October and April, the tides and currents fluctuate and are not possible to determine. The numerous compass roses accommodate the derivation of magnetic north resulting from an individual's geographic location. AS

Escape map worn as a scarf by an Australian Spitfire pilot during World War II

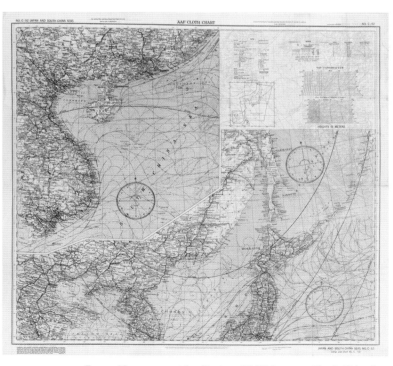

Escape Map, reverse side with view of C-52 Japan and South China Seas

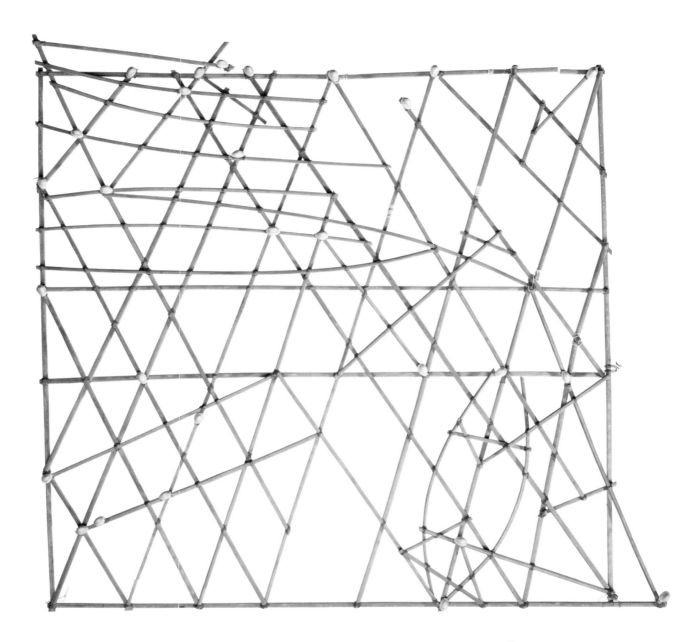

Stick Navigation Chart
Before 1950

↑

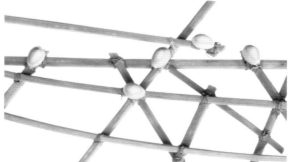

Marshall Islands
Carved wooden sticks, cowrie shells, twine lashing
99.4 x 101.9 x 4.4 cm (39⅛ x 40⅛ x 1¾ in.)
Department of Anthropology
National Museum of Natural History
Smithsonian Institution
Washington, DC, E432083

THE ORGANIZATION OF A SPACE is based on the knowledge of what will take place in that conceptualization or space—sailing, presentations, feasts, worship, dancing. Most important to Micronesians is how the sea, land, and sky intersect. A Micronesian asked about the layout of a space will invariably begin with a discussion of navigation and canoes and how the organization of society and views of the universe were, and are, influenced by relationships with the sea. Survival depended on a familiarity of and rapport with the sea. This in turn required knowledge about how to get across the sea, how to access it for food, and what to do when devastated by it, whether by tidal waves, hurricanes, or other storms.

Micronesians made some of the finest oceangoing vessels in the world: canoes that could sail with either end forward, generally formed of a single asymmetric hull planked by sewing together pieces of wood with coconut-fiber twine; an outrigger; and triangular sails. Navigating by the apparent motion of the Sun and stars, wind direction, ocean currents, wave patterns on the surface of the sea, and the flight of birds, these mariners closely guarded family lore, with this crucial information usually passed from an expert sailing master to a chosen apprentice. Although canoes were built and sailed by men, women usually braided the mat sails.

East of the Caroline Islands, in two parallel north–south island chains known as Radak and Ralik, is the independent nation of the Marshall Islands, famous for its canoes and navigation stick charts. Marshall Islands canoes, with their platforms and thatched houses, were sailed by navigators with secret knowledge, some of which could be visualized in stick charts. By acute observation of the sea, the Marshallese accumulated accurate familiarity with ocean swells: what happens to them as they approach and pass by land, and the characteristics of the interaction of two or more swell patterns in the presence of an island. They also studied reflection, refraction, the shadow phenomenon, and other ancillary wave actions. From this complex information, the Marshallese developed a system of piloting and navigation that they depicted in stick charts in two ways, as models and as piloting instructions.

The data that a stick chart records are indicated by the arrangement of the sticks relative to one another and by the forms given to them by bending and crossing. Curved strips indicate the altered direction taken by ocean swells when deflected by the presence of an island; the strips' intersections are nodes representing where the swells meet and tend to produce a confused sea, which is regarded as a valuable indication of the whereabouts of the voyager. Currents in the neighborhood of islands are sometimes shown by short straight strips, whereas long strips may indicate the direction in which certain islands are to be found.

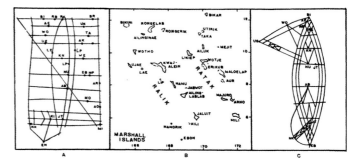

A and C illustrate two different types of Marshall Island stick charts. They relate to the actual map of the Marshall Islands in the center. Island names are indicated on the stick charts with the first and last letter. They show that the Marshallese cartographer-navigator illustrates only the positions and orientations of islands based on observable wave action. Actual distance and sailing time were secondary concerns.

The scientific models, or *mattang*, are constructions that illustrate the concept of swell movements and interactions in the vicinity of small islands. *Mattang* are for instructional use. They represent a simple problem, such as that of a single island, at the center of a chart, with curved swell fronts arranged in four quadrants. The construction is generally symmetrical in order to present a simple set of conditions. The piloting instructions, or *meddo*, illustrate the layout of the islands of the Marshall group, or an area of the Marshalls, and the distinct characteristics of their waves. *Meddo* are similar to maps: shells or coral pieces tied to sticks represent islands and possible navigation courses between them. Their position relative to one another is considerably accurate, but the distances among islands are approximate. The charts are not made to scale: they are mnemonic devices made for their specific owner and are usually unintelligible to others.

Neither the *mattang* nor the *meddo* was taken onboard a canoe, for the information existed primarily in the navigator's memory. The possession of detailed awareness of the behavior of ocean swells when they meet familiar islands or groups of islands make the islanders keepers of knowledge—and confident navigators. **AK**

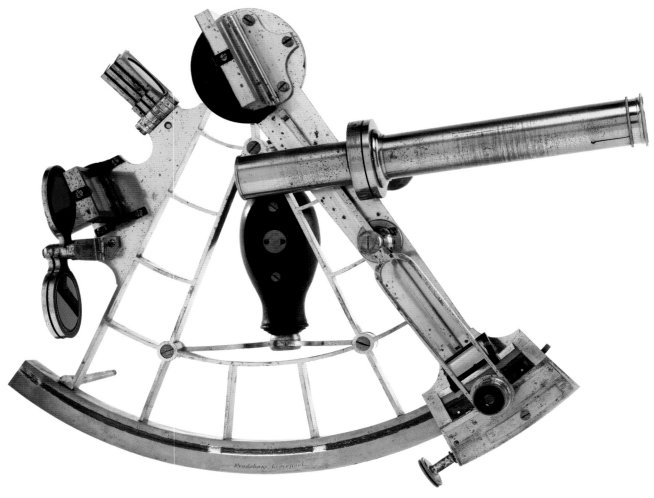

Sextant and Case

ca. 1865

Manufactured by Charles Frodsham & Company
(Liverpool, England)
Sextant: brass, silver, glass
Case: mahogany, brass, felt
Sextant: 27.1 x 31.7 x 10.7 cm (10¹¹⁄₁₆ x 12½ x 4³⁄₁₆ in.)
Case: 28.4 x 33 x 12 cm (11³⁄₁₆ x 13 x 4¾ in.)
Smithsonian Institution
National Museum of American History
Washington, DC, Cat. 1980.0318.03

THE SEXTANT IS a navigation instrument, invented in the mid-eighteenth century to help sailors determine their position at sea. It was designed specifically to determine longitude, the east–west component of position, although it could also be used to measure latitude, the north–south component.

Navigating at sea has always been a challenge, especially when ships venture out of sight of land. With no other points of reference, early seafarers had only their compass, the objects in the sky, and a rough measurement of their speed to enable them to find their way. Over time, instruments such as the backstaff, the cross-staff and the mariner's astrolabe were also developed. These allowed latitude to be measured at sea—an important development—but determining longitude at sea continued to be a problem.

In 1707, an entire British fleet of four large ships was wrecked when it ran aground in stormy weather off the coast of Cornwall. It was one of the worst naval disasters in British history, and more than 1,400 sailors lost their lives. An inquiry later determined that the cause of the disaster was the navigators' inability to calculate their position, a finding that finally brought the problem to widespread public attention.

Among the many proposed solutions for determining longitude, the one that proved workable was the measurement of lunar distances. In this method, the angle between the moon and the Sun, or a selected star, was measured and checked against a printed table of lunar "distances" and the times at which they would be visible at a given location. By comparing this time with the local time of the ship, a navigator could make a precise calculation of its position.

The principal challenge posed by the lunar-distance method was taking the actual measurement. This was the problem that the sextant was invented to solve. The sextant employs the technique of double reflection: by using two small mirrors, one of which is on a movable arm, it is possible to look at two objects at the same time. The observer moves the arm until the reflections of the two objects appear to touch; the angle between them is then determined by reading the position of the arm on a curved, graduated scale. The sextant, which appeared in the early 1730s, was the most complicated navigation instrument of its time, and the most expensive. It also required navigators to purchase a number of other tools, such as astronomical tables, tables of corrections,

Student learning how to determine latitude by using a sextant, 1942. Navigation classes were part of school programming during World War II.

and charts, and to learn to use them to make a complicated series of calculations and corrections. By the 1760s, the sextant's usefulness was well established and it remained the primary method of determining longitude at sea until the mid-nineteenth century.

The importance of this tool is evident in the details of its construction. Because of the many moving parts and the need to make the instrument as accurate as possible, sextants were almost always made of metal, with brass or bronze being preferred because of their resistance to corrosion. To employ a sextant, a navigator had to look at the moon and the Sun in all kinds of weather, so colored eyeshades were placed in front of both mirrors to maximize contrast and protect the user's vision. Also to assist the user, the movable arm was furnished with a clamping screw to lock it down once the two objects were brought into position. A small magnifier, which could be swung out of the way when not needed, was provided to help read the scale. Sextants were always sold in a curved and carefully fitted case, with designated places for all the accessories; the distinctive, irregular shape immediately identified the object within as a sextant, to discourage anyone from placing anything on top of it.

Although eventually supplanted by other navigational instruments and today by Global Positioning Systems (GPS), sextants are still carried on many ships, both as a backup for emergencies and as a symbol of the mariner's skill. **ST**

Book: *Astronomicum Caesareum* (The astronomy of the Caesars)

Facsimile 1969, ©1967

Originally published 1540

↓ →

Written by Peter Apian (German, 1495–1552)
Published by McGraw-Hill
(New York, New York, USA)
Leather-bound paper boards, paper, string
Open:45.8 x 63.9 x 14.2 cm
(18 ¹⁄₁₆ x 25 ¹⁄₁₆ x 5 ⁹⁄₁₆ in.)
Courtesy of Smithsonian Libraries
Washington, DC
Gift from the Margery Masinter Foundation
Endowment for Illustrated Books
f QB41 .A64 1540ab

ASTRONOMICUM CAESAREUM (The astronomy of the Caesars), created by the German printer, mathematician, and cartographer Peter Apian, is one of the most lavish books on astronomy of all time. This folio, printed over an eight-year period, contains detailed astrological and astronomical data and charts, including twenty-one movable disks called "volvelles." The volvelles, sewn one atop another, can be rotated to align such givens as planetary positions and eclipses on calendars. Apian's work was an important tool, employed to calculate future astrological/astronomical events. For example, the volvelle on the opposite page, adorned with a many-headed dragon, can be rotated to predict solar eclipses, while the volvelle below calculates the position of Jupiter in the night sky for a given latitude, time, and date. SVD

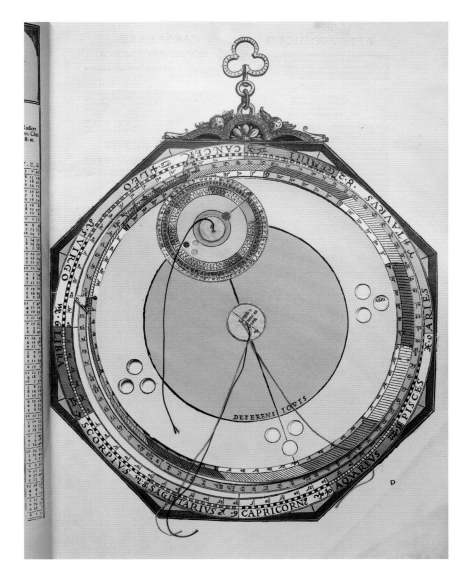

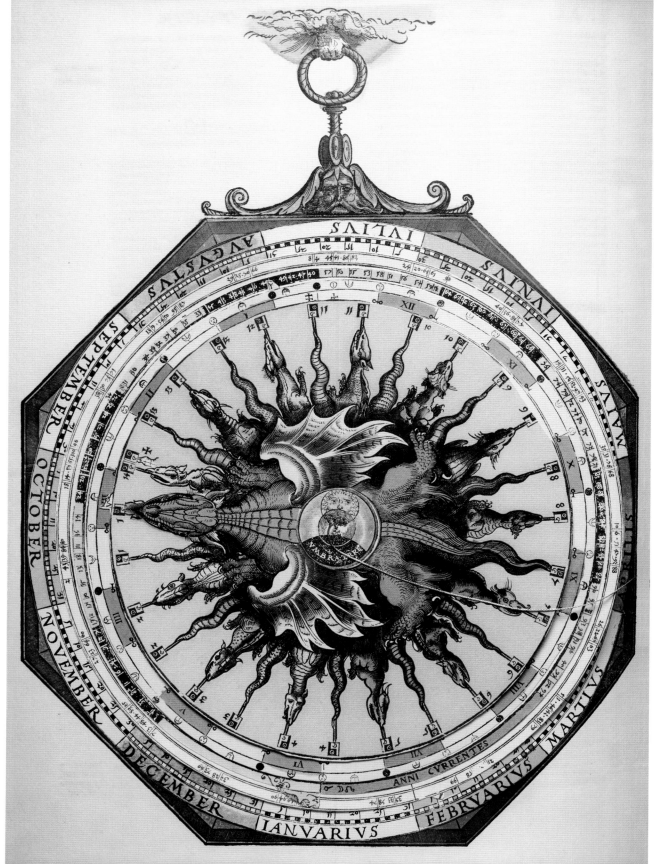

Mariner's Astrolabe
(Replica)

1963
Original 1602

Made by Laurits Christian Eichner
(American, b. Denmark, 1894–1967)
Bronze
22.2 x 17.1 x 6 cm (8¾ x 6¾ x 2⅜ in.)
Smithsonian Institution
National Museum of American History
Washington, DC, Cat. 323719

Using a mariner's astrolabe to measure the angle of the Sun or a star above the horizon

IN THE FIFTEENTH CENTURY, Europeans began to transform marine navigation from a mostly coastal enterprise to sailing on the open seas with the aid of astronomy. Portuguese seamen pioneered this new kind of celestial navigation and prepared the way for the great European voyages of exploration and trade. Simple tables for calculating a ship's position from the Sun and stars were published, and instrument makers devised new tools for observation to use on the rocking decks of oceangoing ships.

One of these devices was the mariner's astrolabe, a streamlined version of the astronomer's planispheric astrolabe, a calculating device originally introduced to Europe by Muslim scholars in the tenth century to display how the positions of many stars shifted with changes in time and latitude. The first documented use of a mariner's astrolabe was by Diogo d'Azambuja of Portugal on a voyage along the west coast of Africa in 1481. The Portuguese and Spanish dominated

the making of astrolabes, but examples attributed to Dutch, French, German, and English artisans also survive. Evidence from wrecks suggests that a single ship might carry more than one astrolabe, with the instruments complementing other celestial navigation aids such as quadrants and, later, cross-staffs.

In 1963, Laurits Christian Eichner made this replica of an original mariner's astrolabe. Eichner was a respected New Jersey maker and restorer of scientific instruments who crafted careful historical reproductions. The National Museum of American History (NMAH), then the National Museum of History and Technology, commissioned Eichner's copy of the astrolabe for study and display, and in 1975 received the original instrument as a donation.

When Eichner cast his copy, fewer than twenty authentic mariner's astrolabes were known worldwide. In the interven-

Engraving, Amerigo Vespucci finding the Southern Cross with a mariner's astrolabe, ca. 1591, Jan Collaert II

ing years, documentary evidence and examples recovered from shipwrecks have shown how common these instruments were, because they were crucial for finding latitude on the open seas from the end of the fifteenth into the eighteenth century.

The mariner's astrolabe evolved over time, and the NMAH's examples, both the original and the replica, have features that were standard in the early seventeenth century. This instrument consists of a very heavy bronze wheel attached to a pivoted suspension ring. An arm, the alidade, rotates over a scale of degrees stamped on the wheel's upper quadrants. The arm has two sighting vanes, each with a pinhole, that the navigator aligned with either the polestar or the Sun.

The navigator held the device at arm's length by its pivoted ring, rotated the alidade to sight a specific star or the Sun, and read on the scale the degrees of altitude indicated by the alidade. The scale could be numbered to measure from either the horizon or the zenith. The navigator then determined the ship's latitude from the measured angle and astronomical tables.

The NMAH's astrolabe and replica are marked with the date, 1602, and a degree scale on the two upper quadrants of the circle. The zenith scale and its diameter of 17.6 cm (7 in.) are typical of Portuguese instruments from the period, but the instrument's origin is unknown.[1] CS

[1] The NMAH's original mariner's astrolabe was reportedly dredged up from the bottom of Manila harbor around 1917. Although research has not linked the instrument to a particular ship or shipwreck, the Manila location associates the astrolabe with a crucial trade route. Founded in 1571, Manila quickly became the hub of direct and continuous global trade linking China, the Americas, and Spain; in the early seventeenth century, Portugal was a dependency of Spain. Spanish galleons made annual trips across the Pacific between Manila and Acapulco, Mexico, carrying mainly Chinese silks and ceramics and South American silver. The trade continued until Mexico's independence from Spain in 1815.

Portable
Equatorial Sundial
and Compass
1748

Made by Jacob Emanuel Laminit
(German, 1719–1760)
Augsburg, Germany
Gilt and engraved brass, cut and blued
steel, blown sheet glass
2 x 6.4 x 6 cm (¹³⁄₁₆ x 2½ x 2⅜ in.)
Cooper Hewitt, Smithsonian Design
Museum, New York, Gift of the Estate
of James Hazen Hyde, 1960-1-12

SUNDIALS, WHICH MEASURE TIME BY THE SUN'S ANGLE, are not usually portable, whereas compasses often are. The latter are for navigating; today their principal use is for sailing and hiking. This pocket-size combination instrument that tells time and direction is specifically part equatorial sundial, with its flat surface aligned with the celestial equator and a post called a gnomon perpendicular to the surface and directed to the North or South Celestial Pole. It is also a status symbol: the small size, complexity (a plumb bob below the dial levels it), and classically sourced decoration indicate that it was a prized personal accessory— as a pocket watch used to be, and a smartphone is today.

In Augsburg, Germany, a center of scientific learning, instrument making, and the metalsmithing arts, an elegant eighteenth-century gentleman might have pulled this sundial-compass from his waistcoat and unfolded it to show off its mechanism and refined engraving. The depictions of allegorical representations of the four continents at the corners, and a mermaid and Neptune engraved on the steel face, suggest a learned owner and virtuoso creator. The maker Jacob Emanuel Laminit, who became a master goldsmith in 1748, applied his skills to this brass, steel, and glass object at the height of the fashion for these accessories in Augsburg. SDC

Radio Compass Loop Antenna Housing
ca. 1940

USA
Rag-filled Bakelite, metal
67 x 23 x 35 cm
(26⅜ x 9¹⁄₁₆ x 13¾ in.)
Smithsonian Institution
National Museum of American
History, Washington, DC
Cat. 1977.0368.65

AT FIRST GLANCE, one might think this object belongs in a stadium. In actuality, it's a World War II radio-antenna housing. Found on almost all airplanes during that conflict, it was one of many projections that peppered the surface of aircraft. Not surprisingly referred to as a "football" by flight crews, it contained a loop antenna used for navigation. The early radio-direction-finder antennas of the 1920s and '30s consisted of wire coils over a circular form mounted on top of the airplane. However, as the speed of airplanes increased, so did the drag, or wind resistance. A streamlined antenna cover became a necessity.

That explains the shape of the antenna housing but not why it was made of Bakelite, the first totally synthetic plastic. Bakelite was created in the laboratory of Leo H. Baekeland, a Belgian organic chemist and entrepreneur who immigrated to the United States in 1889 to pursue a career in the chemical industry. In 1899, he sold an invention, Velox, a photographic paper that could be developed in artificial light, to George Eastman. Now independently wealthy, Baekeland moved his growing family to Snug Harbor, an estate overlooking the Hudson River in Yonkers, New York. There, he turned a barn into a laboratory. Baekeland was aware of work done by other chemists that combined phenol, a by-product of coal tar, and formaldehyde, derived from wood alcohol. The resulting hard, insoluble substance seemed to have no practical application. Baekeland thought that by refining the process he might obtain a usable product, a synthetic shellac.

Natural shellac is harvested from lac, which is secreted by an insect native to South Asia. It was a familiar component of varnishes and other finishes. Because it is easy to mold, it was also used for phonograph records and for electrical insulation and fixtures. It was a limited resource, and could not keep pace with increasing demand from the expanding electrical industry.

The radio loop antenna is located on the top of the plane toward the front. 1940s.

In 1907, Baekeland prepared a mixture of phenol and formaldehyde and drove the reaction under both heat and pressure. The product was a lump of resinous material that was both infusible and insoluble. The resin, when ground to a powder, could be molded into any shape. Once formed, the resin became hard and could not be melted and remolded—it was what we now call a thermosetting plastic. Its properties were nothing short of amazing. It was resistant to heat, cold, water, as well as most acids, and it was a superb electrical insulator. The brittleness of the resinous "Bakelite" could be offset by the addition of fillers such as fabric, wood flour, or asbestos.

Baekeland immediately realized the potential of this new material, particularly for the electrical industry. He worked with Richard Seabury, president of Boonton Molding Co., to develop applications for molded Bakelite products. Boonton was doing a brisk business with electrical companies molding parts from hard rubber, but Seabury saw the advantage of switching to Bakelite. Hard rubber, like shellac, deteriorates when subjected to heat, cold, or wet, clearly serious shortcomings for electrical insulators, switches, and other parts.

In 1910, Baekeland formed the General Bakelite Co. It was not long before investors saw the profits that could be made from this new material, and several companies started to produce their own version of Bakelite. Baekeland spent years in patent litigation and finally won against his two most serious competitors. The three companies merged in 1923 and became the Bakelite Corporation. By this time, the radio, telephone, and automobile industries had embraced this synthetic plastic, which also appeared as jewelry and in household goods.

Baekeland, a marketing genius, didn't overlook the nascent aviation industry. Bakelite was used in airplane parts as early as World War I and continued to be used through World War II. Until the invention of Bakelite, loop antennas were not housed and thus imparted substantial aerodynamic drag. Housing them in an aluminum fairing would have disrupted signal reception, so designers had to wait until a composite manufacturing technology—like Bakelite—became practical enough to support a structure that could withstand aerodynamic stresses.[2] This radio-antenna housing is molded from cloth-filled Bakelite. The addition of cloth to the Bakelite powder provides strength and increases its moldability. In addition to its thermal properties, Bakelite is also lightweight and transparent to radio waves, making it the perfect material for this purpose. AMS

[2] Roger Connor, email message to MM and author, April 17, 2014.

Box Clock
ca. 1816

Designed and made by Eli Terry
(American, 1772–1852) in Connecticut, USA
Wood case with painted dial on glass door,
lead weights, paper
53.3 x 35.6 x 8.9 cm (21 x 14 x 3½ in.)
Smithsonian Institution, National Museum
of American History, Washington, DC
Cat. 317044

THE MECHANICAL CLOCK was invented somewhere in Europe just before 1300, and for centuries it remained an uncommon machine for telling time and a costly symbol of a person's wealth and social standing. In 1700, the rich were still the most likely to own clocks and watches. By 1800, timepieces were becoming less expensive and more widely available to a growing American middle class that included artisans, shopkeepers, and professionals.

In the early nineteenth century, a handful of Connecticut inventors and entrepreneurs transformed how clocks were made in the United States. Recognizing a vast potential market for low-cost domestic clocks, Eli Terry and his associates, Seth Thomas and Silas Hoadley, applied water-powered machinery to clock making. One of the proving grounds of the industrial revolution in the United States, clock making changed from a craft to a factory process, in which machines mass-produced uniform, interchangeable parts. This manufacturing technique appeared in other industries about this time and became known as the "American system."

The process called for a whole new kind of clock. The first mass-produced clocks had movements of wood, instead of scarce and expensive brass. Although the earliest of these wooden clocks had long pendulums and fitted into the traditional tall cases, Terry devised a distinctly American clock small enough to set on a mantel or shelf.

This clock demonstrates Terry's determination to make his clocks as economical as possible. The case is a simple wooden box, while the glass door bears reverse-painted numbers that serve as a dial. Terry began to mass-produce his austere but serviceable shelf clock in 1816, and immediately proceeded to refine the design. The plain box case acquired a slender pillar on either side, scrollwork on top, and a set of graceful feet. A dial was added, and the lower portion of the glass door was decoratively reverse-painted.

In the wooden movement, Terry experimented with modifications of the escapement, revised the gear trains, and replaced the rack-and-snail striking mechanism with the more economical count wheel. The result of these efforts, patented in 1823, was a wooden, weight-driven, hour-striking, thirty-hour clock, which soon became widely known as the "Connecticut pillar-and-scroll clock."

With the design of his clock perfected, Terry set about organizing its manufacture. Production was underway in 1822. By 1825, Terry, in partnership with his brother Samuel and his sons Eli Jr. and Henry, was operating three factories, each turning out two to three thousand pillar-and-scroll clocks a year. Originally, Terry's clock cost fourteen dollars, but before long its price dropped to less than ten.

Terry's success spawned imitators eager to capture part of the market for lower-cost clocks. By 1830, western Connecticut was home to more than one hundred firms, large and small, making clocks with wooden movements. The output of the industry soon became too large to be absorbed by the local market. Scores of traveling salesmen were dispatched to the West and South. Sold largely to rural buyers by these itinerant merchants, the clocks played an early and significant role in transforming the rural North from overwhelmingly agricultural to a modern market society.

Wooden clocks from Connecticut were among the earliest consumer products in the United States. Regarding the Yankee clock peddlers, reported an English traveler in the 1840s, "in Kentucky, in Indiana, in Illinois, in Missouri, and here in every dell of Arkansas, and in cabins where there was not a chair to sit on, there was sure to be a Connecticut clock."[3]

The wooden-movement shelf clock enjoyed a brief but intense boom, abruptly curtailed by the national financial panic of 1837. The crisis hit the Connecticut wooden-clock makers so hard that they feared the entire industry would collapse. Chauncey Jerome, a successful manufacturer who had once produced cases for Eli Terry's clocks, devised a new process, patented by his brother Noble in 1839, for using stamped brass to make inexpensive movements. The Jeromes, their imitators, and their rivals were soon making hundreds of thousands of brass-movement clocks for a world market. CS

[3] George W. Featherstonhaugh, *Excursion Through the Slave States, from Washington on the Potomac* (New York: Harper & Brothers, 1844).

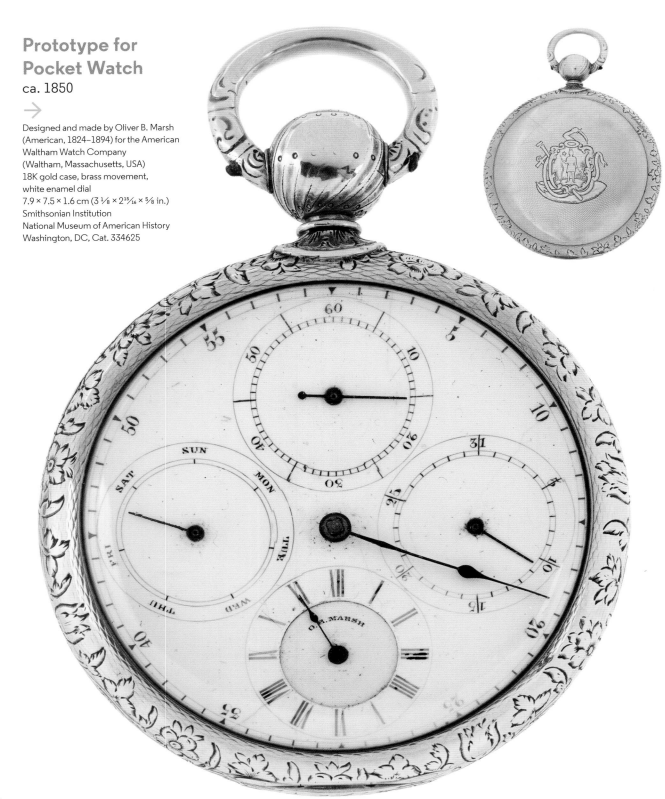

Prototype for Pocket Watch
ca. 1850

→

Designed and made by Oliver B. Marsh
(American, 1824–1894) for the American
Waltham Watch Company
(Waltham, Massachusetts, USA)
18K gold case, brass movement,
white enamel dial
7.9 × 7.5 × 1.6 cm (3 ⅛ × 2¹⁵⁄₁₆ × ⅝ in.)
Smithsonian Institution
National Museum of American History
Washington, DC, Cat. 334625

WATCHES HAVE ALWAYS BEEN more than tools to keep time. Over the centuries, they have served as fashion items, status symbols, and valued heirlooms with personal connections. They are also complex wearable technologies.

The appetite for watches in the United States in the early nineteenth century was huge: about $46 million worth were imported between 1825 and 1858, especially from England and Switzerland. To tap into this market, a few Americans attempted to produce watches domestically, but probably no more than two thousand such timepieces were made in the United States before the 1850s.

In that decade, watchmakers at a succession of companies that would become the American Waltham Watch Company of Waltham, Massachusetts, developed the world's first machine-made watches. The firm, launched in 1849, started life in a corner of the Howard & Davis clock factory in Roxbury, near Boston. The Waltham designers, in particular, Edward Howard and Aaron Dennison, completely reimagined the watch so that its movement could be assembled from interchangeable parts made on specialized machines invented for the purpose. The designers also conceived a highly organized, factory-based work system to speed production and cut costs. With help from a cadre of experienced mechanicians and funding from Howard's father-in-law, the Boston mirror maker Samuel Curtis, the enterprise got under way.

During a visit to the Springfield (Massachusetts) Armory, Dennison had observed techniques for the mass production of firearms with interchangeable parts. Taking arms making as their model, the new firm's founders adopted a tight organization, elevated the role of an expert machine shop, and eventually settled on a manufacturing system that relied on prototypes. Waltham designers made a model watch and a master set of gauges to fit it, and every watch part made thereafter was measured against the corresponding model part.

In its first decade, the firm's work was largely experimental. By late 1852, however, Howard and Dennison had samples to show—two prototypes and seventeen watches marked "Howard, Davis & Dennison"—handmade by Oliver and David Marsh, watchmaker brothers from Calais, Vermont. One of the prototypes, made by Oliver Marsh, survives in the collections of the Smithsonian Institution. Its white enamel dial indicates minutes around the rim and features four smaller dials displaying the hour (at six o'clock), the second

(at twelve o'clock), the day of the week (at nine o'clock), and the date (at three o'clock).

After reconsidering the prototypes and consulting with the jewelers who would be selling the new watches, the firm's management changed direction. The design of the first watches—eight-day movements with two mainsprings—gave way to a simpler timepiece that ran on one mainspring for slightly longer than a day. Although superficially similar to English watches, the new American watch featured a mainspring in a "going barrel," that is, without the traditional fusee and chain to equalize the force of the unwinding spring. This was a watch with fewer parts to make. The next hundred watches, built on the new model, took until the fall of 1853. The third batch of nine hundred sold for just forty dollars each, cased; at the time, a watch buyer would have purchased the movement and case separately from a jeweler. An imported movement of the same quality cost twice as much.

The firm's early years were financially unsteady, but unexpected success came during the Civil War, when the William Ellery movement, selling for an unbelievable thirteen dollars, became a fad among the Union soldiers. Just as itinerant peddlers had aroused the desire for inexpensive clocks, so roving merchants sold thousands of inexpensive watches like this to eager customers in wartime encampments.

Waltham would remain an important innovative force in both watch and machinery design for the rest of the century. The Waltham factory became a paragon of production, a highly publicized marvel of American know-how and enterprise. The firm spawned a raft of American competitors, who turned out movements by the millions, and the effect of these sales was international: Swiss watchmakers, who had dominated the world market, saw their exports to the United States peak in 1872 and then crash to a low in 1876. To remain competitive, the Swiss learned American techniques and would gradually mechanize aspects of their own operations. CS

(above right) *Unidentified soldier, possibly Private Florentine Ariosto Jones of Co. A, 13th Massachusetts Infantry Regiment, in Union uniform with pocket watch.*

Abacus
ca. 1900

→

Made by Oh Tani or Oh Ya
(Japanese, n.d.) in Hiroshima, Japan
Wood, bamboo
4 x 46 x 12 cm (1⁹⁄₁₆ x 18⅛ x 4²³⁄₃₂ in.)
Smithsonian Institution
National Museum of American History
Washington, DC, Cat. 1989.0515.01

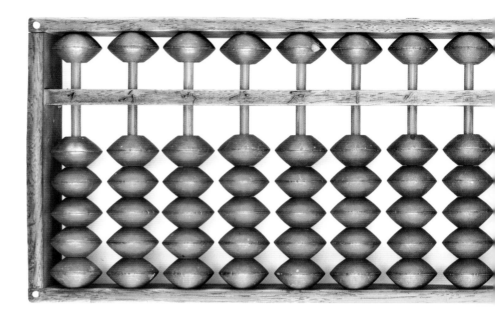

IN ANCIENT TIMES, people employed pebbles and rods to assist with simple calculations. This practice died out in Europe with the introduction of Hindu-Arabic numbers in the sixteenth century and then with the spread of slates and less expensive paper in the eighteenth and nineteenth centuries. In Russia and Central Asia, the beads that moved in grooves, which had been known in classical Rome, became pierced beads moving along the rods of an abacus.

Chinese and Japanese merchants had long availed themselves of sets of sticks to track the results of routine calculations. By the fourteenth century, the abacus began to displace these in China. A few Japanese merchants owned abaci as early as the fifteenth century, but between 1600 and 1800, the Japanese practice increasingly followed the Chinese model and adopted the abacus.

An abacus—the word is of Greek origin—consists of equally spaced rods set in a rectangular frame and beads that slide along the rods. Each column of beads represents a single digit. A horizontal bar divides the columns into two sections. The beads in the upper section represent fives, those in the lower section, ones. In the Chinese abacus, the beads are round; there are two in the upper section and five below, so that any column can represent up to fifteen.

By the mid-nineteenth century, the Japanese modified the design of what they called a *soroban*. Instead of rounded counters, the beads were slightly biconical, with a protruding join that was easier to manipulate. The users also noticed that only one "five" bead was necessary to represent a decimal number. Each column of this Japanese abacus, has only one bead above the crosspiece, so any column can represent up to ten. In the twentieth century, it became common to have, in addition to the single bead above the crossbar, only four beads below it, so that the column could represent the digits up to nine—all one needs for decimal arithmetic.

To operate the soroban, the user pushes all the beads away from the crossbar. The counters are then moved toward it as needed. The smallest place values are on the right, as in Western arithmetic. In the example shown here, the beads on the right side represent (reading right to left) 0,9,8,7,6...1. To add numbers, one moves beads toward the crossbar, making adjustments for fives and for carrying. To subtract, one moves beads outward, accounting for fives and for borrowing. More complicated procedures are used for multiplication and division.

This abacus from about 1900, like many of its time, has a wooden frame and beads and bamboo rods. The use of wood

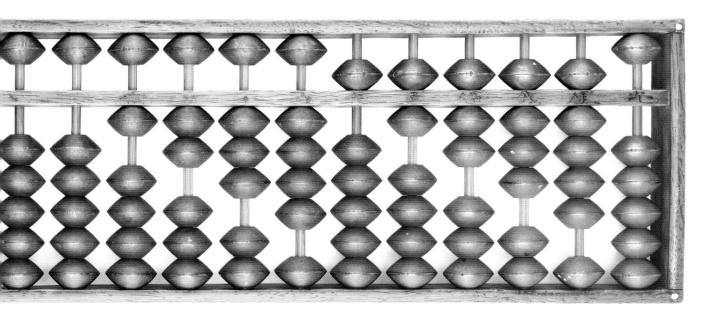

and bamboo was quite common in the nineteenth and early twentieth centuries, but after World War II abaci were often made of molded plastic.

All the columns of this abacus except the center one are labeled with Japanese characters on the crossbar. A mark on the back indicates that the abacus was made by Oh Tani (or Oh Ya) in Hiroshima. An inscription indicates that it was owned by Yoshizaemon Muraoka of the city of Sakata-ken in northern Japan. In 1933, this city became Sakata-shi.

The abacus was of great practical and instructional value in Japan. It was exhibited for international visitors at least as early as 1876, when abaci were shown by the Japanese Department of Education at the International Centennial Exposition in Philadelphia. Examples were imported into the United States by Asian immigrants. Tourists visiting Asia purchased abaci as souvenirs, and Asian visitors might have brought abaci with them, often as goodwill gestures. This abacus was brought to the United States and donated to the Smithsonian Institution by the collector and historian of computing devices, K. Kadokura, in 1989.

In the late nineteenth and early twentieth centuries, Western historians turned their attention to the abacus. Cargill G. Knott published an article on the soroban in 1886.[4] That same year, David Eugene Smith of Teachers College, Columbia University, collaborating with Yoshio Mikami, a Japanese librarian, published a volume that included an extensive discussion of the calculating rods used early in Japanese history and the later introduction of the abacus.[5]

The years following World War II saw a revival of the abacus in Japan and increased interest in the tool among some Americans.[6] Since the introduction of inexpensive electronic calculators in the 1970s, its use has waned. Abacus schools still exist, however, and a contemporary Australian journal of business studies takes its name from the instrument.[7] PK

4 Cargill G. Knott, "The Abacus, in Its Historic and Scientific Aspects," in *Handbook of the Napier Tercentenary Celebration, or, Modern Instruments and Methods of Calculation*, ed. E. M. Horsburgh (London: G. Bell, 1914).
5 Yoshio Mikami and David Eugene Smith, *A History of Japanese Mathematics* (Chicago: Open Court Publishing Company, 1914).
6 Takashi Kojima, *The Japanese Abacus: Its Use and Theory* (Rutland, VT) Charles E. Tuttle Company, 1954).
7 *Abacus: A Journal of Accounting, Finance and Business Studies* was established in 1965.

Calculator:
ET55
1980

Designed by Dieter Rams
(German, b. 1932) and
Dietrich Lubs (German, b. 1938)
Manufactured by Braun AG (Germany)
ABS polymer casing
13.6 x 7.8 x 1 cm (5⅜ x 3¹⁄₁₆ x ⅜ in.)
Courtesy of Cara McCarty

THE GERMAN INDUSTRIAL DESIGNER DIETER RAMS cares about the user's experience. For him, good design means creating practical products that are beautiful and easy to operate. An iconic example of Rams's relentless "less-but-better" philosophy is this Braun calculator; its understated elegance and exacting precision of detail made it an immediate success. Nothing is arbitrary. In addition to the instrument's clarity of function, the smooth texture feels good to touch and the rectangular form fits comfortably into the palm of a hand. The articulated, color-coded, M & M–shaped push buttons, offset against a matte black background, contribute to an intuitive use and add visual appeal, countering the impersonal qualities of most technological objects. Emotive responses are not generally associated with calculating machines, but this is a tool one wants to have and to show—a coveted possession—rather than hiding it away in a drawer until required. As a testament to its enduring legacy, the minimalist form and layout of the keypad were inspirations for Apple's iPhone calculator. CM

Protractor
1889–92

Designed by Alton J. Shaw
(American, n.d.)
Manufactured by Darling, Brown & Sharpe
Manufacturing Company
(Providence, Rhode Island, USA)
Sheet steel
15.7 x 26.1 x 0.2 cm (6³⁄₁₆ x 10¼ x ¹⁄₁₆ in.)
Smithsonian Institution
National Museum of American History
Washington, DC, Cat. 1977.0460.01

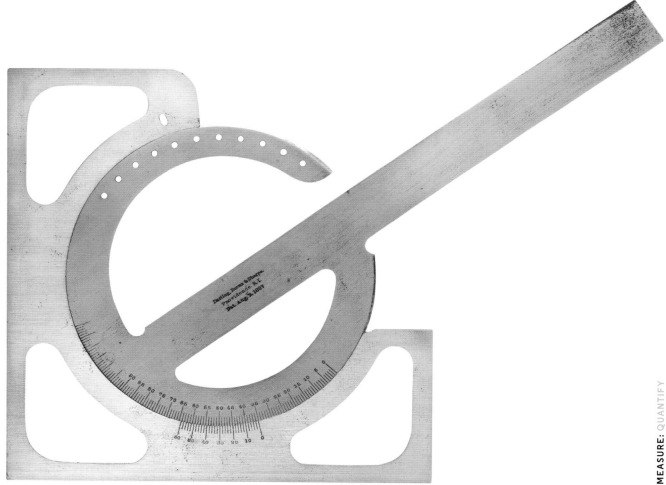

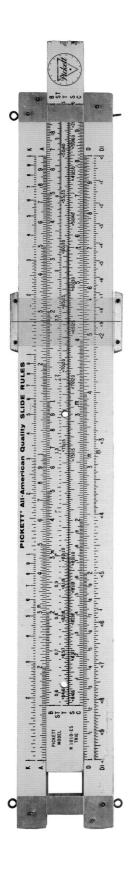

Demonstration Slide Rule: *Pickett N1010-ES Trig Duplex*

ca. 1960

Made by Pickett Industries
(Santa Barbara, California, USA)
Plywood, plexiglass
33 x 213.4 x 3.2 cm (13 x 84 x 1¼ in.)
Smithsonian Institution
National Museum of American History
Washington, DC, Cat. 2010.3095.071

THIS DEMONSTRATION SLIDE RULE represents a small but special class of tools: teaching instruments. These are actual working models that are oversize or otherwise modified to allow teachers to show how the real device functions.

Made around 1960, this slide rule was used in the physics class of an Ohio high school. Fully 2.13 m (7 ft.) long, it's a scaled-up replica of the Pickett N1010-ES Trig, which was popular with high-school and college students. It has all the same scales and is even painted the same "Eye Saver" shade of yellow. Pickett Industries provided these instruments to any school that ordered at least twenty-four standard-size rules.

Slide rules came into wide use around 1950, when new machinable aluminum alloys became available. This suddenly made it possible to manufacture high-precision slide rules that were also compact, lightweight, and durable. The instruments were soon commonplace and quickly came to represent science and technology for an entire generation. In the mid-1970s, with the appearance of powerful, low-cost electronic calculators, the demand for slide rules quickly plummeted and, by 1980, most of the suppliers had left the business. The decline of the slide-rule market was so precipitous that manufacturers still had large inventories when they halted production. Those same inventories now help to supply a small but enthusiastic group of collectors. A few specialized slide rules are still manufactured for very specific purposes, but the many slide-rule apps probably exceed them in total sales. ST

3D Laser Scanner: *Leica ScanStation C10*

2010

Designed and manufactured by Leica Geosystems (Heerbrugg, Switzerland, and Norcross, Georgia, USA)
Compact, pulsed, dual-axis-compensated, very-high-speed laser scanner; integrated camera and laser plummet
39.6 x 35.8 x 23.9 cm
(15⅝ x 14⅛ x 9⅜ in.)
Courtesy of Leica Geosystems

LIKE MOST FORMS OF MEASURING, surveying is being achieved with increasing precision, speed, and ease. The task is performed primarily by people physically marking, measuring, and mapping specific positions and points in an environment. This is more challenging when measuring extremes of scale and detail or working on difficult terrain. Lidar—a conflation of "light" and "radar"—is also known as "3D laser scanning" and "high-definition surveying" (HDS), and is a high-speed measuring tool that helps map and visualize environments and surfaces in rich detail. By moving the Lidar around a site or structure, like a 360-degree panoramic camera, it captures scenes and surfaces, accurately measuring (to ¼ in. [.64 cm]) out to a distance of some 300 m (1,000 ft.)—about three football fields. The Lidar then combines millions of scanned data into a seamless, full-dome digital image from which one can get an instant, precise measurement just by clicking on any two points. The image can be viewed from any perspective. An entire building, for example, can be scanned and the data compiled to produce a 3D computer model that anyone can virtually "fly through." Lidar's range of capabilities is vast: in addition to continuous 3D panoramic images, it can render detailed topographic maps of the Earth's surface, survey a crime scene, or peer into archaeological sites located in dense jungles that are difficult to access, giving us new insights into the world around us. CM

Illustration of Xochicalco (Mexico), UNESCO World Heritage site demonstrating digital preservation process using measurement data generated by 3D laser scanner, produced by CyArk

Photographic detail of Xochicalco (Mexico), produced by CyArk

3D laser scan of Xochicalco (Mexico), produced by CyArk

Tonometer
1876

Designed and made by Rudolph Koenig
(French, b. Germany, 1832–1901)
in Paris, France
Steel, walnut
96.5 x 129.5 x 63.5 cm (38 x 51 x 25 in.)
Smithsonian Institution, National Museum
of American History, Washington, DC
Cat. 315716 (rack, 600 tuning forks)
Cat. 322452 (61 tuning forks)

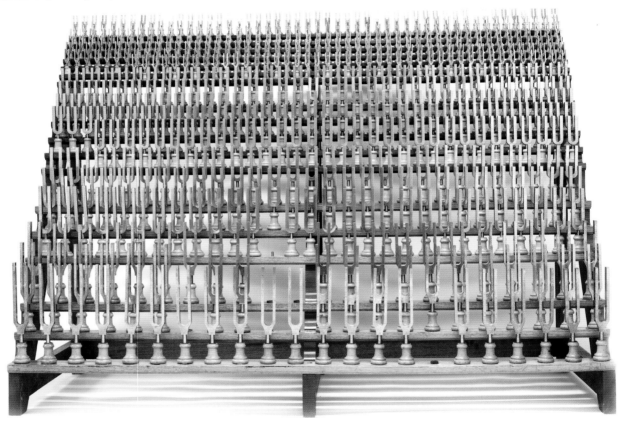

A TONOMETER, as the name suggests, is an instrument for determining the frequency of sounds. It does this by providing carefully measured standards against which other sounds can be compared. It was brought to the heights of mechanical perfection in the late nineteenth century by the great Parisian acoustic-instrument maker, Rudolph Koenig.

The tuning-fork tonometer was first proposed in 1834 by a German silk manufacturer and acoustic researcher, Johann Scheibler. He made many of these instruments over the course of his career, the most ambitious of which consisted of fifty-six forks, tuned at four wavelength intervals, from A220 to A440, that together covered the range of a single octave.

Scheibler's forks, made with the greatest possible accuracy, were tuned with the aid of an acoustic siren as well as with acoustic "beats," the distinctive pulsing sound produced when nearly identical sound waves are combined, but both of these techniques ultimately depended on the human ear, which was considered an inferior organ. By the middle of the nineteenth century, a powerful new technique of optical comparison of sounds had emerged. Koenig used this method, which employed Lissajous figures, to further refine the construction of tuning forks. Starting in the 1860s, he almost single-handedly turned the humble tuning fork into the most precise scientific instrument of the nineteenth century. And over the course of Koenig's nearly forty-year-career, this precision was incorporated into each of the thousands of forks that poured out of his busy atelier.

Koenig's shop was located in one of Paris's quietest neighborhoods, and he lived on the floors immediately above it. He devoted himself to the manufacture of precision acoustic instruments and to the scientific study of sound. On select evenings he opened his workshop to scientists and musicians, and the scientific exchanges he hosted there were luminous and legendary.

As his fame and business grew, Koenig sought to expand into the American market, and so displayed his apparatus at the Philadelphia International Centennial Exposition of 1876. He brought samples of his entire stock with him, including his masterpiece, the Grand Tonomètre, which he demonstrated to a select audience of leading US scientists. The judges' official report described it as consisting of 670 separate forks, "giving as many different shades of pitch extending over four complete octaves, and making equal intervals of eight simple vibrations each for the first octave, and of twelve each for the succeeding octaves; the whole forming an absolutely perfect means of testing . . . the number of vibrations producing any given musical sound, and of accurately tuning any musical instrument."[8] The report went on to echo the general opinion: "Of the exhibit of Dr. Koenig as a whole, it may be said that there is no other in the present International Exhibition which surpasses it in scientific interest," and he was awarded a gold medal of special distinction.[9]

After the Exposition, interest in Koenig's instruments in the United States was so great that Joseph Henry, secretary of the Smithsonian Institution, and other leading figures circulated an appeal to raise the funds to purchase his entire collection. Koenig was persuaded to leave them in storage at the University of Pennsylvania and he returned to Paris with the promise that payment would be forthcoming. Six years later, despite their best efforts, the sponsors reluctantly informed him that they would be unable to complete the acquisition. There was disappointment and "some ill feeling" on both

Rudolph Koenig's clock fork: the unprecedented accuracy of the tuning forks in Koenig's Tonometer was made possible by his use of this master instrument, the clock fork, which he used to make the final adjustments on every tuning fork that he made. The clock fork's accuracy came from using an actual clock to constantly monitor the frequency of a large tuning fork. Instead of a pendulum or a spring, the clock was driven by the motion of the fork itself, which was kept in a temperature controlled room and meticulously adjusted by moving small weights attached to each of its tines. The frequency of the fork being tested was determined by comparing it to the clock fork with a frictionless optical method called "Lissajous figures." By the end of the nineteenth century, Koenig's tuning forks were widely seen as having established a new level of mechanical precision.

sides, and Koenig returned to the United States to retrieve his instruments.[10] Fortunately, what funds had been raised allowed the purchase of the tonometer, along with several other instruments. These were presented to the United States Military Academy at West Point, where they remained until their donation to the Smithsonian Institution in 1958.

Koenig's tonometer represents the pinnacle of mechanical acoustic-instrument manufacture, and, although it was surpassed in the twentieth century by microphones, oscilloscopes, and other electroacoustic tools, it still stands as a monument to the skill, dedication, and vision of both its maker and the age in which he lived. ST

[8] David Pantalony, *Altered Sensations: Rudolph Koenig's Acoustical Workshop in Nineteenth-Century Paris* (Dordrecht, Netherlands: Springer, 2009).

[9] Ibid., 149-200.

[10] Dayton Clarence Miller, "Rudolph Koenig," in *Anecdotal History of the Science of Sound: To the Beginning of the 20th Century* (New York: Macmillan, 1935).

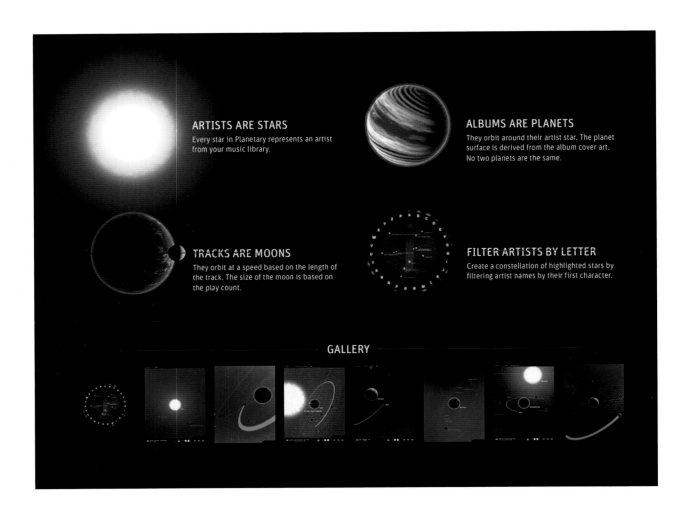

ARTISTS ARE STARS
Every star in Planetary represents an artist from your music library.

ALBUMS ARE PLANETS
They orbit around their artist star. The planet surface is derived from the album cover art. No two planets are the same.

TRACKS ARE MOONS
They orbit at a speed based on the length of the track. The size of the moon is based on the play count.

FILTER ARTISTS BY LETTER
Create a constellation of highlighted stars by filtering artist names by their first character.

GALLERY

Software and Source Code: *Planetary*
2011–12

Designed by Bloom Studio (2010–12) and Robert Hodgin (American, n.d.) in San Francisco, California, USA
C++ and Objective-C source files
File size (not including image files and other assets): 12,779 lines
Cooper Hewitt, Smithsonian Design Museum
New York, Gift of Ben Cerveny, Tom Carden, Jesper Andersen, and Robert Hodgin
2013-14-1

PLANETARY'S ALTERNATIVE MUSIC-PLAYER application for the iPad was designed to represent your music collection as a series of celestial bodies. Songs are moons, albums are planets, artists are suns—and the orbits of each are determined by the length of albums and tracks. Their brightness depends on how often you play them. Written in C++ using the Cinder framework, Planetary is an elegant interactive visualization, the first offering from Bloom, a San Francisco start-up founded to explore new ways to picture data and new forms of interactive products. Planetary was originally developed for the iPad, as there were no alternatives at the time. Today there are many more hardware and software environments in which Planetary may be implemented.

The source code for the app and its previous public versions is available online from Cooper Hewitt's website, cooperhewitt.org, along with programming notes and design sketches. SC

Helios

Mima

Hope Valley Hill

The Red Truth

Caesura

Shoulder To Hand

Glimpse

Fourteen Drawings

Backlight

Come With Nothings

Hollie

A Mountain Of Ice

Helios • Caesura • Come With Nothings

MADE IN U.S.A.

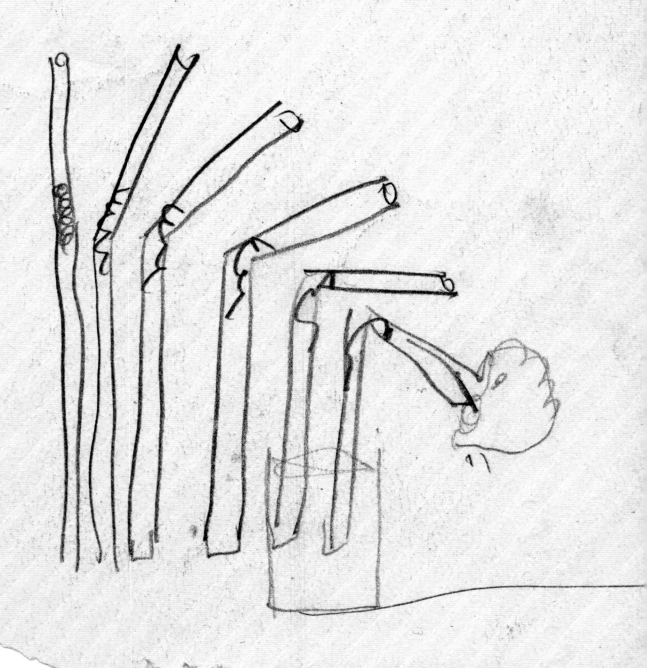

TINKERING, SKETCHING, MODELING, prototyping, and playing are all essential parts of the design process. They are tools that help designers push a notion, often to a tangible solution that can test its validity and feasibility. For inventors, sketches and models stake a claim to a specific concept that may ultimately result in a patent. The imagination of the American inventor Joseph Friedman flowed into notes on memo pads and other stationery, including used envelopes, and even onto chocolate packaging. His notes were reminders to himself of ideas needing further development, as much as the speculations of an active mind.

Designers and innovators solve problems and evaluate a product's performance along the way. Earl S. Tupper, who devised the airtight plastic containers called "Tupperware," reflected on his role as an inventor in his diary/inventor's log, "My Purpose in Life": "To take each thing as I find it and 'put it on the spot,' so to speak, and see how I can improve it, practically to better serve its present purpose,—or to serve a better purpose."[1] Equally significant was Tupper's comment about users, whom he wanted to understand better so that he could both appeal to them and help them. Tupper intended to do this by seeing himself as a "super coordinator, with [an] observatory and workshop high above this world, where I can look down and take in many things."[2]

Tupper's skill at observing the world around him in order to make more informed and better products is essential in all areas of design. With 3D printing, we can make prototypes, test them, refine the design, and then produce an improved prototype. The technology is ideal for creating affordable and customizable objects such as prosthetic limbs or for empowering the user to design unique objects. Just as the Internet transformed communication, 3D printing is bringing about the next revolution in manufacturing.

One of the most recent and intelligent purposes for this new technology is making tools and parts in space. Made In Space, Inc., had to completely rethink how a 3D printer could serve in a zero-gravity environment. When the printer arrives on the International Space Station, the Station's occupants will almost dispense with waiting for the next shuttle from Earth to deliver parts, and come closer to achieving self-sufficiency off-planet.

It may seem as if the human hand has become more removed from making and that digital skills will soon replace the fine craftsmanship represented, for example, by the patent models in this section. But the contribution of the Tangible Media Group has come full circle, finding a way to use our hands to communicate physically even when miles apart. At the forefront of user-interaction design, Tangible Media Group's project, inFORM, enables virtual participants to share visual information by means of what is essentially a sensor-activated pegboard. As one participant manually shapes the three-dimensional information, the keyboard translates the gestures into form and mass, to which the other participants can respond immediately with their own modifications. In effect, the users' hands are doing the work of a 3D printer, without the material waste, and with the collaborative tool of human interaction.

(opposite) *Sketch for Flexible Straw, 1930s; Made by Joseph B. Friedman (American, 1900–1982); Pencil on paper; Sheet (irreg.): 16.5 x 13.8 cm (6½ x 5⁷⁄₁₆ in.); Joseph B. Friedman Papers, Archives Center, National Museum of American History, Washington, DC, 2001.3031*

[1] Earl S. Tupper, "My Purpose in Life" (notebook, ca. 1935), Earl S. Tupper Papers, Series 2: Early Business, Paper and Scientific notes, Invention Diary and Sketchbook, Box 4, Folder 2, Archives Center, National Museum of American History.
[2] Ibid.

THE PATENT MODEL COLLECTION at the Smithsonian's National Museum of American History comprises more than 10,000 patent models, housed within different divisions at the Museum. The objects in the collection date from 1836 to the early twentieth century, and range from simple devices such as clothespins to elaborate machines such as printing presses and the then-new nineteenth-century technology of electricity. The history of the collection illustrates how models, like many useful tools, have performed a wide variety of functions over time, from demonstrating design and function, to inspiring inventors, to helping us understand our past.

For most of the nineteenth century, the Patent Office required inventors to submit a model with their patent application. Inventors placed great importance on their models, viewing a well-executed one as the key to obtaining a patent. They might hire a professional model maker to turn a two-dimensional paper drawing into a three-dimensional miniature machine or turn to another skilled artisan, such as blacksmith, watchmaker, or cabinet maker. Some inventors built their own.

A model's construction depended primarily on what the patented feature was. Many patents issued in the nineteenth century were for minor improvements to existing devices rather than for wholly new technologies; the inventor could show the complete machine or only the device submitted. Models could be fine miniatures of their commercial counterparts (like printing presses or plows) or the actual manufactured machines (like sewing machines or firearms) with the patented feature added. While the models did not have to work, many of them did. In general, they tended to adhere to the Patent Office's condition that they not exceed one foot (30.48 cm) in any dimension.

In the second half of the nineteenth century, the US Patent Office Model Room and its four halls showcased thousands of models, drawing researchers, inventors, the curious public, and manufacturers. To the inventor, the idea of manufacturers and investors studying his or her patent model offered a great incentive to present a striking, handsome model that would stand out on the crowded Model Room shelves.

In 1880, the Patent Office dropped the requirement to submit models, except in unusual circumstances—the Office had simply run out of space in which to display or even store an ever-rising flood of models. Inventions were also becoming more complex and less amenable to representation by models. Once the requirement to submit a model was rescinded, a decline in the large number of professional model makers in Washington, DC, was inevitable.

The models suffered two major fires at the Patent Office. The first, in 1836, destroyed the approximately 7,000 models submitted up to that date. Not only were the models lost, but all the patent drawings and records of patent applications and grants were destroyed. A second fire, in 1877, destroyed 75,000 models out of a collection of 200,000.

In June 1908, the Smithsonian acquired 284 models from the Patent Office. The strength of this selection was firearms; smaller categories included printing presses, sewing machines, typewriters, telegraphs, electric lamps, locomotives, gas and steam engines, agricultural instruments, and textile machinery. Before the summer ended, curators made further selections, this time of photography, musical instruments, lighting and heating, more firearms, and other mechanical devices, bringing the total to just over 1,000.

The Patent Office packed the remaining models into more than three thousand crates, which they moved several times. In 1926, Congress decided to dispense with the stored collection of models, and the subsequent bill gave the Smithsonian Institution first choice. By one report, curators at the Smithsonian's US National Museum selected as many as 15,000 out of the 352,000 available, with the rest sold by the Treasury Department as "useless government property." The National Museum gave away an unknown number of models to schools, universities, other museums and industries, and to the descendants of inventors.

The fame and success of inventions such as Eli Whitney's cotton gin and Elias Howe's sewing machine spurred Americans to attempt to patent almost everything imaginable. This national mania is illustrated in the diversity and size of the Smithsonian's patent-model collection. Their profusion testifies to the enthusiasm of Americans to conceive a better idea, create an improved machine, and try to mechanize America efficiently, from home to farm to factory. During the nineteenth century, patent models were proudly exhibited as icons of American invention. In the twenty-first century, they serve as tools for understanding not only the ingenious wonders of an earlier era, but also our relationships to the complexity of technology and technological change. **BJ & BCL**

Hansen
Writing Ball
(Commercial)
1878

Designed by Rasmus Malling-Hansen
(Danish, 1835–1890) in Denmark
Brass, ferrous alloy, paper
22.9 x 22.2 x 20.3 cm (9 x 8¾ x 8 in.)
On deposit from Wyckoff, Seamans
& Benedict, Smithsonian Institution
National Museum of American History
Washington, DC, Cat. 181005

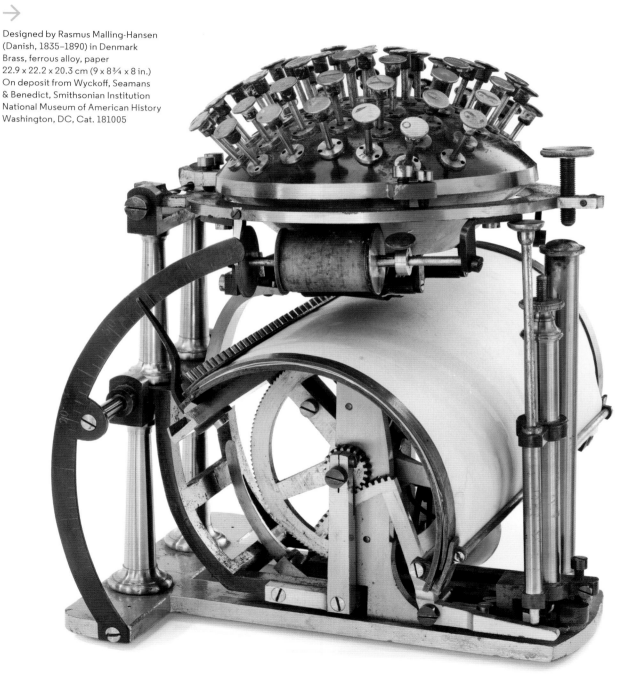

SCHREIBKUGEL IST EIN DING GLEICH MIR:VON

EISEN

UND DOCH LEICHT ZU VERDREHN ZUMAL AUF REISEN.

GEDULD UND TAKT MUSS REICHLICH MAN BESITZEN

UND FEINE FINGERCHEN UNS ZU BENUETZEN.

Poem by Friedrich Wilhelm Nietzsche (German, 1844–1900), typed with a Hansen writing ball, February 16, 1882: "The writing ball is a thing like me: made of iron/Yet easily twisted on journeys/ Patience and tact are required in abundance/As well as fine fingers to use us."

ONE OF THE MOST COMPLEX instruments of the nineteenth century was the typewriter. Beginning in the early eighteenth century, there had been scores of efforts to make a mechanical writing tool. Among the first such devices to have some commercial success, especially in Europe, was the "writing ball," invented by Rasmus Malling-Hansen, a Danish teacher of the deaf, beginning in 1865. Initially inspired to provide a mechanical means of communication for his deaf and mute charges, Malling-Hansen strove for more than two decades to develop a workable model, finally patenting his writing machine in Denmark, England, and Sweden in 1870. He continued improving his "writing ball," named for the sphere-shaped part holding the machine's keys, and made several revisions. He received three US patents, in 1872, 1875, and 1878.

With the application for his "Type Writing-Machine" (US Patent 125,952, granted April 23, 1872), Malling-Hansen submitted a model, which survives in the Smithsonian collections. The model shows only a portion of a working machine: a brass hemisphere atop a wooden box holds keys for the three letters O, L, and F. Two hinged doors open to reveal a partial mechanism. The patent description explains how type-carrying plungers converge on a moving surface to make an imprint on paper wrapped on a cylinder; in addition, the machine's spring-driven mechanism for rotating the cylinder line by line and advancing it horizontally letter by letter could be either controlled by a pendulum or powered by electricity. The inventor further suggested in the patent

description that the "types"—today called "keys"—should be arranged in two clusters, vowels together for the fingers of the left hand, consonants for the right. The user could not see the paper while typing, a characteristic of all such devices until "visible" machines were introduced in the 1890s.

The Smithsonian's second Hansen machine is from about 1878. A commercial example of the "writing ball," it features a full set of fifty-two characters, with capital letters only, gleaming brass components, and a curved paper carrier.

Ironically, the 1878 Hansen machine was given to the Smithsonian by the writing ball's principal competitor, the firm of Wyckoff, Seamans & Benedict, which provided the machine for display in 1891. The firm had acquired the rights to manufacture and sell Remington typewriters, which had originated in the work of the inventor Christopher Latham Sholes, a Wisconsin newsman and political figure. With various partners, Sholes had built a series of writing machines beginning in 1867. By 1872, he had a prototype that went into production at the Remington arms factory in Ilion, New York. That machine, on the market in 1874, became the basis of the modern typewriter. Its QWERTY keyboard, introduced on the earliest Sholes machines to prevent the type bars from clashing during typing, ultimately displaced the comely and ergonomic Hansen sphere.

It wasn't entirely clear to their inventors who would use the new machines. Early advertisements appealed to authors and clergymen. The most famous early adopter of the

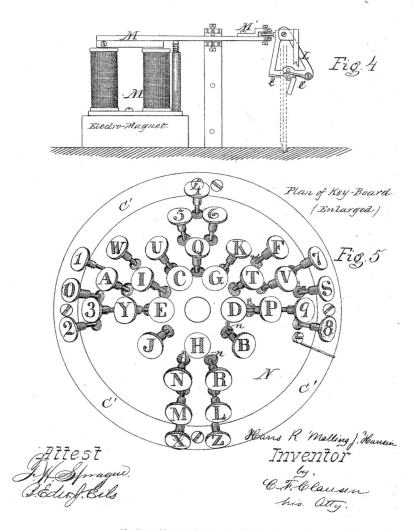

3 Sheets--Sheet 3.

HANS R. MALLING J. HANSEN.
Type-Writing Machine.

No. 125,952.

Patented April 23, 1872.

Fig. 4

Electro-Magnet.

Plan of Key-Board.
(Enlarged)

Fig. 5

Attest

Inventor

Keyboard layout drawing by Malling-Hansen for one of his many type-writing machines, 1872.

Hansen writing ball was the German philosopher Friedrich Wilhelm Nietzsche. Mark Twain used a Remington.

But it was business offices that made the typewriter a successful invention, albeit slowly at first. Sales increased in the 1880s, especially in the United States, when other manufacturers began to challenge Remington, and corporate and government paperwork multiplied. Specialized versions of the typewriter were employed for dictation and bookkeeping. With the expansion of clerical work and the introduc-

tion of the typewriter, a new profession emerged. Offices were hiring "type writers" for the first time and, although the position was initially gender neutral, women took clerical positions as never before, quickly outnumbering men. By the late 1890s, numerous manufacturers were producing hundreds of thousands of machines for worldwide markets. Except for personal letters, which remained mostly composed by hand, the typewriter had become the implement for most forms of writing. CS

Patent Model for Wire Rope-making Machine, Patent No. 2,720

July 16, 1842

Made by John A. Roebling
(American, 1806–1869) in USA
Brass, steel
27.9 x 26.7 x 24.1 cm
(11 x 10½ x 9½ in.)
Smithsonian Institution
National Museum of American
History, Washington, DC
Cat. 308790

THIS PATENT MODEL was included with John A. Roebling's "Method of and Machine for Manufacturing Wire Ropes," an application that received US Patent 2,720 on July 16, 1842. The entirety of Roebling's patent claims detailed how to manufacture wire rope, and this model demonstrated the phase of wrapping greased insulating wire around the rope. The strength and durability of Roebling's invention made it superior to hemp rope in many industrial applications, but its utility went far beyond replacing traditional cord.

John A. Roebling & Sons Company was the preeminent manufacturer of wire rope during the late nineteenth and early twentieth centuries. Roebling, an engineer as well as an inventor, was responsible for the Niagara Falls Suspension Bridge; the Roebling Suspension Bridge, which spanned the Ohio River from Cincinnati to Covington, Kentucky; and, most famously, the Brooklyn Bridge. Roebling & Sons also supplied the wire rope for the George Washington and Golden Gate bridges. Wire rope had a starring role in the mechanization and electrification of modern America, due to its use in cable cars, elevators, telephones, telegraphs, and electrical systems. GK

Patent Model for Sewing Machine, Patent No. 9,041

June 15, 1852

↓

Made by Allen B. Wilson
(American, 1824–1888) in
Watertown, Connecticut, USA
Metal, wood
12.7 x 16.5 x 30.5 cm (5 x 6½ x 12 in.)
Smithsonian Institution
National Museum of American
History, Washington, DC
Cat. T06055

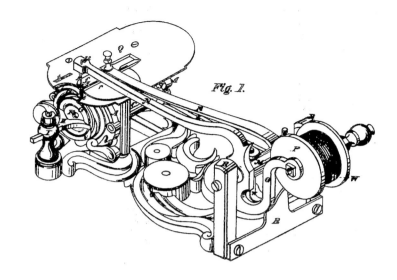

Fig. 1.

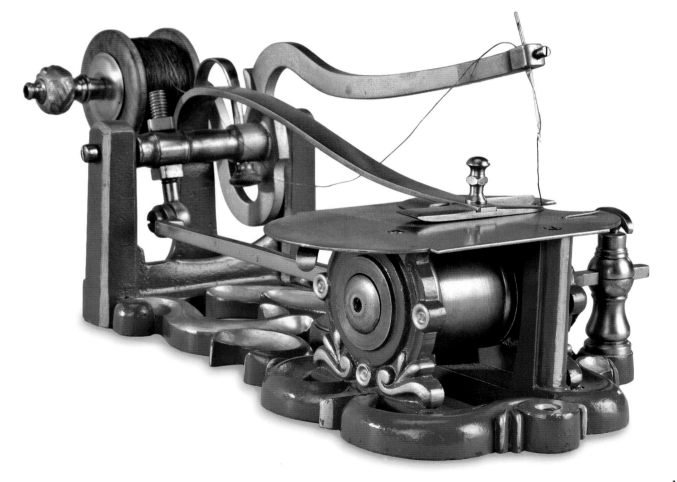

Patent Model for Lock, Patent No. 32,330

May 14, 1861

Made by Linus Yale, Jr.
(American, 1821–1868) in USA
Brass, iron
19.1 x 15.2 x 9.5 cm (7½ x 6 x 3¾ in.)
Smithsonian Institution
National Museum of American History
Washington, DC, Cat. 309165

TOOLS

184

WE USE LINUS YALE JR.'S nineteenth-century designs for locks today. He was thirty years old when he gave up painting portraits to follow his father into lock making in 1850; his earliest efforts were directed mainly to improving locks for bank safes. Yale's handmade, expensive mechanical devices established his reputation as a gifted designer, while his ideas evolved continuously in an effort to stay one step ahead of clever lock pickers and determined safe crackers. In the 1860s, Yale turned to designing and patenting the locks and key so familiar to us—the cylinder lock, the narrow serrated key that opens it, and the modern combination lock.

This model from 1861 is an example of a Yale design. In 1868, he established the Yale Lock Manufacturing Company with Henry R. Towne in Stamford, Connecticut, where the manufacture of locks was transformed from craft to mass production. CS

Patent Model for Carpenter's Combination Tool: Bevel and Try Square, Patent No. 70,547

November 5, 1867

Made by John Graham
(American, n.d.) in Ludlow,
Vermont, USA
Steel, brass
12.7 x 14.9 cm (5 x 5⅞ in.)
Smithsonian Institution
National Museum of American History
Washington, DC, Cat. 210834.01

THIS COMBINATION TOOL served as a model for patent application number 70,547, granted to John Graham on November 5, 1867. The carpentry tools listed in the patent include a bevel, marker, gauge, try square, and level—what Graham described as an "indicator." When the square was placed upon a surface, the indicator pointed vertically to twelve o'clock if the surface was level, varying to the left or right if not. The indicator was Graham's main claim to invention in his patent, but he also claimed "the combination of one or more supplemental movable or adjustable squares, with a try-square." This claim made Graham's invention a multitool, a carpenter's Swiss Army knife of bevels, levels, and squares. GK

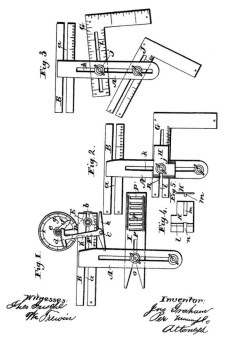

Patent Models for Clothespins

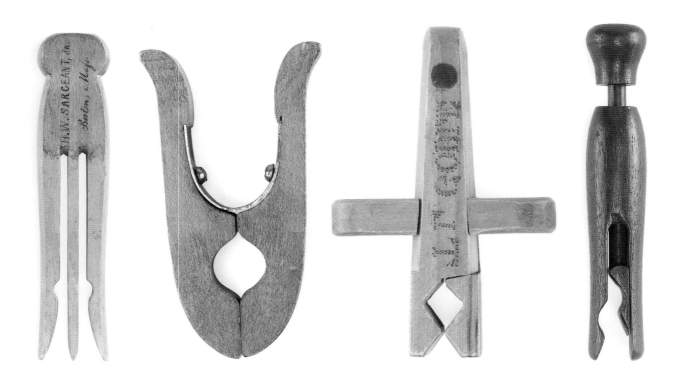

Patent No. 47,223
April 11, 1865

Made by Henry W. Sargeant, Jr.
(American, n.d.) in USA
Wood
11.4 x 2.5 x 1.1 cm
(4½ x 1 x ⁷⁄₁₆ in.)
Smithsonian Institution
National Museum of American
History, Washington, DC
Cat. T11393.037

Patent No. 141,740
August 12, 1873

Made by Vincent D. Urso
(American, b. Italy, ca. 1850)
and Benjamin Charles
(American, n.d.) in USA
Wood, metal
7.9 x 1.9 x 1.3 cm
(3⅛ x ¾ x ½ in.)
Smithsonian Institution
National Museum of American
History, Washington, DC
Cat. T11393.025

Patent No. 60,627
December 18, 1866

Made by T. L. Goble
(American, 1823–1890) in USA
Wood
7.6 x 5.1 x 1.6 cm
(3 x 2 x ⅝ in.)
Smithsonian Institution
National Museum of American
History, Washington, DC
Cat. T11393.012

Patent No. 45,119
November 15, 1864

Made by Jeremiah Greenwood
(American, 1832–1897) in USA
Wood
10.2 x 1.9 cm
(4 x ¾ in.)
Smithsonian Institution
National Museum of American
History, Washington, DC
Cat. T11393.005

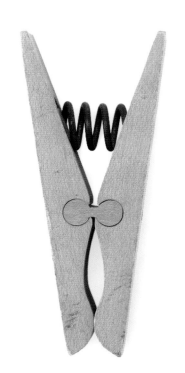

Patent No. 119,938

October 17, 1871

Made by Henry Mellish
(American, 1804–1878) in USA;
Wood
7 x 2.5 x 1.6 cm
(2 ¾ x 1 x ⅝ in.);
Smithsonian Institution
National Museum of American
History, Washington, DC
Cat. T11393.011

Patent No. 76,547

April 7, 1868

Made by A. L. Taylor
(American, 1841–ca. 1910)
in USA
Wood, metal
10.5 x 2.2 x 1.7 cm
(4 ⅛ x ⅞ x ¹¹⁄₁₆ in.)
Smithsonian Institution
National Museum of American
History, Washington, DC
Cat. T11393.035

Patent No. 63,759

April 9, 1867

Made by David M. Smith
(American, 1809–1891) in USA
Wood, metal
7.1 x 3.2 x 1.4 cm
(2 ¹³⁄₁₆ x 1 ¼ x ⁹⁄₁₆ in.)
Smithsonian Institution
National Museum of American
History, Washington, DC
Cat. T11393.039

Patent No.272,762

February 20, 1883

Made by Richard B. Perkins
(American, 1842–d. 1920–30)
in USA
Wood, metal
12.9 x 2.5 x 1.7 cm
(5 ¹⁄₁₆ x 1 x ¹¹⁄₁₆ in.)
Smithsonian Institution
National Museum of American
History, Washington, DC
Cat. T11393.040

→

Made by Francis M. Comstock
(American, n.d) in USA
Metal
14 x 21.6 x 25.1 cm
(5½ x 8½ x 9⅞ in.)
Smithsonian Institution
National Museum of American
History, Washington, DC
Cat. T11410.031

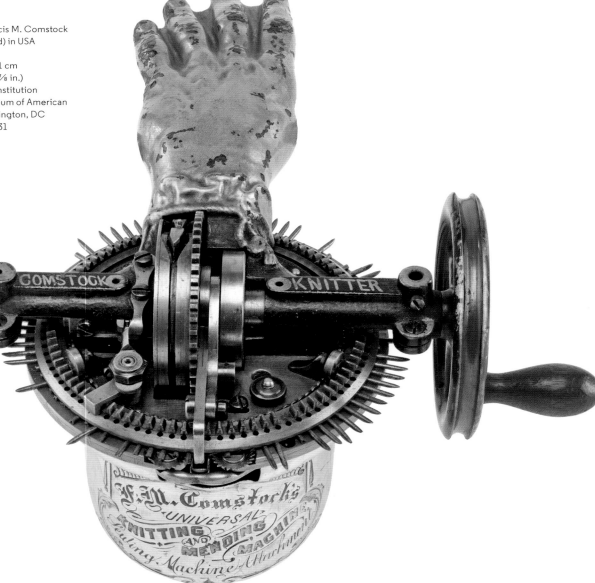

F. M. COMSTOCK.
Improvement in Knitting Machines.

No. 125,543.   Patented April 9, 1872.

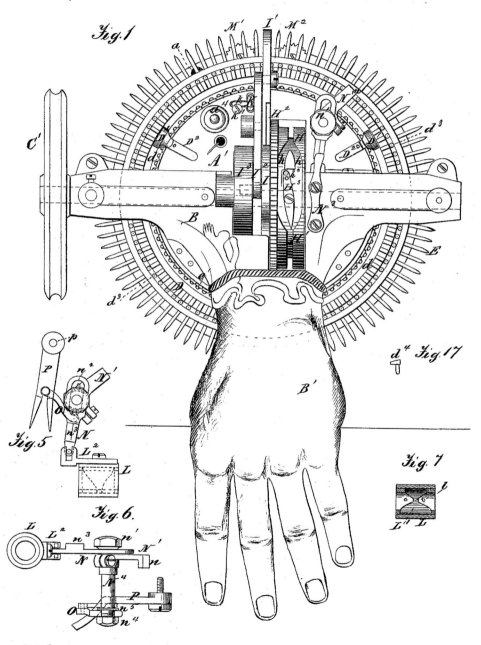

Fig.1

Fig.5

Fig.6

Fig. 17

Fig. 7

Witnesses.
A. Ruppert.
B. Eder J. Eils

Inventor.
F. M. Comstock

Edison Lamp
1880

Designed by Thomas Alva Edison
(American, 1847–1931)
Bamboo, glass, wood, brass,
plaster, platinum, cork
H x Diam: 17.8 x 6 cm (7 x 2⅜ in.)
Smithsonian Institution
National Museum of American
History, Washington, DC
Cat. 310579.01

IN 1880, THOMAS EDISON and his team began selling their newly invented electrical lighting system, which incorporated lamps like the one shown here. An electrical current heated a filament of baked bamboo, thereby making the filament glow, or "incandesce." These early Edison lamps provided the same amount of light as gas lamps but they glowed steadily, rather than flickering, and gave off no fumes. With no open flame, incandescent lamps could be used where candles or gas lamps would be dangerous, such as mines and textile factories. They also invited flexibility in lighting design, since they could be installed without regard to fuel flow or flame path. Simple in construction, Edison's lamps lasted about 650 hours and, unlike gas lamps, could be lit and turned off with just the flick of a switch. The new lighting provided a practical and, ultimately, inexpensive way to extend the day, for both work and play. HW

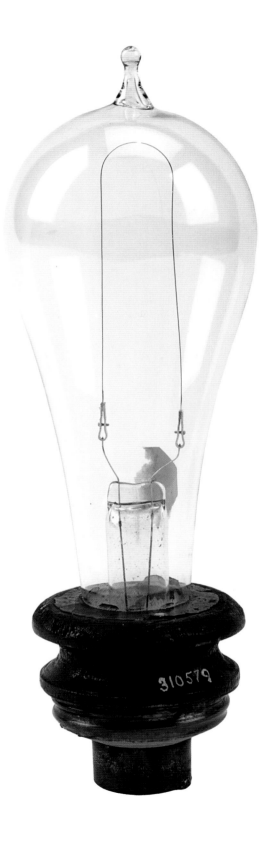

Book: *Les Raisons des forces mouvantes avec diverses machines tant utilles que plaisantes*
(Explanations of motive forces, with various machines as useful as they are pleasing)
1615

Written by Salomon de Caus
(French, 1576–1626)
Published by Jan Norton (Frankfurt, Germany)
Vellum over paper boards, paper
Open: 40.5 x 51.1 x 13.1 cm
(15 15/16 x 20 1/8 x 5 3/16 in.)
Courtesy of Smithsonian Libraries
Washington, DC, f TJ144 .C37 1615

SALOMON DE CAUS, a French architect and engineer, studied and wrote about such diverse subjects as landscape design; mythological and allegorical figures; water; steam and solar power; sundials; and the creation of pipe organs. His innovative theories and inventions were employed when he directed the construction of the palaces and grounds at Heidelberg for Elector Frederick V around 1613. At that time, Caus chronicled his inventions in the three books that comprise *Les Raisons des forces mouvantes avec diverses machines tant utilles que plaisantes*, which include the ornamentation of palace grottoes and fountains, the manufacture of pipe organs, and the application of steam, hydraulic, and solar systems—important tools for powering machines, musical instruments, and fountains. Illustrated here is an innovative tool for augmenting the power of a fountain, whereby water is heated as the sun streams through glass disks mounted by the window (A, B). The heated water then rises into a pipe (C, D), through the wall, and out from the fountain in the adjoining chamber. **SVD**

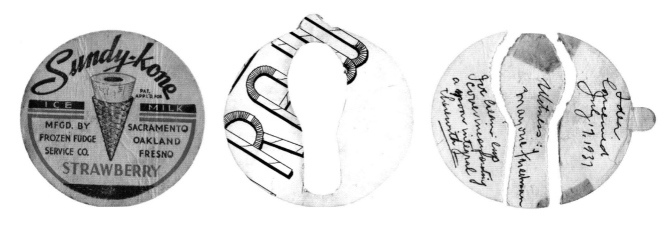

Cardboard Mock-ups for Ice-cream Cup and Spoons, ca.1937; Made by Joseph B. Friedman (American, 1900-1982); Ink on paper; Approximately 15.9 x 18.4 cm (6 1/4 x 7 1/4 in.) each; Joseph B. Friedman Papers, Archives Center, National Museum of American History, Washington, DC, 2001.3031

SKETCHING HAS LONG BEEN an effective tool to help people imagine, think about, define, refine, and realize ideas. Inventors, in particular, often depend on this resource to explore concepts, brainstorm, test approaches, clarify and explain their notions, and document their creative method. Artistic skill is neither the point nor the standard; rather, there seems to be a mysterious alignment between the mind and the hand that stimulates the imagination. For many, the very gestures involved in moving pen or pencil across paper produce a thought, to be further developed in gradually more finished drawings. Inventors may follow the first visual notes on their concepts with scale or measured drawings and in time build a model or prototype. A series of sketches can illustrate the whole "invention biography" of an item. Once completed, a sketch can provoke responses, sparking discussions and other dynamic engagement with an inventor's work. These jottings are a significant part of the invention record, providing insight into how innovative ideas take shape, from first inkling to concrete result. And these sometimes fugitive drafts may be the only remaining evidence of an idea that disappeared or one that was never realized.

Most inventors keep written records of their work, and many of the sketches shown here include text describing functionality and the types of raw materials intended for creating a model. However, words alone are not adequate. Sketches make it possible to imagine what something will look like and how it might work, before the inventor, investor, or both, commit time and money to building or manufacturing the item or even a prototype.

Some of the familiar attributes and properties of sketching are: unpolished, quick, direct, clear, accidental, without details, open ended—later versions will come—and plentiful. As the examples presented here attest, sketches are made in both pencil and ink. Invention sketches are often collected in bound notebooks, and they are as diverse as their makers. For example, Earl S. Tupper's notebook is part invention log, part diary. Joseph B. Friedman preferred scraps of paper and favored envelopes, while others innovators captured their ideas on the back of documents or even on napkins.

The drawings in this section are swift and summary, demonstrating that in the early stages of the process an inventor seeks to grasp and explore the notion rapidly, with the intention of returning to it for further development. The sketches make clear that the individuals who made them found the activity pleasurable in itself. Friedman and Tupper produced hundreds of drawings that reveal the joy of recording ideas in this medium. Some of the tools shown here were eventually patented and manufactured. Friedman's flexible drinking straw, Brannock's shoe-measuring device, Watson's "telescope" shopping cart, and Tupper's container have changed little from their original inception. It is intriguing to be able to plot the course of these familiar objects from first thought to store shelves. **AO**

(see appendix page 258 for transcriptions of sketches)

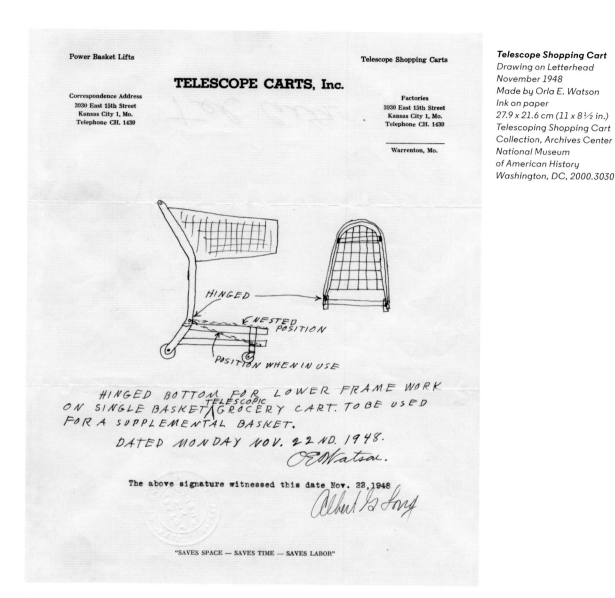

TELESCOPE CARTS, Inc.

Power Basket Lifts

Telescope Shopping Carts

Correspondence Address
3930 East 15th Street
Kansas City 1, Mo.
Telephone CH. 1439

Factories
3930 East 15th Street
Kansas City 1, Mo.
Telephone CH. 1439

Warrenton, Mo.

HINGED

NESTED POSITION

POSITION WHEN IN USE

HINGED BOTTOM FOR LOWER FRAME WORK
ON SINGLE BASKET TELESCOPIC GROCERY CART. TO BE USED
FOR A SUPPLEMENTAL BASKET.
DATED MONDAY NOV. 22ND. 1948.
OEWatson.

The above signature witnessed this date Nov. 22, 1948

"SAVES SPACE — SAVES TIME — SAVES LABOR"

Telescope Shopping Cart
*Drawing on Letterhead
November 1948
Made by Orla E. Watson
Ink on paper
27.9 x 21.6 cm (11 x 8½ in.)
Telescoping Shopping Cart
Collection, Archives Center
National Museum
of American History
Washington, DC, 2000.3030*

ORLA E. WATSON (AMERICAN, 1896–1983)

THE SHOPPING CART is used worldwide. Although Orla Watson did not invent it, his improvements to this versatile tool are significant and a standard in the industry today. He introduced permanently attached hinged baskets, which allow the carts to nest for compact storage (US Patent 2,479,530) thus conserving valuable floor space. The telescoping shopping carts debuted at Floyd Day's Super Market, in Kansas City, Missouri, in 1947. Watson was a tinkerer at heart. He made his own air conditioners, mechanical valves, pumps, and gauges—none of which he ever manufactured or licensed.

Watson's pencil sketches represent his process of solving such details as the dimensions of the basket, while the simple side view conveys the overall design. Here, the inventor was thinking visually and spatially. Today's cart is bigger, made of different materials, such as plastic, and has a cup holder and a child's seat, but the concept has changed little since 1947. AO

MAKE: SKETCHES

CHARLES F. BRANNOCK (AMERICAN, 1903–1992)

CHARLES BRANNOCK WAS A CLASSIC AMERICAN INVENTOR, often waking in the middle of the night to jot down written and sketched notes to capture his concept and using any available paper, rather than a formal invention notebook. The sketches here offer insights into the process that resulted in his Brannock Device, a foot-measuring instrument he patented in 1928 (US Patent 1,682,366, granted August 28, 1928). The now-ubiquitous tool was adopted by shoe stores across the United States and by the United States military to outfit its troops. Brannock refined his device over two years, with a sequence of models, from one made with his childhood Erector® set, to a cardboard example displaying calibrations, to a pattern in wood. The final production model was of cast aluminum and assembled by hand. Brannock began manufacturing it in 1925, and in 1926 he offered his invention to shoe retailers, first for rent and then for sale. AO

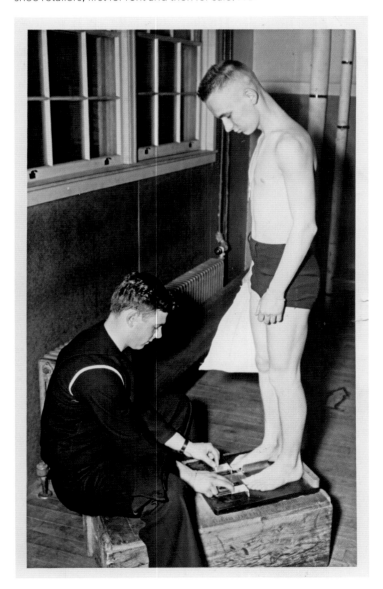

(left) *Soldier Being Fitted for Boots Using Brannock Device Double Unit,* June 1945
Silver gelatin on paper; 20.8 x 12.7 cm (8 3/16 x 5 in.)
Brannock Device Company Records, Archives Center, National Museum of American History Washington, DC, 1999.3007

(opposite)

1.*Sketch for Mechanism for Measuring Width of Foot,* 1940s; Made by Charles F. Brannock
Pencil on paper; 25.2 x 20.2 cm (9 15/16 x 7 15/16 in.)
Brannock Device Company Records, Archives Center, National Museum of American History, Washington, DC, 1999.3007

2. *Sketch for Stool for Use with Brannock Device*
ca. 1947; Made by Charles F. Brannock
Pencil on paper; 31.8 x 20.3 cm (12½ x 8 in.)
Brannock Device Company Records Archives Center, National Museum of American History, Washington, DC, 1999.3007

3. *Copy of Patent Drawing for Foot Measuring Device,* 1960, made by Charles F. Brannock

4. *Sketch for Brannock Device,* ca. 1920s; Made by Charles F. Brannock; Pencil on paper; 28 x 21.6 cm (11 x 8½ in.); Brannock Device Company Records, Archives Center, National Museum of American History, Washington, DC, 1999.3007

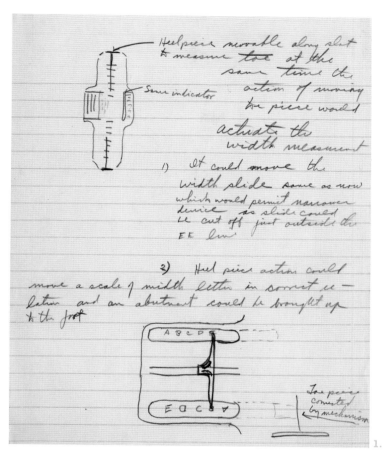

June 28, 1960   C. F. BRANNOCK   2,942,344

FOOT MEASURING DEVICE

Filed Nov. 21, 1958

INVENTOR.
Charles F. Brannock
BY
D. Emmett Thompson
ATTORNEY

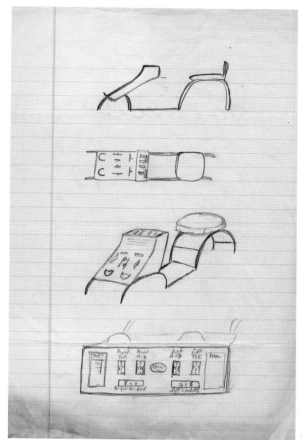

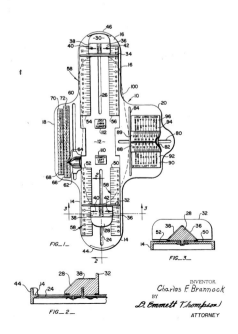

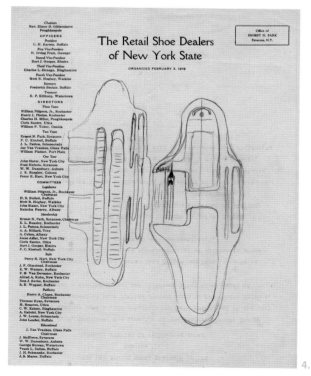

The Retail Shoe Dealers of New York State

ORGANIZED FEBRUARY 3, 1919

Office of
ERNEST N. PARK
Syracuse, N.Y.

Chaplain
Rev. Elmer D. Gildersleeve, Poughkeepsie

OFFICERS
President
C. H. Barton, Buffalo
First Vice-President
H. Irving Pratt, Oswego
Second Vice-President
Burt J. Gosper, Elmira
Third Vice-President
Charles L. Strange, Binghamton
Fourth Vice-President
Mott B. Hughey, Watkins
Secretary
Frederick Becker, Buffalo
Treasurer
R. P. Ellthorp, Watertown

DIRECTORS
Three Years
William Pidgeon, Jr., Rochester
Harry J. Phelan, Rochester
Charles H. Miller, Poughkeepsie
Chris Santor, Utica
William F. Tober, Oneida
Two Years
Ernest N. Park, Syracuse
P. C. Kimball, Buffalo
J. L. Patton, Schenectady
Jay Van Vranken, Glens Falls
William Platner, Fort Plain
One Year
John Slater, New York City
Fred Nichols, Syracuse
W. W. Duxenbury, Auburn
J. S. Burgher, Cohoes
Percy E. Hart, New York City

COMMITTEES
Legislative
William Pidgeon, Rochester, Chairman
H. S. Bullett, Buffalo
Mott B. Hughey, Watkins
John Slater, New York City
Malcolm Fearey, Albany
Membership
Ernest N. Park, Syracuse, Chairman
E. L. Beasley, Rochester
J. L. Patton, Schenectady
A. A. Millard, Troy
A. Cohen, Albany
Jesse Adler, New York City
Chris Santor, Utica
Burt J. Gosper, Elmira
F. C. Kimball, Buffalo
Sale
Percy E. Hart, New York City, Chairman
J. P. Olmstead, Rochester
K. W. Wasters, Buffalo
P. M. Van Deventer, Rochester
Alfred A. Kohn, New York City
Don J. Burke, Rochester
S. E. Wygant, Buffalo
Publicity
Harry A. Chase, Rochester, Chairman
Thomas Ryan, Syracuse
H. Beacom, Utica
C. W. Kelsey, Binghamton
A. Gabriel, New York City
J. W. Loane, Schenectady
John Leader, Buffalo
Educational
J. Van Vranken, Glens Falls, Chairman
J. McElwee, Syracuse
W. W. Duxenbury, Auburn
George Bureau, Watertown
Frank L. Dolins, Buffalo
J. H. Schmanke, Rochester
J. S. Meyer, Buffalo

JOSEPH B. FRIEDMAN (AMERICAN, 1900–1982)

JOSEPH FRIEDMAN'S BEST-KNOWN INVENTION

is the flexible straw, but the range of his inventive activities encompassed writing implements, improvements to engines, and household products. He received nine United States patents and several foreign ones. The flexible straw and the company he formed to manufacture it became the focus of his inventive life.

Friedman frequently sketched on loose scraps of paper—he was especially fond of envelopes—working out ideas and solving problems. His pencil sketch of the flexible straw (p.176) captures his method at its very best. Dating from the 1930s, it is the first example of Friedman experimenting with this idea. The pencil lines were drawn quickly but with purpose, but the sketch is whimsical, too, at first glance recalling a flower wilting in a vase. Friedman's flexible straw, called a "Drinking Tube," was granted US Patent 2,094,268 on September 28, 1937. The sketches here reflect his wide range of inventive interests. AO

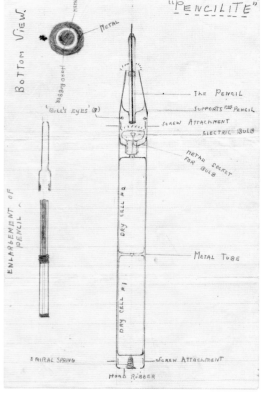

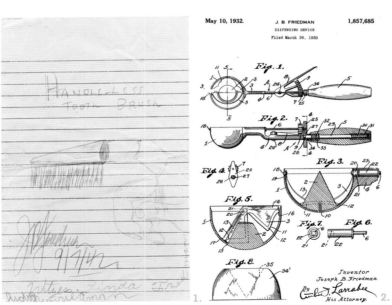

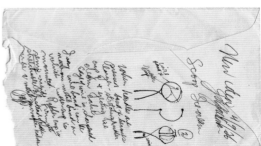

1. **Sketch for Handle-less Tooth Brush,** September 7, 1942; Made by Joseph B. Friedman; Pencil on paper; 19.7 x 12.5 cm (7¾ x 4¹⁵⁄₁₆ in.); Joseph B. Friedman Papers, Archives Center, National Museum of American History, Washington, DC, 2001.3031

2. **Copy of Patent Drawing for Dispensing Device,** May 10, 1932, Made by Joseph B. Friedman; Ink on paper; 28 x 21.6 cm (11 x 8½ in.); Joseph B. Friedman Papers, Archives Center, National Museum of American History, Washington, DC, 2001.3031

3. **Sketch for New Idea for Ice-cream Scoop,** 1936; Made by Joseph B. Friedman; Ink on paper; 9.2 cm x16.5 (3⅝ x 6½ in.); Joseph B. Friedman Papers, Archives Center, National Museum of American History, Washington, DC, 2001.3031

4. **Sketch for Pencilite,** ca. 1915; Made by Joseph B. Friedman; Pencil on paper; 20 x 12.7 cm (7⅞ x 5 in.); Joseph B. Friedman Papers, Archives Center, National Museum of American History, Washington, DC, 2001.3031

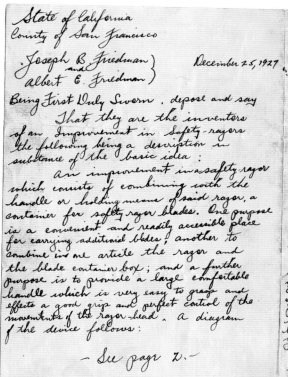

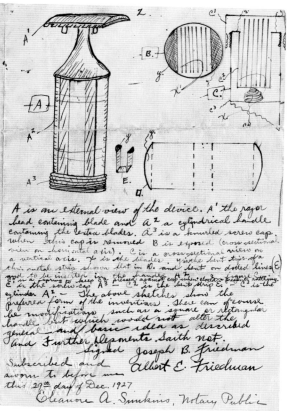

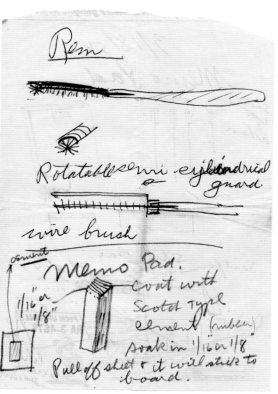

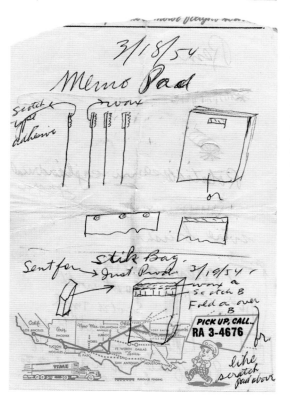

Sketch for a Safety Razor with Notes
December 1927
Made by Joseph B. Friedman
Ink on paper
21 x 28 cm (8 1/4 x 11 in.)
Joseph B. Friedman Papers
Archives Center
National Museum of American History, Washington, DC
2001.3031

Sketches for Memo Pad with Adhesive Strip
March 18, 1954
Made by Joseph B. Friedman
Ink and pencil on paper
15.5 x 10.8cm (6 1/8 x 4 1/4 in.)
Joseph B. Friedman Papers
Archives Center
National Museum of American History, Washington, DC
2001.3031

MAKE: SKETCHES

197

(above left) **Sketch for Inflatable Umbrella,** January 19, 1954; Made by Joseph B. Friedman; Pencil on paper; 21.3 x 8.5 cm (8⅜ x 3⅜ in.); Joseph B. Friedman Papers, Archives Center, National Museum of American History, Washington, DC, 2001.3031

(above right) **Pocket Notebook of Inventions,** 1958; Made by Joseph B. Friedman; Ink on paper; Open: 25.2 x 7.5 cm; (9¹⁵⁄₁₆ x 2¹⁵⁄₁₆ in.); Joseph B. Friedman Papers, Archives Center, National Museum of American History, Washington, DC, 2001.3031

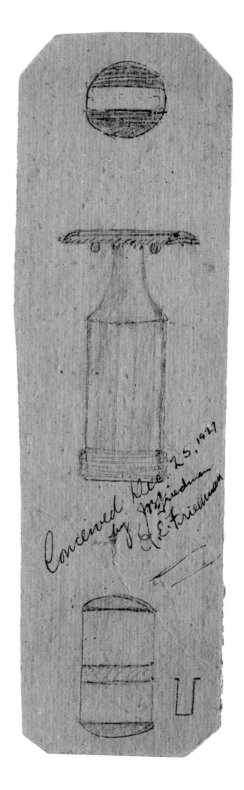

Friedman executed this sketch for a safety razor on Christmas Day on the back of a package of chocolates: *Sketch for Safety Razor,* December 25, 1927; Made by Joseph B. Friedman; Pencil on cardboard; 23.5 x 6.7 cm (9¼ x 2⅝ in.); Joseph B. Friedman Papers, Archives Center, National Museum of American History, Washington, DC, 2001.3031

EARL S. TUPPER (AMERICAN, 1907–1983)

EARL TUPPER IS BEST KNOWN FOR HIS "TUPPERWARE," its airtight "Tupper Seal" (US Patent 2,816,589, granted December 17, 1957) for food containers giving rise to an entire industry. Many of his earliest designs—for corsets, a water motorcycle, and a dental-floss cleaning fork, among others—reflect the flexibility of his ingenuity. Tupper's ideas, visualized in an invention notebook, are clearly laid out, but in it he also advised himself on such matters as "How to Invent" and "My Purpose in Life." His sketches for various hair combs, each slightly different in size, color, style, and functionality, demonstrate Tupper's attention to detail and his interest in considering multiple approaches. He captured not only the idea, but his entire methodology: list every invention; date it; note it in a diary/notebook; begin a folder on it as work starts; place all bills, letters, and sketches relating to it in the folder; and make an outline of progress for each one. **AO**

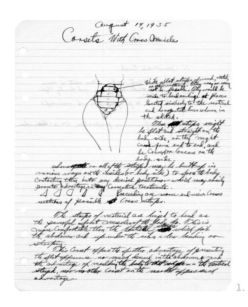

1.

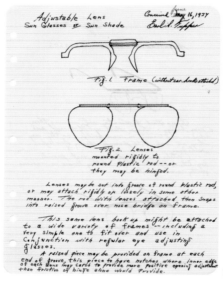

2.

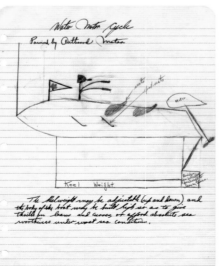

3.

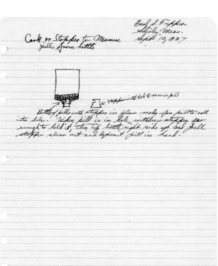

4.

1. *Pages from Tupper Notebook: Sketch for "Corsets with Cross Muscles,"* August 14, 1935
Made by Earl S. Tupper
Ink on paper; 28 x 21.4 cm (11 x 8 7/16 in.)
Earl S. Tupper Papers, Archives Center
National Museum of American History
Washington, DC, 1992.3213

2. *Sketch for "Adjustable Lens Sun Glasses or Sun Shade,"* June 16, 1937
Made by Earl S. Tupper
Ink on paper; 28 x 21.5 cm (11 x 8 7/16 in.)
Earl S. Tupper Papers, Archives Center
National Museum of American History
Washington, DC, 1992.3213

3. *Sketch for "Water Motor Cycle,"* undated; Made by Earl S. Tupper
Ink and pencil on paper
28 x 21.6 cm (11 x 8 1/2 in.)
Earl S.Tupper Papers, Archives Center
National Museum of American
History Washington, DC, 1992.3213

4. *Sketch for "Cork or Stopper to Measure Pills from Bottle,"*
September 10, 1937
Made by Earl S. Tupper
Ink on paper
28 x 21.5 cm (11 x 8 7/16 in.)
Earl S.Tupper Papers, Archives Center
National Museum of American History
Washington, DC, 1992.3213

(opposite)
Sketch for "Adjustable Lens Glasses,"
June 16, 1937
Made by Earl S. Tupper
Ink on paper
28 x 21.5 cm (11 x 8 7/16 in.)
Earl S. Tupper Papers, Archives Center
National Museum of American History
Washington, DC, 1992.3213

June
May 16, 937

Adjustable Lens Glasses

Lenses attach to plastic rod running thru nose bridge. Lenses attach rigidly to rod and depend on rod turning in nose bridge; or they may hinge on rod to provide raising for eye shades.

Notches on side of nose rest provide cog-like adjustment for holding lenses in various partly raised positions.

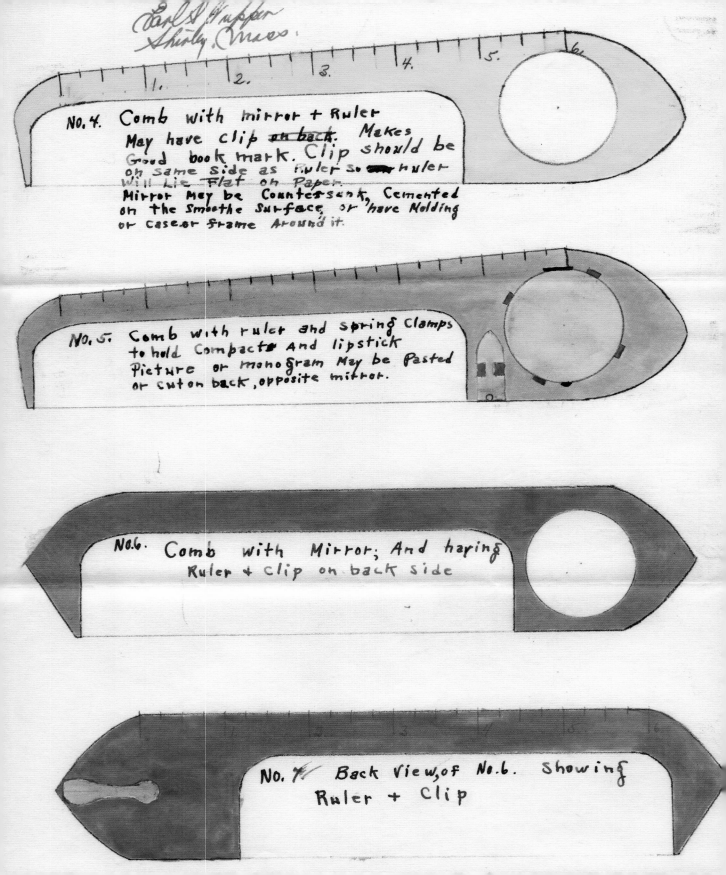

Carl A. Wupper
Shirley, Mass.

NO. 4. Comb with mirror + Ruler
May have clip on back. Makes
Good book mark. Clip should be
on same side as Ruler so Ruler
Will Lie Flat on Paper.
Mirror May be Countersunk, Cemented
on the Smooth Surface, or have Molding
or case or frame Around it.

NO. 5. Comb with ruler and spring clamps
to hold Compacts And lipstick
Picture or monogram May be Pasted
or cut on back, opposite mirror.

NO. 6. Comb with Mirror; And having
Ruler + clip on back side

NO. 7. Back View, of No. 6. Showing
Ruler + Clip

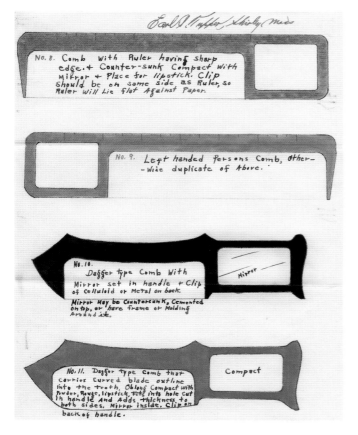

No. 8. Comb with Ruler having sharp edge. + Counter-sunk Compact with Mirror + Place for lipstick. Clip should be on same side as Ruler, so Ruler will Lie flat Against Paper.

No. 9. Left handed Persons Comb, Other-wise duplicate of Above.

No. 10. Dagger type Comb with Mirror set in handle + Clip of Celluloid or Metal on back.
Mirror May be Countersunk, Cemented on top, or have frame or Molding Around it.

Mirror

No. 11. Dagger type Comb that carries curved blade outline into the teeth. Oblong Compact with Powder, Rouge, lipstick. Fits into hole cut in handle And Adds thickness to both sides. Mirror inside. Clip on back of handle.

Compact

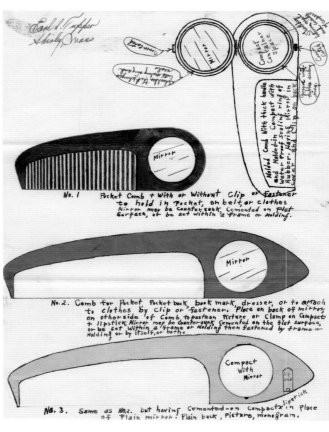

No. 1 Pocket Comb + with or without Clip or Fastener to hold in Pocket, on belt, or clothes. Mirror may be counter-sunk, Cemented on Flat Surface, or be set within a frame or Molding.

Mirror

No. 2. Comb for Pocket Pocket book, book mark, dresser, or to attach to clothes by Clip or fastener. Place on back of mirror on other side of Comb to paste on Picture or Clamp on Compact + lipstick. Mirror may be counter-sunk Cemented on the flat surface, or be set within a frame or Molding then fastened by frame or Molding or by itself, or both.

Mirror

No. 3. Same as No. 2. but having Cemented-on Compact + lipstick in Place of Plain mirror. Plain back, Picture, monogram.

Compact With Mirror

(opposite and above) *Sketches for Comb Designs, March 1937; Made by Earl S. Tupper; Ink on paper; 27.9 x 21.6 cm (11 x 8½ in.);*
Earl S. Tupper Papers, Archives Center, National Museum of American History, Washington, DC, 1992.3213

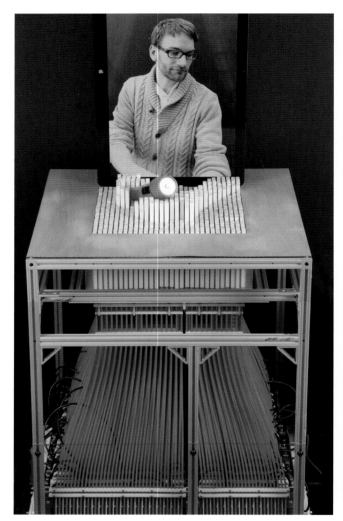

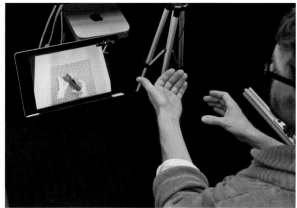

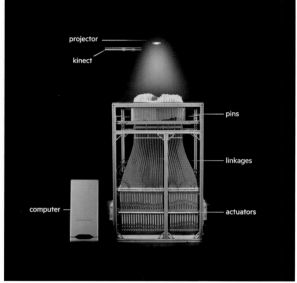

projector
kinect
pins
linkages
computer
actuators

inFORM

2013

Designed by Tangible Media Group:
Daniel Leithinger (Austrian, b. 1980),
Sean Follmer (American, b. 1987),
Philipp Schoessler (German, b. 1986),
and Hiroshi Ishii (Japanese,
b. 1956)
(Cambridge, Massachusetts, USA)
Electromechanical assembly, aluminum
frame, Microsoft Kinect Sensor,
Apple Mac mini, display
182.9 x 66 x 66 cm (6 ft. x 26 in. x 26 in.)
Courtesy of Tangible Media Group
and MIT Media Lab. This installation was
generously supported by Stealcase.

IMAGINE MANIPULATING OBJECTS VIRTUALLY and physically
with your hands in real time and from thousands of miles away. The Tangible Media
Group, led by Hiroshi Ishii, at the MIT Media Lab, is working on this new type of user
interaction and transforming how we may communicate and work in the future.

One of their current projects is inFORM, a dynamic-shape display that gives physical
form to digital information: physical "pixels" on a table surface move in real time, in
accordance with data from a motion-sensing input device. A depth-sensing camera
sends signals from a remote location to the motorized-pin surface, where objects can
be handled by the virtual participants in a videoconference. This ability to interact physically creates a strong sense of presence. In addition, future three-dimensional designs
will be physically prototyped, albeit at low resolution, without the need for 3D printing.
Architects and urban planners will be able to share and discuss their designs immediately
with clients—even miles apart. MM

Sketchbot

2012

Designed by Tellart
(Providence, Rhode Island, USA)
Graphic design by B-Reel (UK)
Industrial design by
Universal Design Studio (UK)
for Google Creative Labs (USA)
Aluminum, plastic, assorted
electrical components
JavaScript, HTML, CSS,
and Python source files
137.2 x 137.2 x 137.2 cm
(54 x 54 x 54 in.)
Cooper Hewitt,
Smithsonian Design Museum
New York, Gift of Google, Inc.

THE SKETCHBOT INCORPORATES A PROCESS: first a camera takes a picture, then software extracts a human face from it and sends a series of commands to a robot, which reproduces the face as a contoured line drawing. Sand was chosen because it is reusable and sustainable—in its first year alone, Sketchbot drew over 10 million images. Sand also enables the portraits to be easily erased. The software may also be considered a tool. It is made up of three parts—a Web-based user interface to take and select images, a server that queues the images and drawings, and a controller that operates the robot arm to make the drawing. The separation of these tasks allows the Sketchbot to be reimagined to work with devices other than the robot arm. The Sketchbot was originally commissioned by the Science Museum, London, for the Chrome Web Lab exhibition in 2012. The source code for the Sketchbot, including instructions for building your own version with Lego bricks, is available online from Cooper Hewitt's website, cooperhewitt.org. SC

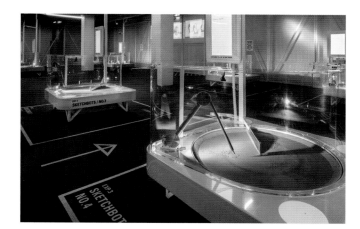

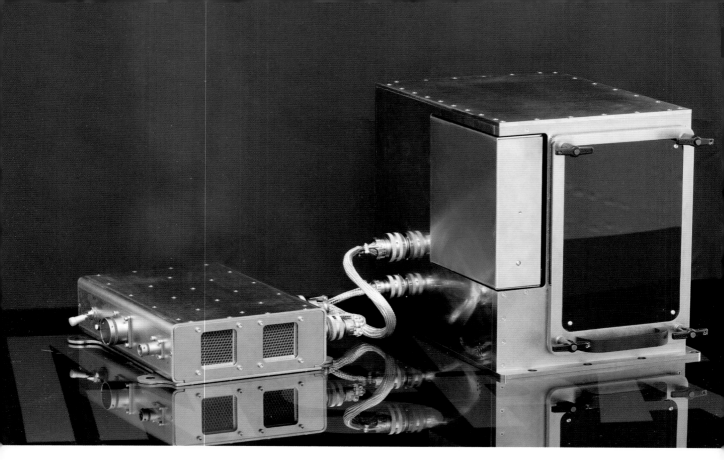

3D Printing
in Zero-G
Experiment
2013–14

Designed and manufactured by
Made In Space, Inc. (Moffett
Field, California, USA) and NASA
Marshall Space Flight Center
(Huntsville, Alabama, USA)
Aluminum, steel, plastic
40 x 44.1 x 44.6 cm
(15 ¾ x 17 ⅜ x 17 ⁹⁄₁₆ in.)
Courtesy of Made in Space, Inc.
and NASA

A FUTURE IN WHICH SPACE missions will be mostly self-sufficient will soon be here. Made In Space, Inc. has partnered with NASA's Marshall Space Flight Center to launch the first 3D printer built specifically for use in microgravity to the International Space Station (ISS). The printer, dubbed the "3D Printing in Zero-G Experiment"—or, in some circles, "the flying factory"—will demonstrate manufacturing capabilities in space. Normally, 3D printers use an additive extrusion-based process to build objects layer by layer out of polymers, composites, and other materials. The challenges of designing for space are numerous; the printer must account for the movement, or "float," of components during liftoff and in microgravity, survive vibrations and changes in pressure during launch, and be provided with adequate electrical power and ventilation. Thus far, all space missions have been completely dependent on Earth and the launch vehicles that send equipment to space. The greater the distance from Earth and the longer the duration of the mission, the more difficult it is to resupply materials. The 3D printers will allow the current supply chain from Earth to space to be largely bypassed, with astronauts able to create the parts and tools they need. At present, these include common instruments and replacement parts, but they will eventually comprise more complex necessities, such as the small, deployable satellites known as CubeSats. Made In Space's 3D printer is generating a selection of ABS-plastic test parts, the very first objects to be manufactured off planet Earth. CM

TOOLS

1. Functionality Test
2. Vertical Column
3. Tensile Coupon
4. Torque Coupon
5. Crowfoot
6. Cubsat Clip
7. Container
8. Wrench
9. Buckle (Male)
10. Buckle (Female)
11. Cable End Cap (Half)
12. Mold Base
13. PicoSat

"Imagine an astronaut needing to make a life-or-death repair on the International Space Station. Rather than hoping that the necessary parts and tools are on the station already, what if the parts could be 3D printed when they needed them?"

AARON KEMMER, CEO of Made In Space, Inc.

Related Tools and Test Parts, 2013–14; Designed by Made In Space, Inc. engineers, including Mike Snyder, Noah Paul-Gin, Deejay Riley, Matt Napoli, and American Society for Testing and Materials (ASTM); Thermoplastic; Variable dimensions: 5.6 × 16.4 × 16.7 mm (¼ × ²¹⁄₃₂ × ²¹⁄₃₂ in.) to 60.3 × 52.5 × 51.5 mm (2 ⅜ × 2 ¹⁄₁₆ × 2 ¹⁄₃₂ in.)

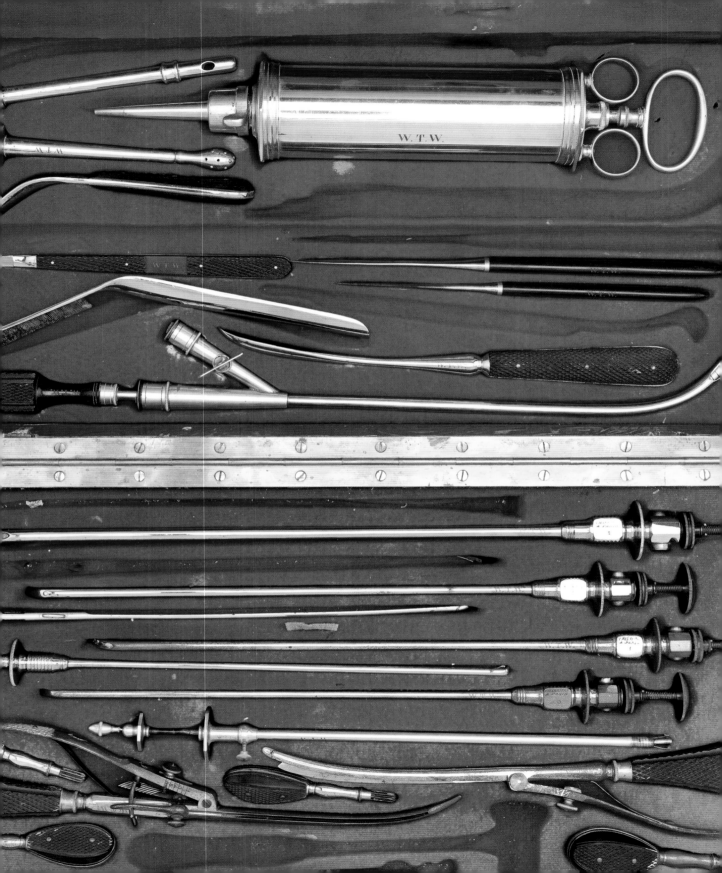

A TOOLBOX IS AS UNIQUE and personal as its owner. The box and implements inside bespeak the profession and personify the character, status, and skill of its owner. A nineteenth-century state-of-the-art European surgical set, which would have been coveted by any doctor, was not only a status symbol but reflected the owner's expertise. The fact that each instrument was stamped with his initials reinforced a sense of pride and possession that could only be captured through fine craftsmanship. The Iñupiat of northwest Alaska, like many indigenous people, exquisitely carved their awls and other tools to show respect for the material—the plant or animal from which it came.

Oftentimes, the craftsmanship and delicate embellishment conceal the function of the tools inside. The elegantly decorated enameled writing box and meticulously incised needle case belie their practical applications as containers for writing and sewing instruments. For the Aleut of southwest Alaska, incorporating different colored threads in the seams of a gut work bag was both ornamental and a way of personalizing a possession. Such toolboxes tended to be compact and highly portable because its user might be days away from any supply source. Today, a trip into space could turn into a disaster without the right tools for repairing a problem. Because there was no precedent for a spacecraft toolbox, NASA engineers looked to familiar wrenches and screwdrivers for the Skylab tool kit, but tailored them and their container for an antigravity environment. Velcro®, snugly molded cavities, and covered drawers helped to keep the tools from floating away.

The twenty-first-century toolbox has retained the portability of its earlier counterparts and still relies on the ingenuity of an "interior" designer and engineer to conceptualize the intricacies of spatial compartmentalization. The Swiss Champ SOS Kit includes tools that someone stranded in the wilderness might need to survive, find their way home, or even prepare an emergency campsite, all tucked inside a palm-size case. The MacBook Air, with its sleek, wafer-thin profile, defines the portable office or studio and can manage filing, calculating, and researching, once the job of a personal assistant. In fact, the MacBook's intuitive interface and tactile keyboard make it enjoyable to tackle these tasks. It also comes closer than any other electronic device to being the universal toolbox, completely customizable inside with apps and wallpaper, and outside with stickers and cases. Although many variables influenced the design of toolboxes over the 250 years represented in this section, their individuality remains a constant.

TOOLBOXES

(opposite) *Lithotomy surgical set, 1833–42, made by Joseph-Frédéric-Benoît Charrière*

Child's Tool Chest
1900–24

Manufactured by R. Bliss
Manufacturing Company
Company, est. 1845
(Pawtucket, Rhode Island, USA)
Wood, metal, paint, paper, ink
33 x 43.2 x 22.9 cm (13 x 17 x 9 in.)
Smithsonian Institution
National Museum of American History
Washington, DC, Cat. 1977.1101.0167

MINIATURIZING OBJECTS TO A SCALE accessible to children has held a special fascination for designers and makers over the centuries. This child's tool chest declares carpentry to be boys' work, a commentary on early-twentieth-century society and its gender expectations. Inside the lid is a color lithograph of boys building a small house beneath a banner that reads, BLISS UNION TOOL CHESTS FOR BOYS. R. Bliss Manufacturing Company, originally a producer of wood screws and clamps for piano and cabinet makers, became well known for their lithographed wooden toys around the turn of the twentieth century.

The chest, complete with a hinged lid and a removable top tray, contains functional tools, including a metal plane, chisel, hammer, and saw. Only the size of the tools and the adjustments made to the grips for smaller hands distinguish the contents from their adult versions. GK

Traveling Dressing Table Set

1875

Retailed by Asprey & Co.
(London, England)
Silversmith: Thomas Whitehouse
(British, act. 1848–d. 1898)
Coromandel-veneered joined wood;
silk; gilt and tooled calfskin;
raised, chased, and engraved silver;
cut glass; mirrored glass; carved
mother-of-pearl; cut and engraved brass;
gilt metal; forged steel
Closed: 21.3 x 32.4 x 23.3 cm
(8⅜ x 12¾ x 9³⁄₁₆ in.)
Cooper Hewitt, Smiths〔
Design Museum, New Y
Gift of Danny J. H. Kauf
1984-133-1-a/i

VOYAGES OCCASION THE NEED for customized tool kits. Unlike today, when air travel requires carry-on toiletry liquids to fit in clear plastic bags and other containers, in the nineteenth century, this elegant dressing-table box would have held stylish and functional implements. The owner probably had someone to carry it for him or her, so practical considerations such as weight and sturdiness were not paramount. While men and women alike availed themselves of such boxes, with minor variations of implements, this example appears more likely to have been a man's. In 1870s London, a man might well have had creams for his hair and wax for his moustache, colognes and manicure equipment, and button hooks and other items needed for dressing. Both sexes of the more educated classes were likely to communicate by mail, often several times a day, so this traveling case provides places for stationery, pen, inkwell, and sander, as well as a surface in the concealed drawer below the area with the toiletries for composing (and perhaps hiding) correspondence. SDC

Machinist's Tool Chest

Early 20th century

Made by Union Tool Chest Company, Inc.
(Rochester, New York, USA)
Used by Albert Latham and his son
Harold Albert Moore Latham
at United Shoe Machinery Company
(Beverly, Massachusetts, USA)
Wood, metal, felt, mirror, approximately 250 tools
Closed: 33 x 50.8 x 21.3 cm (13 x 20 x 8 ⅜ in.)
Smithsonian Institution
National Museum of American History
Washington, DC, Cat. 1989.0259.348

ALBERT LATHAM AND HIS SON Harold Albert Moore Latham used these machinist's tools and toolbox during their careers at the United Shoe Machinery Company (USMC) in the early twentieth century.[1] The seven-drawer chest contains nearly 250 machinist's instruments, all well protected in felt-lined drawers. The bottom tray, actually the front of the box, swings up to keep the drawers from opening. The box could also be locked to secure the owner's tools, his or her most prized possessions.

The history of the USMC is emblematic of how industry became mechanized, enabling the mass production of a uniform shoe cheaper and faster than ever before. In the early twentieth century, it took more than 150 machine operations to produce a typical welt shoe, and any breakdown during the workday would halt production, making immediate repair imperative and skilled mechanics a necessity. GK

[1] Richard Roe, "The United States Shoe Machinery Company," *Journal of Political Economy* 21, no. 109 (1913): 941.

(above) *The United Shoe Machinery Company opened an industrial school in 1909 that taught young men factory work while they completed high school. Here, an instructor teaches young men the use of machines between 1915 and 1938.*

(top) *Harold Albert Moore Latham began working at the United Shoe Machinery Company during the 1920s and wore this badge when performing his duties as a supervisor in the 1940s.*

Skylab Tool Kit #2

1973–74

↓

Manufactured by McDonnell Douglas
Astronautics Co. (USA)
Aluminum, anodized aluminum,
steel, cardboard, ink
Closed: 24.8 × 39.4 × 28.6 cm
(9¾ × 15½ × 11¼ in.)
Smithsonian National Air and Space
Museum, Washington, DC
Transferred from NASA
Marshall Space Flight Center
A20110451000

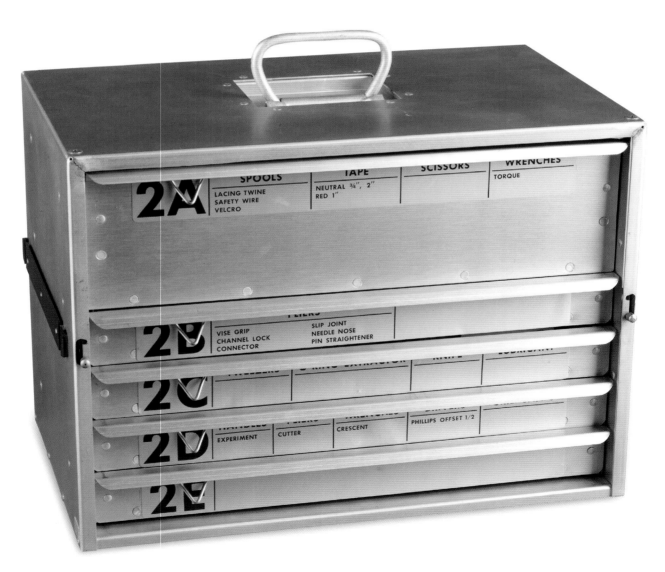

Astronaut making repairs on the Hubble Space Telescope

WHEN THE SKYLAB ORBITAL WORKSHOP—the United States' first space-station—was launched into low Earth orbit in May 1973, planners at NASA had to imagine the kinds of tools crew members might require for lengthy stays on the spacecraft. Three separate crews of three astronauts each occupied the spacecraft until February 1974, with the last and longest stay eighty-four days. The lack of experience provisioning crews for long-duration spaceflight meant turning to familiar tool kits, resembling those commonly found in garages and workshops all over the country. Added features such as Velcro® tabs on the implements and incised trays in the drawers helped to secure the tools in a zero-gravity environment.

NASA provided several onboard kits, which contained a variety of tools and supplies that the planners anticipated might be needed to maintain the spacecraft and the equipment within it. This kit was a backup for the one used on Skylab Orbital Workshop, now displayed at the National Air and Space Museum in Washington, DC. AAN

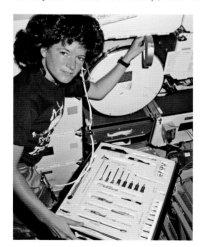

(above left) *Astronaut Sally Ride displays some of the in-flight maintenance tools on board Challenger during her first space mission in 1983.*
(above right) *STS-130 pilot Terry Virts lets a wallet of small tools float on the International Space Station.*

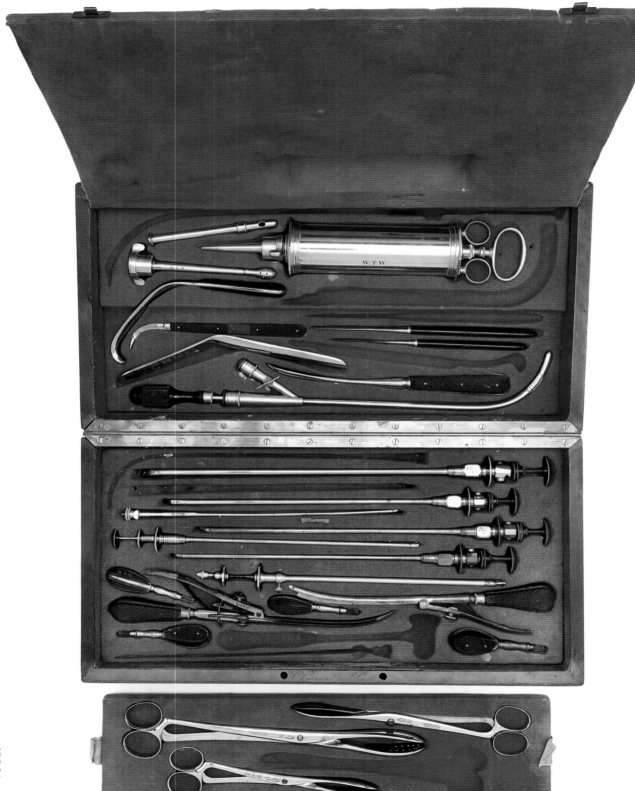

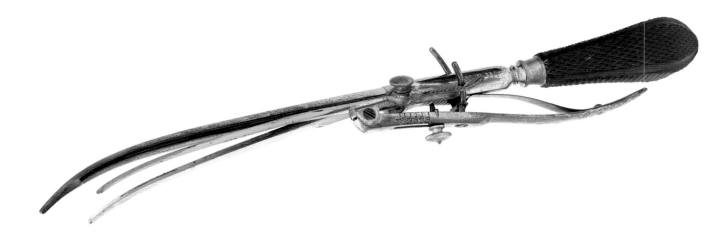

Lithotomy Surgical Set
1833–42

Made by Joseph-Frédéric-Benoît Charrière
(French, b. Switzerland, 1803–1876)
Case: mahogany, brass, chamois
Instruments: steel, ebony
Closed: 11.2 x 44.5 x 22.8 cm
(4⁷⁄₁₆ x 17½ x 9 in.)
Smithsonian Institution
National Museum of American History
Washington, DC, Cat. 302606.773

THIS HANDSOME LITHOTOMY SET is an early example of a collection of instruments made for a specific surgical specialty—in this case, the removal of stones from the kidney or bladder. The twenty-six instruments, used for cutting, grasping, or crushing stones, as well as irrigating the bladder, are housed in a brass-trimmed mahogany case lined with red chamois.

The instruments made by Joseph-Frédéric-Benoît Charrière were status symbols, extraordinarily precise and far more elegant than anything produced by his American counterparts. This set is one of three Charrière surgical sets owned by William Thomas Wilson, a wealthy Baltimore physician who graduated from the University of Maryland School of Medicine in 1842. It is not known whether Wilson procured these surgical tools in Europe or in the United States through a surgical-instrument maker or an apothecary acting as an agent for Charrière. What is clear, however, is Wilson's pride in his profession and in the tools of his trade, each of which is stamped with his initials. JC

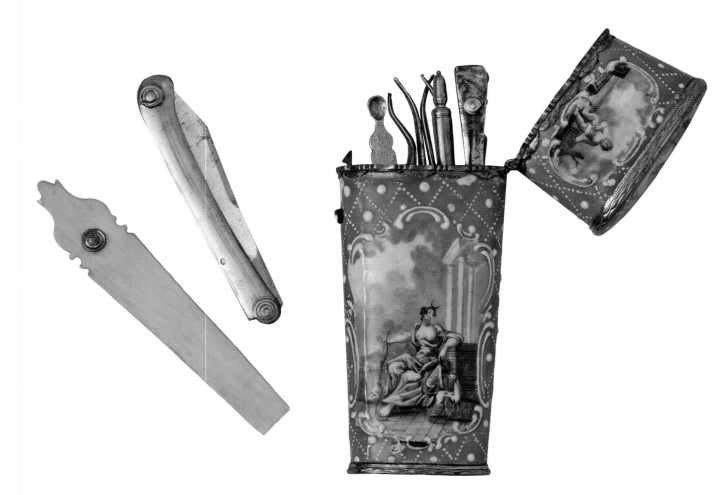

Etui with Writing and Grooming Instruments

1770–80

Staffordshire, England
Enamel on copper, gilt copper,
steel, ivory, cut wood
10 x 4.3 x 2 cm (3¹⁵⁄₁₆ x 1¹¹⁄₁₆ x ¹³⁄₁₆ in.)
Cooper Hewitt, Smithsonian
Design Museum, New York
Bequest of Sarah Cooper Hewitt
1931-6-105-a/h

THIS ETUI, OR CASE, also called a *nécessaire*, holds scissors, a needle case, thread, penknife, tweezers, pencil, and ivory tablet, all "necessary" to eighteenth-century women of social status or pretensions. The same artisan probably also made cutlery, but almost certainly did not enamel the case. While some of the objects suggest delicate sewing and grooming, the small pencil and ivory tablet could have served both for domestic lists and as a reusable dance card.

The enameled copper case states its femininity with scrolls and images of Venus and Cupid, as well as of Diana the huntress and a dog, a symbol of faithfulness. These symbols of love and fidelity imply that this was likely a gift from husband to wife. The materials and techniques employed show it to be a product aimed at a merchant class newly rich from the industrial revolution, centered in the middle of England, where the case was made. It was thus more affordable than the high-style gold work done in London or crafted by foreign goldsmiths. SDC

Writing Toolbox

1750–75

Staffordshire, England
Enamel on copper, gilt copper,
glass, wood
5.1 x 6.4 x 3.8 cm (2 x 2½ x 1½ in.)
Smithsonian American Art Museum
Washington, DC, Gift of John Gellatly
1929.8.245.26

DECORATIVE ENAMEL BOXES blossomed in the second half of the eighteenth century as objects of exchange among wealthy Britons, passing from hand to well-manicured hand, before coming to rest on a proper Georgian's table. Some might hold snuff or beauty spots, implying a place in a life of leisure. Despite the intensive craftsmanship and skillfully wrought motifs, most commonly frolicking figures and pastoral scenes, these containers were referred to as "trifles." Indeed, this box fits snugly in the palm and, viewed closed, does nothing to disrupt the impression of frivolousness. Yet its interior is tightly packed with compartments for writing tools, including an adjustable brass quill-pen holder and two cut-glass vials with enameled lids. The scale of these—each is barely more than 2.5 cm (1 in.) long—makes clear the gender and class of the intended author, as well as, perhaps, the length of the texts that might flow from them: calling cards, thank-yous, and invitations to tea, innocent (and possibly less virtuous) notes on the eve of a revolution in which the pen would play an outsize role. **NRB**

Woman's Workbox with Lid

Created before 1870s

Yup'ik, Yukon-Kuskokwim Delta
(Alaska, USA)
Carved wood, walrus-ivory inlay
10.2 x 24.1 x 10.2 cm (4 x 9½ x 4 in.)
Collection of Edward W. Nelson, 1879
Gift of Edward W. Nelson, Department
of Anthropology, National Museum
of Natural History, Smithsonian
Institution, Washington, DC, E36240

A YUP'IK WOMAN'S TOOLBOX safeguarded some of her most precious instruments and materials. Small scrapers and awls; sinew, fiber, and scraps of yarn to sew with; and needle cases and other small objects would have been found in this personal container (*gungasvik*).

Yup'ik men made the chests, each one unique. This well-crafted box has a solid top and base, with an oval body that was formed by boiling and bending a narrow lath of wood. The walrus-ivory handle and inlays are incised with concentric circles, a Yup'ik design that symbolizes levels of the cosmos. The container's other function—as a heavily used cutting board—is revealed by the numerous scratches on the bottom.[2] The chest's owner simply turned the box over to cut pieces of skin or sinew for sewing. AC & MM

[2] Artifact consultation, April 17–18, 2010, National Museum of Natural History, Washington, DC, on the occasion of the opening of the exhibition, *Yuungnaqpiallerput (The Way We Genuinely Live): Masterworks of Yup'ik Science and Survival* (April 17–July 25, 2010)

Work Bag

Created before 1880s

Unangax̂ (Aleut), Atka Island,
Aleutian Islands (Alaska, USA)
Stitched and embroidered sea-lion intestine
25 x 22.5 cm (9 ¹¹⁄₁₆ x 8 ⁷⁄₈ in.)
Collection of Lucien M. Turner, 1882
Department of Anthropology
National Museum of Natural History
Smithsonian Institution
Washington, DC, E65272

WATERPROOF AND WINDPROOF, gut was an essential material in the indigenous communities of northwest Alaska. The extremely laborious process of making it into a cloth that could then be stitched into parkas, floats, work bags, and even windows was reserved for women, who washed the intestines of ocean mammals and inflated the intestines for drying. The material was then cut into strips 5 cm to 10 cm (2–4 in.) wide and as long as 61 m (200 ft.); finally, the fabric was cut into panels for sewing.[3]

This beautiful translucent and waterproof bag for sewing materials (*imguĝdax̂*), made of sea-lion intestine, consists of four panels sewn with the fibrous sinew of a sea mammal. Blue, red, and green threads are delicately incorporated into the seams; such pouches might also be personalized with caribou hair, seal fur, bird feathers, or strips of dyed esophagus. Before Russian fur merchants brought iron needles in the eighteenth century, women employed bird- or fish-bone needles, with notches instead of eyes to hold the thread. AC & MM

[3] Lucien M. Turner, *An Aleutian Ethnography*, ed. Raymond L. Hudson (Fairbanks: University of Alaska Press, 2008), 70.

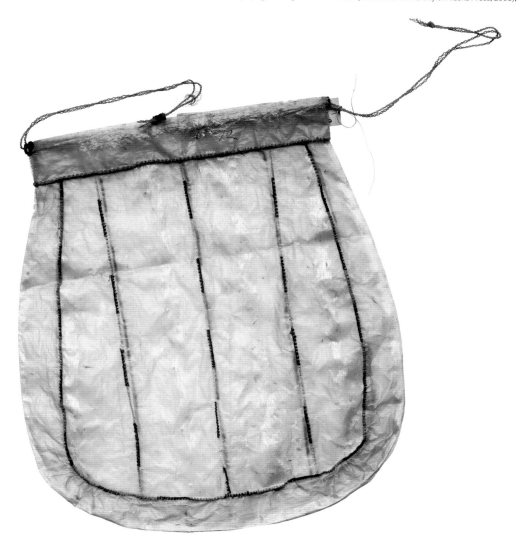

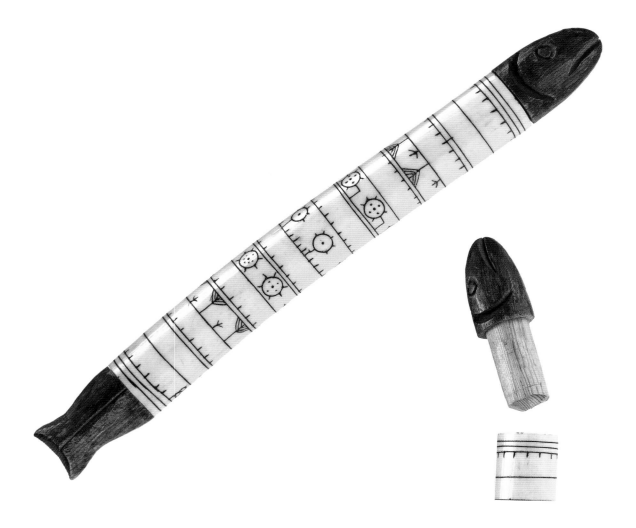

Needle Case
Created before 1947

↑

Kuskwogmiut Yup'ik (Kuskokwim Eskimo)
Calista Native Corp., Doyon Native Corp.
(Alaska, USA)
Carved, incised, painted wood; incised
Tundra Swan wing bone (humerus)
14.5 x 1.6 x 1.3 cm (5¹¹⁄₁₆ x ⅝ x ½ in.)
National Museum of the American Indian
Smithsonian Institution
Washington, DC, 21/800

A YUP'IK WOMAN'S ABILITY TO SEW was critical to her family's survival—just as men had to master hunting skills, women had to learn to sew and mend before they married. This exquisite case housed a woman's essential needles, which were of bone and with or without eyes. Women used a fine-pointed bodkin, or awl, of bone, ivory, or deer horn, to pierce sea-mammal gutskin or land-animal skins, then stitched the seam closed.

This case was made from a section of the hollow wing bone of a swan and has wooden stoppers at each end, one representing the head of what is probably a blackfish and the other the tail. The bone is delicately incised with crosshatching, rings, and spurred lines—patterns frequently employed in the Yup'ik community. The remarkable skill the carver applied to an extremely utilitarian object speaks to the connection between maker, user, and environment: the expertise and the decoration honor the swan that provided the material and the blackfish, which gives sustenance to the people. MM

Awl and Cord
Created before 1916
↓

Iñupiaq (Alaskan Iñupiat Eskimo)
Arctic Slope Native Corp.
(Point Barrow, Alaska, USA)
Carved and perforated bone, hide cord
Awl: 13.2 cm (5¼ in.)
Cord overall: 14.9 cm (5⅞ in.)
National Museum of the American Indian
Smithsonian Institution
Washington, DC, 4/8457

WOMEN USED AWLS to make the holes in gut or skin through which they would then thread sinew or other fibers to stitch the pieces of material together. Awls came in a variety of sizes, suitable to the variety of materials to be sewn. The shapely bone and ivory points on this page and the next would have been used to perforate different thicknesses of skins or gut. MM

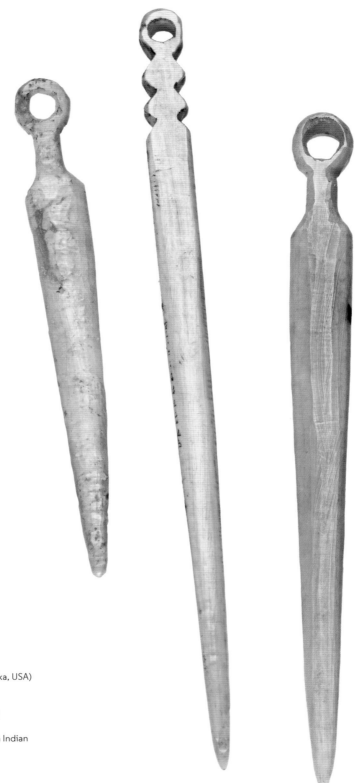

Awls
Created before 1914

↑

Iñupiaq (Alaskan Iñupiat Eskimo)
NANA Native Corp. (Candle, Alaska, USA)
Carved ivory
Left: 5 x 0.6 cm (1¹⁵⁄₁₆ x ¼ in.)
Center: 7.3 x 0.5 cm (2⅞ x ³⁄₁₆ in.)
Right: 6.4 x 0.6 cm (2½ x ¼ in.)
National Museum of the American Indian
Smithsonian Institution
Washington, DC, 3/6271

Pocket Knife/Multitool: *Swiss Champ SOS Kit*

ca. 1985

Designed and manufactured by
Victorinox (Switzerland)
Stainless steel, cellulose acetate-butyrate
(Cellidor®), variable materials
Case (closed): 11.1 x 6.4 x 4.4 cm
(4⅜ x 2½ x 1¾ in.)
Cooper Hewitt, Smithsonian Design Museum,
New York, Gift of Victorinox, 2013-56-1-a/x

ONE OF THE SMALLEST AND MOST COMPACT multifunction tool kits in the world, the Victorinox Swiss Champ SOS Kit boasts 101 features. In addition to the standard implements—blades, scissors, file—the collection also includes many other outdoor and survival items, such as a can opener, fish scaler, awl, wire cutters, and screwdrivers. More than thirty retractable implements nestle neatly inside the compact red handle marked with the inlaid Victorinox cross and shield. The SOS Kit evolved from the knife designed in the late nineteenth century by Karl Elsener—the founder of Victorinox—for the Swiss Army. After World War II, the Victorinox knife was widely used among American soldiers, who popularized it and renamed it the "Swiss Army" knife. Today, these tool kits are ambassadors of their country of origin, underscoring precision, functionality, and innovative design. CT

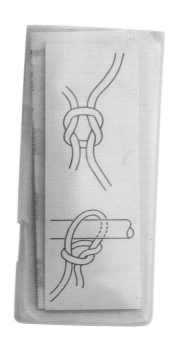

(above and opposite) *Swiss Champ SOS contents*

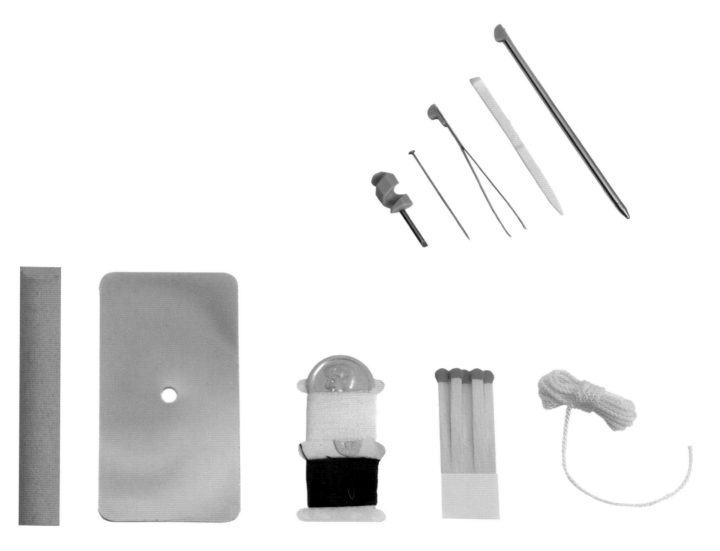

Laptop Computer:
MacBook Air
2014

Designed by Jonathan Ive (British, b. 1967)
and Apple Industrial Design Team
Manufactured by Apple Computer, Inc.
(Cupertino, California, USA)
Anodized, CNC-milled, drilled,
and laser-pierced aluminum;
arsenic-free glass; polycarbonate
Cooper Hewitt, Smithsonian
Design Museum, New York
Gift of Apple

ONCE UPON A TIME, the tools sitting on a designer's worktable were simple implements for drawing, erasing, carving, cutting, gluing, sculpting, and so on. This basic toolbox sat in a larger studio or workshop equipped with drafting boards, T-squares, parallel rules, power tools, photostat cameras, hot-wax machines, and more, depending on the designer's field of endeavor, and those tools were made to communicate with printing and manufacturing plants near and far. Today, many of these tools have been swallowed up by computers and transformed into software. They are ready at hand wherever the user happens to be working. Designers manipulate software applications with input devices such as Wacom pens and Cintiq drawing surfaces, and they send their data to 2D and 3D printers; more often than not, the designer's output is simply a network of other computers. Designers work in their studios on desktop machines, but as portable laptops become more powerful and more connected to cloud-based storage and resources, they can take their tasks anywhere. The toolbox has become a movable studio at the nexus of a global network.

The first laptop computer was designed by Bill Moggridge for GRiD Systems Corporation in 1981, well before the introduction of user-friendly electronic design tools. Priced at about $8,000 a unit, the GRiD was reserved for elite business, government, and military applications and for NASA space missions. Apple's Macintosh, introduced in 1984, offered a new set of instruments, available to individuals. The first adopters developed raw and quirky digital languages suited to the low-resolution output and tiny storage capacity of the early models. By the start of the 1990s, a sea change had swept the graphic-design field, and nearly everyone in the profession was obliged to augment their old set of hand tools with the new ones bubbling out of Apple's beige boxes. Adobe Photoshop, originally intended for professional photographic retouchers, became basic literacy for designers in every field, from illustration to architecture, allowing its users to mix, alter, and simulate the supposed realities of the photographic image. Software for setting type, editing video, and creating 3D models revolutionized professional practices, simultaneously opening the floodgates of digital creation to everyday citizens.

The old tools didn't disappear. In the 1920s, Constructivist artists had embraced the camera as the revolutionary symbol of the new mechanical age, while continuing to wield their pencils and brushes in the service of their new vision—they often took up lithography crayons to simulate the texture and contrast of photography. Designers today still employ pencils and brushes, but more often than not they also apply digital simulations of the old implements in software applications. Digital tools, represented as the analog pen, brush, magnifying glass, and eraser, are grouped together in the "toolbar," a strip of icons loosely based on the toolbox of yore. The behaviors of many of these digital implements bear little relation to the physical objects to which they refer. For example, designers use the "pen" tool in Adobe Illustrator to construct Bezier curves anchored by points; mastering this instrument requires a leap of understanding into a very specific paradigm of drawing.

The first MacBook Air was introduced in 2008. Remarkably thin and light, the Air was prized for its portability. In the years that followed, the technology contained within its sleek, minimal box achieved greater speed and capacity. In a market enlivened by smartphones and small, cheap "netbooks," the compact Air became more popular than Apple's heftier MacBook Pro. The-wafer-thin Air has no drive for reading CDs and DVDs, but users can download files and applications wirelessly and can plug in an external superdrive as needed. The integral multitouch trackpad has replaced the mouse, and it responds—sometimes unexpectedly—to gestures such as pinching, swiping, and rotating.

The input devices of the laptop computer may soon be as quaint and charming as rubber erasers and wooden pencils. Digital tools with haptic feedback are vying to replace the keyboard and mouse; they allow designers and artists to push, pull, and carve virtual materials by means of direct physical gestures. New materials will allow digital screens to bend and flex; before long, the portable design office may fold up and fit in your pocket. The vocabulary of design will continue to evolve alongside the technology, as designers learn to master and remake the processes enabled by an ever-changing toolbox. EL

IN 1850, WHEN HERMANN VON HELMHOLTZ invented the ophthalmoscope for looking into the eye, it was the first time scientists and doctors could see inside a living body. The simple handheld instrument, with its precisely ground lenses, changed their comprehension of how the body worked and spawned a variety of scopes and other devices for exploring it. Today, capsule endoscopy, which employs a tiny camera inserted into a pill-size capsule, such as the Pill-Cam® SB 3, provides the same real-time feedback as gastrointestinal surgery but without invasive means. These two tools of observation, although separated by more than 150 years, remain similar in their ability to augment our sense of sight and to satisfy our desire for exploration—one physically, the other virtually—of unfamiliar territories.

Satellites and microscopes have allowed us to travel to equally extreme environments without leaving our chair. A journey into the world of microorganisms is documented beautifully in seventeenth-century drawings from Anton van Leeuwenhoek's microscope, much as the Solar Wall relays extraordinarily high-definition images of the Sun's surface from telescopes and data transmitted by NASA's Solar Dynamics Observatory. Charles and Ray Eames captured this extreme travel by using scale in their film *Powers of Ten*, which transports viewers from Earth to the edge of the known universe and back, and then deep inside the human body.

The effectiveness of these groundbreaking tools begins with the designer's and scientist's own skills of observation in determining the problem to be solved and creatively identifying the resources for a solution. Nature is a perpetual inspiration, which is especially apparent in examples in this section. By emulating a bee's behavior, the RoboBee, a flying robot, offers a strategy for reviving these valuable insects' increasingly depleted colonies. Biological sonar in bats and other animals allows them to "see" with sound. White-cane tips perform the same function by providing essential information about the terrain to the visually impaired user.

As we continue to journey farther, deeper, and longer, our tools will have to respond to performance demands by becoming more efficient, economical, and sustainable. While our five senses remain the primary way we understand the world around us, the tools of observation in the following pages ultimately make us more knowledgeable travelers.

OBSERVE

(opposite) *Film*, Powers of Ten, *1977, written and directed by Charles and Ray Eames*

Autofold Cane

1980s

↓ →

Designed by Hycor
Manufactured by Mahler
(Brooklyn, New York, USA)
Rubber, elastic cord, aluminum,
iron, reflective tape
Extended (incl. cord): 107.3 x 2.5 cm
(42¼ x 1 in.), Folded: 10.5 × 27.3 × 2.5 cm
(4⅛ x 10¾ x 1 in.)
Smithsonian Institution
National Museum of American History
Washington, DC, Cat. 306619.10

(opposite)
Metal Glide Cane Tips, 2000
Rubber, metal
Diam: 2.8 cm (1⅛ in.)
Smithsonian Institution
National Museum of American History
Washington, DC, Cat. 2001.0324.01-03

FOR A PERSON WHO IS BLIND or has low vision, a white cane is an observational tool, a navigation device, and a symbol. It is a simple yet sophisticated means for observing and traversing terrain. In the way it integrates detection and navigation, it is a mechanical analog to the echolocation employed by other species. A white cane conveys essential information about the ground surface, such as solidity, moisture, and changes in texture. For example, it can pick up the raised dots at the edge of a train platform, or the sound of a tap may indicate transition from concrete to gravel, allowing the user to act accordingly.

The primary information exchange takes place at the tip, where the cane meets the ground. The hand–cane connection is secondary: the cane extends the hand to where interactions take place. Once the person is moving, feedback from the tip is essential for ascertaining what is unfolding underfoot, so the condition of the tip matters. Tips—like shoe soles or car tires—wear down and have to be replaced. The metal bottom falls off, the rubber disintegrates. If a person uses a roller-ball tip, the plastic gets nicked and worn. The old tip unscrews to make way for the new.

People have used long canes as a tool for centuries. Observation and travel were relatively safe until fast-moving trolleys, automobiles, and streetcars began to crowd roadways and clog intersections in the last half of the nineteenth century. Street life dramatically changed as vehicles took over public space and pushed people onto sidewalks.

Collisions between vehicles and between people and automobiles were frequent, as pedestrians and drivers adapted to new etiquette and thoroughfare conventions. Instead of gathering, playing, and working in the middle of roads, as had been the norm for thousands of years when the pace was slower, pedestrians were now forced to make way. People with limited mobility or sensory impairment were especially in danger of being hit and injured in the paved and faster-paced urban environment. In the 1920s, communities across the country adopted "white cane" laws as a way to raise awareness and counter these dangers. Under these laws, people using a distinctively white cane (not simply a long cane) had the right of way. Those in moving conveyances had to stop or yield and were at fault when accidents occurred. As a consequence, the white cane also became a symbol of consideration toward people who were blind, many of whom were soldiers injured in World War I, and an indirect symbol of disability rights. Fraternal and civic clubs collected donations to support people with vision loss who needed canes. They passed out small white lapel canes in exchange.

A white-cane culture gradually developed among those who used the instruments and, with it, certain features of the canes took on additional symbolism. With shifts in materials and designs, canes have become consumer products that reflect preferences and taste. The style of a white cane sometimes conveys the personal politics of the owner. Just as people in the 1880s interpreted the image of a hammer and muscular forearm of an artisan to mean fraternity or a red *B* on a navy-blue late-twentieth-century baseball cap as a belief in Boston's athleticism, white-cane users interpret a person's choice as a sign of something more. Long, rigid canes may indicate a wish to assert one's presence; rigid canes also produce a distinctive tapping sound. The National Federation for the Blind runs "boot camps" for people with vision impairments in which students learn to downhill-ski, iron, and navigate their daily routes using rigid canes. Folding or telescoping canes are good for riding a bus or in a theater or restaurant when the user does not desire to make a statement or otherwise attract attention. Sighted people generally do not notice a folded cane, so the user blends into a crowd more easily until they get up and go. The next generation of canes, designed for social, political, and landscape changes, will be equally complex and culturally intricate. **KO**

Hearing Aid: *Zon*
2008

Designed by Stuart Karten (American,
b. 1957), Paul Kirley (American, b. 1967)
and Dennis Schroeder (American, b. 1963)
for Stuart Karten Design
Manufactured by Starkey Laboratories, Inc.
(Minnesota, USA)
Injection-molded nylon, chromed metal,
high-gloss metallic paint
3.3 x 1.7 x 0.7 cm (1⁵⁄₁₆ x ¹¹⁄₁₆ x ⁵⁄₁₆ in.)
Cooper Hewitt, Smithsonian Design Museum
New York, Gift of Starkey Laboratories, Inc.
2011-5-1

TO ADDRESS THE STIGMA sometimes associated with traditional hearing aids, Stuart Karten Design created this stylish and empowering tool. Individuals with hearing impairments often wait as long as eight years before getting their first hearing aid, because they associate the conventional shrimp-shaped beige hearing aid with age and weakness, even disability. Borrowing visual cues from modern architecture, jewelry, and automotive design, Karten transformed the hearing aid into a visually appealing object. Available in a palette of six understated colors that blend with various hair and skin tones, Zon is virtually invisible when worn behind the ear and bears closer resemblance to a piece of jewelry than to a medical device. The Zon hearing aid was a 2008 recipient of the Cooper Hewitt, Smithsonian Design Museum's People's Design Award. JP

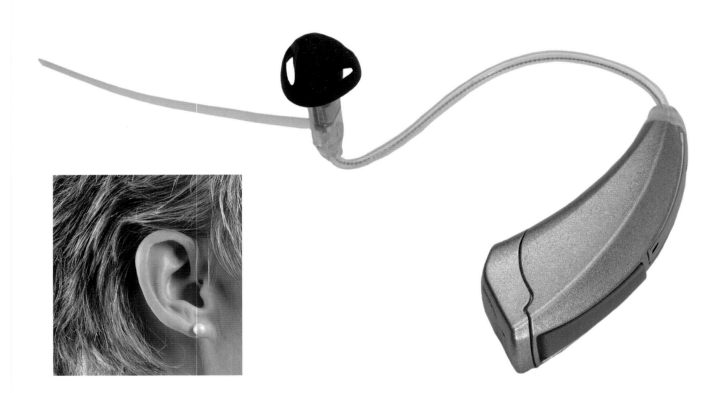

PillCam® SB 3

2001

Invented by Gavriel Iddan (Israeli, n.d.)
Manufactured by Given Imaging, Ltd.
(Yoqneam, Israel)
LED light source, lens, battery,
antenna, transmitter, imager
2.6 x 1.1 cm (1 x ⅟₁₆ in.)
Courtesy of Given Imaging
A Covidien Company

TOOLS THAT ENTER THE HUMAN BODY for observation must be minimally invasive. Similar to backpacking in a fragile ecosystem, where any disturbance to the field may result in harm, such devices present unique challenges. For patients and physicians, maintenance of bodily integrity is both an ethical and a technological issue. Practically speaking, physicians are better able to diagnose and treat a person when they have reliable information, and direct observation is usually preferred over mediated data. Patients desire freedom from pain, discomfort, and risk. PillCam capsule endoscopy was created to meet physician and patient needs when it is necessary to observe the gastrointestinal (GI) system.

Interest in looking at the GI tract dates back hundreds of years, but the relative techniques have undergone steady design improvements only since the nineteenth century. The tools inserted into the body went from rigid to flexible tubes to fiber optics. Engineering the optics and illumination and the techniques for guiding the instruments led to further medical specialization.

In traditional diagnostics, the physician may examine the GI tract by means of radiological images, including fluoroscopic monitoring; exploratory surgery; "push" endoscopy; the transnasal insertion of a scope into the digestive tract; colonoscopy; and the barium enema. Capsule endoscopy was invented to improve upon and sometimes replace these practices. With this procedure, the patient swallows a small digital video camera with light-emitting diodes (LEDs) that illuminate what is around it and a transmitter that exports the pictures of the small intestines. The camera sends images—approximately fifty thousand over the course of its route, or two to six frames per second—to a wireless data recorder that the patient wears on her or his waist for eight hours. The

data are then downloaded into a computer and analyzed by the physician. The tiny, pill-size camera is used once and disposed of after excretion. The PillCam can image places, such as parts of the intestines, that other techniques have difficulty reaching and it works best in tight areas, but less well in the stomach, for example. It can identify such conditions as bleeding, tumors, and vascular lesions and diagnose malabsorption disorders.

Gavriel Iddan, a military missile designer, invented the PillCam. Iddan was a mechanical engineer in the Israeli Ministry of Defense when, in the 1980s, he took a series of sabbaticals to the United States to study imaging. He eventually devised a way to miniaturize the then-current imaging system. After Iddan underwent a colonoscopy in the early 1990s his interest intensified, and he imagined a tiny vessel with a camera traveling through the intestine. The first of his several patents was granted in 1994. To perfect the device and set up a commercial enterprise to market it—the procedure costs around $1,500—Iddan worked with a team that included the gastroenterologist Paul Swain of the United Kingdom. The PillCam was approved for commercial use by the United States Food and Drug Administration in 2001.

Although still relatively new in clinical use, this technology has captured the lay imagination. It combines fantasy for miniaturization, science-fiction travel within the body, and crossing forbidden frontiers. Elegantly, it relies on the body's own intestinal motility to move it through the system. It is, to be sure, an innovation in existing diagnostic imaging, but in an era of anxiety about out-of-control, nonconsensual observation, the tiny camera provides surveillance of the most intimate human geographies. KO

Leeuwenhoek
Microscope
(Replica)

1961
Original ca. 1670

↓

Original made by Anton van Leeuwenhoek
(Dutch, 1632–1723)
Brass
9 x 2.3 x 3 cm (3⁹⁄₁₆ x ⅞ x 1³⁄₁₆ in.)
Smithsonian Institution, National Museum
of American History, Washington, DC
Cat. M-09840

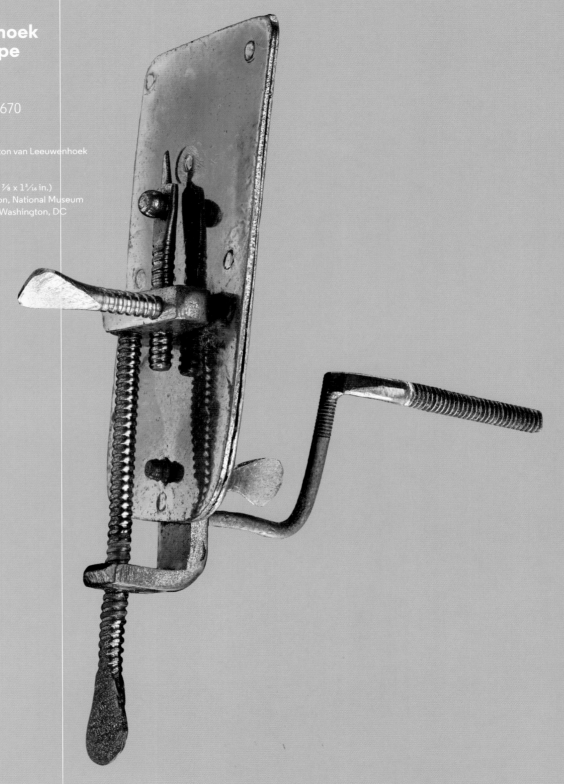

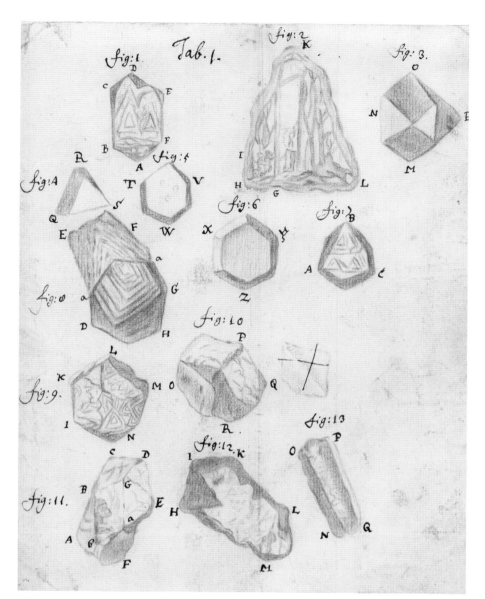

ALLOWING ONE TO SEE what was previously invisible, Anton van Leeuwenhoek's device was one of the earliest applications of a simple (single-lens) microscope for the examination of living things. Far superior to anything available at the time, his microscopes could magnify the view 250 times or more. The instrument was very basic—a brass plate with a lens mounted in a tiny hole. The specimen was mounted on a sharp pin in front of the lens, and its position and focus were adjusted by turning the two screws. The entire instrument was only 7.5 cm to 10 cm (3–4 in.) long, and had to be held close to the eye; it required good lighting and great patience to use.

One of Leeuwenhoek's special skills was grinding the lenses, which produced the superior magnification. He was one of the first scientists to observe and describe single-celled organisms, which he originally referred to as "little animalcules." JP

(above left) *Anton van Leeuwenhoek's red chalk drawings of grains of sand, from a letter to The Royal Society, December 4, 1703*

(above right) *Looking through a replica of Leeuwenhoek's microscope*

Ophthalmoscope and Case

1860

↓ →

Designed by Richard Liebreich
(German, 1830–1917)
Ophthalmoscope: metal, wood, optical glass
Case: leather, velvet
Case (closed): 1.5 x 13.8 x 6.2 cm
(⁹⁄₁₆ x 5⁷⁄₁₆ x 2⁷⁄₁₆ in.)
Smithsonian Institution
National Museum of American History
Washington, DC
Cat. 314016.231.01-02

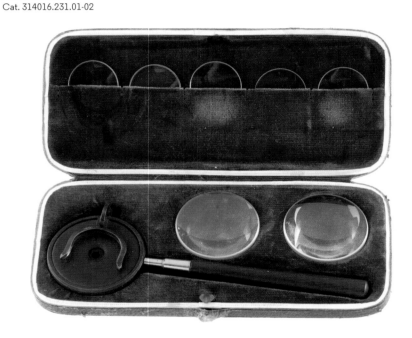

THE HUMAN BODY PRESENTS many intriguing spaces that invite exploration. Tools for observing and comprehending holes, openings, crevices, edges, and surfaces abound in the history of medicine. The dark circle in the middle of the eye and where that enticing opening—the pupil—might lead has intrigued lovers, poets, scientists, and countless idle narcissists. A great leap in knowledge about this mystery occurred in 1850, when Hermann von Helmholtz, a physiology professor in Königsberg, devised an instrument for looking into the eye. His first eye mirror used reflection to direct light rays for illumination, and within a year he had added a lens to sharpen the image. Von Helmholtz was not the first to see the fundus—the back of the eye—but he was the one who wrote about what he had done. The optical basis for his instrument was straightforward: the rays from sunlight, a candle, or a lamp entered the eye and were reflected back. This simple tool afforded observers the first opportunity to see living tissue in action (other than in wounds and injuries). The fundus displays blood vessels and the throbbing substance of life, visible as it functions in real time within the human body. Until the ophthalmoscope, the interior examination of an opened human body was possible only in cases of traumatic injury, dissection, or autopsy. Data from cadavers skewed comprehension about how organs and tissue functioned. Motion had long ceased, colors had faded, and textures had transmuted. Von Helmholtz's tool expanded understanding of the circulatory system, hypertension, diabetes, and other conditions.

This new information was as stimulating and far-reaching in medical circles as the realization a few decades later that microscopic "bacteria" could cause disease. Physicians excited by the idea of directing light into the body and using a magnifying lens to enhance sight began exploring the corporal terra incognita of the throat, stomach, ears, and nose. The success of the ophthalmoscope fostered the invention of implements such as endoscopes, laryngoscopes, otoscopes and, eventually, the fiber optics of the 1960s. Physicians immediately started to fiddle with the ophthalmoscope to improve its range of effectiveness. The original tool had three basic parts—a source of illumination, a means to reflect light into eye, and a method for making the image of the fundus clear. The need for a reliable light source received a great deal of attention. Von Helmholtz used a candle. Others followed with oil lamps, then gas lamps, then incandescence, after Thomas Edison's bulb. A New England ophthalmologist, William S. Dennett, added an electric bulb to his device in 1885, but the bulb's brief life made it impractical in those early days of electricity. In addition, the angle of reflection had to be properly aligned with both the light source and the observer for anything to be visible. The possibility of placing the source of illumination within the instrument spurred another burst of inventive options: the first practical electrical device, by Henry DeZeng of Camden, New Jersey, was made in 1914.

In seeking how best to deliver light into the eye, the physician-designers tried tilted and fixed mirrors, as well as altering the size and composition of the reflecting surface. To sharpen the image they experimented with the power of the viewing lenses, the use of concave and convex lenses, and the position of the lens. Some practitioners preferred an individual lens, others a disk (set) of lenses or detachable disks. By 1913, there were some two hundred variations on the ophthalmoscope.

Richard Liebreich's 1860 alteration was one of several early modifications. His model directed a beam of light to the back of the eye and had removable lenses that could flip out of the way. Liebreich, who had studied with von Helmholtz, went on to an illustrious career in ophthalmology.

In Liebreich's time, the examiner had to be extremely physically close to the patient. The small, flat device required

intimacy between the participants, but this was nothing new: in the mid-nineteenth century, physicians felt skin, sniffed bodily odors, and held wrists without intervening instruments. In fact, patients were just beginning to get used to a therapeutic experience mediated by diagnostic tools such as the clinical thermometer and stethoscope. The ophthalmoscope expanded that relationship. As with other newly devised tools of the time, it added to a doctor's aura of expertise, as much as to her or his mastery of human physiology. KO

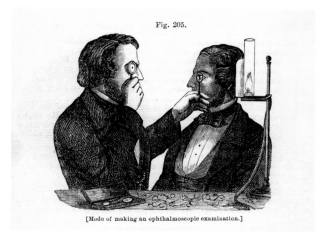

Fig. 205.

[Mode of making an ophthalmoscopic examination.]

"Mode of making an ophthalmoscopic examination," in Robert Druitt, The Principles and Practice of Modern Surgery (Philadelphia: Henry C. Lea, 1867), 376.

FIG. 49.—Ophthalmoscopic examination. Method of the upright image. Obser and patient in the correct position.

. . .Ophthalmoscopic examination in G. E. de Schweinitz, Diseases of the Eye; A Handbook of Ophthalmic Practice for Students and Practitioners (Phil: W.B. Saunders Co., 1906), 120.

Spencer
Microscope
1849–59

Designed by Charles A. Spencer
(American, 1813–1881)
Manufactured by C. A. & H. Spencer
(New York, USA)
Brass, glass
47 x 41.5 x 20 cm (18½ x 16⁵⁄₁₆ x 7⅞ in.)
Smithsonian Institution
National Museum of American History
Washington, DC, Cat. 1990.0183.01

UNTIL CHARLES A. SPENCER began making microscopes in Canastota, New York, in 1838, the only high-quality microscopes available in the United States were imported from Europe. Spencer gained fame among American scientists for his fine objective lenses, which provided stronger magnification and sharper resolution than many European models. In 1847, J. W. Bailey, professor of chemistry at the United States Military Academy, remarked, "I look upon the results obtained by Mr. Spencer as a proud triumph for American art."[1] Spencer microscopes quickly became standard instruments, required by most medical schools. This brass monocular microscope, equipped with a mirror to reflect light through the slide, could be used with either a compound or simple lens. JP

[1] J. W. Bailey, quoted in C. R. Gilman, "An Account of a Compound Achromatic Microscope, Made by Charles A. Spencer of Canastrota, N.Y.," *The American Journal of Science and Arts*, 2nd ser., (May 1848): 239.

Telescope:
Transit of Venus
1873

Made by Alvan Clark
(American, 1804–1887) in USA
Brass, iron, glass
Telescope in box: 25.4 cm x 2.03 m x 38.1 cm
(10 in. x 6 ft. 8 in. x 15 in.)
Base and mount in box:
88.9 cm x 1.98 m x 101.6 cm
(35 in. x 6 ft. 6 in. x 40 in.)
Smithsonian Institution
National Museum of American History
Washington, DC, Cat. 2006.0182.02-03

IN THE EIGHTEENTH AND NINETEENTH
centuries, one of the most difficult problems in astronomy was ascertaining the size of the solar system.
Although the *relative* distance of each planet from
the Sun was known, their *actual* distances were not.

The most promising solution seemed to be to measure the "Transit of Venus"—the passage of the planet
Venus across the face of the Sun. The plan called for
observers at two different points to each register the
time the transit began. Because they were in separate places, they would see it start at slightly different
times and, knowing that time difference along with
the distance between the two locations, it would be
possible to calculate the distance to the Sun. For a
variety of reasons, however, these measurements
were almost impossible to make.

In 1874, the United States government sent eight
expeditions to observe the transit, stationing them
across the globe and equipping them with identical
sets of equipment, including eight of these exquisite
telescopes, specially made by the American telescope maker Alvan Clark. Although not completely
successful, the expeditions were a bold assertion
that American science—and American scientific-
instrument making—had come of age. ST

Film:
Powers of Ten
1977

→

Written and directed by Charles Eames
(American, 1907–1978) and
Ray Eames (American, 1912–1988)
Running time: 9 minutes
© Eames Office, LLC

POWERS OF TEN is a short film written and directed by the designers Charles and Ray Eames. An adaptation of Kees Boeke's 1957 book *Cosmic View*, it depicts the relative scale of the universe in powers of ten.

More specifically, the film is about scales of observation. Ranging from the infinitesimal to the cosmic, as well as orders of magnitude in between, it provokes rich, interdisciplinary thinking from multiple perspectives. Beginning a mythical journey into space with a lakeside picnic in Chicago as its starting point, the film transports viewers to the outer edges of the known universe by increasing the distance from Earth ten times every ten seconds. Returning to Earth with breathtaking speed, the film then pictures a voyage into the human body, ending inside a carbon atom in the hand of a man sleeping at the picnic. Its message about the role of scale in shaping our understanding of the world is as relevant today as when the orginal version was first made in 1968. JP

1 meter

100,000 million meters

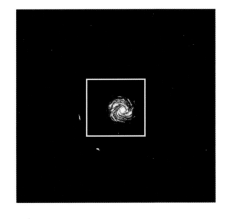

10 meters

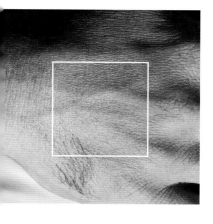

10,000 meters

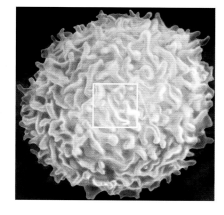

10 million meters

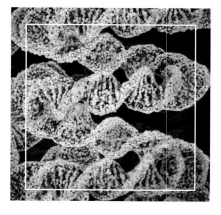

1 meter

1 millimeter

1 micron

RoboBee
August 2012

→

Designed by Kevin Y. Ma (American, b. 1988)
and Robert J. Wood (American, b. 1977)
with Pakpong Chirarattananon, Sawyer B. Fuller,
Harvard School of Engineering and Applied
Sciences (Cambridge, Massachusetts, USA)
Carbon fiber composite, piezoelectric ceramic,
Garolite glass fiber composite, alumina ceramic,
polyimide film, polyester film, acrylic film adhesive,
cyanoacrylate adhesive, epoxy adhesive
Manufacturing processes: laser micromachining;
high-temperature, high-pressure lamination;
manual assembly with tweezers
Mass: 80 mg (about the weight of a honeybee)
L: 2 cm (¾ in.), wingspan: 3 cm (1⅛ in.)
Electrical power requirement: 20 mW
Courtesy of Harvard School of Engineering
and Applied Sciences and Wyss Institute
for Biologically Inspired Engineering

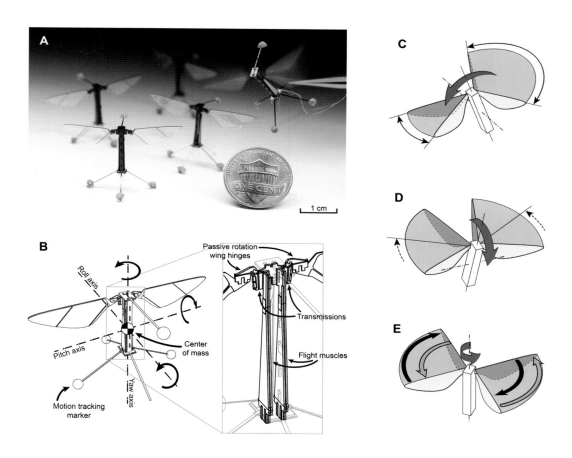

A. Five RoboBees with penny for scale; B. Illustration of how each wing is independently driven by a separate flight muscle; C. Roll torque; D. Pitch torque; E. Yaw torque

THE ROBOBEE IS THE WORLD'S FIRST insect-scale flying robot. Weighing 80 mg (approximately the weight of a honeybee) and with a wingspan of a little more than 3 cm (1⅛ in.), the RoboBee was imagined and designed by researchers at Harvard University's School of Engineering and Applied Sciences. The team was interested in creating a robotic bee colony in order to investigate the alarming collapse of bee colonies worldwide over the past few years. The goal was to replicate the unique behavior that emerges from interactions among thousands of bees.

Facing the difficult challenge of producing such small mechanical devices, the researchers looked to the process of manufacturing pop-up books. To build the individual bees, sheets of laser-cut materials such as carbon fiber are layered and sandwiched together into a thin, flat plate that then folds up (like a child's pop-up book) into the complete electromechanical structure.

Swarms of RoboBees could be in our not-too-distant future. They will not only have the capacity to artificially pollinate flowering crops, but could also participate in search-and-rescue missions, act as environmental sensors, or conduct covert surveillance. MM

Satellite:
Explorer 1 (Replica)

1958
Original launch date February 1958

Manufactured by Jet Propulsion Laboratory
California Institute of Technology (USA)
Metal shell
L x Diam (excluding antennas):
174 x 15.2 cm (68½ x 6 in.)
Smithsonian National Air and Space Museum
Washington, DC, Transferred from
the US Army Ordnance Museum
A19890568000

EXPLORER 1 WAS THE FIRST SUCCESSFUL US Earth-orbiting satellite. As with many tools of exploration, the satellite's design was determined by its history and use. After successful launches from the Soviet Union and a failed American attempt, *Explorer 1* was rapidly developed to achieve orbit. It was mounted externally on top of a modified sounding rocket, an arrangement that required the satellite to incorporate its own rocket booster—which took up the back half—to achieve final orbit. The launch method also called for a conical nose to minimize drag during ascent through the atmosphere. *Explorer 1*'s front half contained detectors for cosmic rays and micrometeorites, electronics, batteries, and communication equipment. Four radio antennas extended from the middle of the satellite.

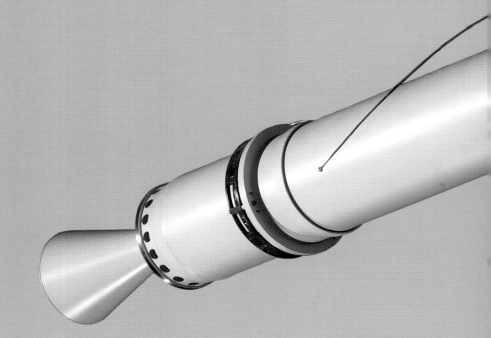

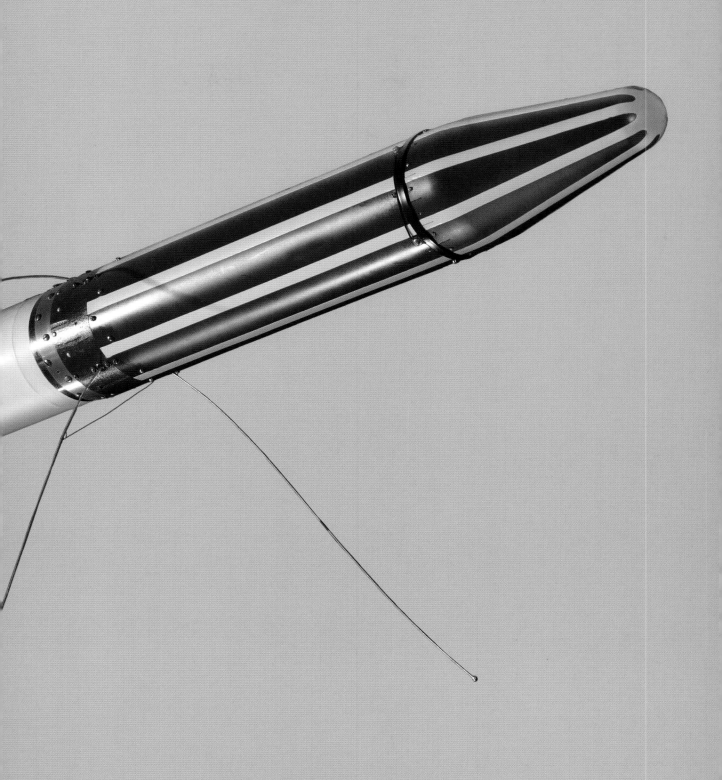

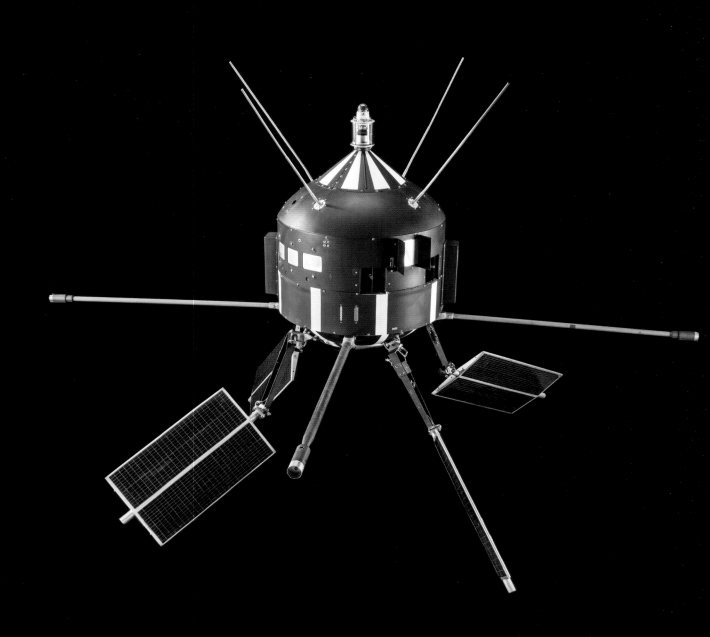

Satellite: *Ariel 2* (Replica)

1970s
Original launch date March 27, 1964

Designed by Goddard Space Flight Center (USA)
Manufactured by Westinghouse Electric
Corporation (USA) and NASA (USA)
Epoxy-bonded fiberglass, aluminum, other light metals, plastics
Overall: 2.31 m x 154.9 cm x 2.31 m (7 ft. 7 in. x 61 in. x 7 ft. 7 in.)
Smithsonian National Air and Space Museum
Washington, DC, Transferred from NASA, A19751411000

Engineers at the NASA Goddard Space Flight
Center in Greenbelt, Maryland, constructed the
Ariel 2 from parts of *Ariel* test models. NASA
transferred the *Ariel 2* to the Smithsonian National
Air and Space Museum in 1975.

WHEN THE INTERNATIONAL ionosphere satellite *Ariel 1* launched on April 26, 1962, it represented three years of effort on the part of the United Kingdom and the United States to integrate British experiment packages into a United States spacecraft. *Ariel 2* followed less than two years later, launching from NASA's Wallops Flight Facility on Wallops Island, Virginia. *Ariel 2* carried four experiments designed to study the ionosphere, a region in the upper atmosphere at an altitude of roughly 75 km to 1,000 km (46–621 mi.) that is ionized by solar radiation. The spacecraft was the first radio-astronomy satellite, listening for radio waves from the galaxy as well as from natural Earth events. The *Ariel 2* experiments also measured levels of ozone and oxygen, the flow of micro-meteorites, radiation, and the temperature and density of electrons in the ionosphere. These experiments furthered the investigation of the ionosphere measured by *Ariel 1* and by earlier American *Explorer* satellites.

Powered by solar cells feeding nickel-cadmium batteries, *Ariel 2* was designed to function for one year, circling the Earth every 101 minutes in an elliptical orbit that varied between 290 km and 1,355 km (180–842 mi.). It was launched in the nose cone of a multistage *Scout* rocket, designed at NASA's Langley Research Center in Hampton, Virginia. The main body of the satellite is 58.4 cm (23 in.) in diameter and 55.9 cm (22 in.) high. The Broad Band Ozone Detector extends only a few centimeters off the top of the satellite, and the 111.8 cm (44 in.) experiment booms and the solar arrays fold tightly to allow the 69.5 kg (153 lb.) spacecraft to fit into the cone. Once in orbit, rockets spun the *Ariel* to approximately 160 revolutions per minute, with the spin diminishing as the spacecraft extended the experiment booms and solar arrays.

Over time, the satellite's spin would decrease to fewer than 50 revolutions per minute.

In the Cold War spirit of the International Geophysical Year (1957–58), the United States announced that it would launch scientific experiments or even complete satellites built by other countries. The offer came through the Committee on Space Research of the International Council of Scientific Unions. Within that same year the British National Committee on Space Research submitted proposals to NASA in response to the offer, an effort that would produce six successful international satellites named after the magical, airy spirit in William Shakespeare's *Tempest* (1611–12). By early 1960, NASA and the British Committee had agreed on the division of responsibilities for the first *Ariel*. The United Kingdom was responsible for the design, fabrication, and testing of the flight sensors and scientific experiments and their associated electronics. Engineers at NASA's Goddard Space Flight Center designed, fabricated, and tested the "bus," or main vehicle; integrated the British experiment packages; and provided the spacecraft's power-supply telemetry, command receiver, thermal control, and data storage. NASA was also responsible for the launch. *Ariel 2* followed the same division of labor, except that the Westinghouse Electric Corporation fabricated the fiberglass spacecraft using NASA's designs.

Following the successful launch and deployment from Wallops Island, *Ariel 2* operated until November 1964. As *Ariel 2* had no onboard rockets to correct its orbit, the orbit continued to decay until the spacecraft burned up as it reentered the atmosphere on November 18, 1967. DD & HH

Earth-Sun to Scale

Solar Wall
2010

←

Designed by Mark Weber
(American, b. 1969) and Henry "Trae"
Winter III (American, b. 1972)
Video display of the sun's surface from
the Atmospheric Imaging Assembly
aboard NASA's Solar Dynamics Observatory
Satellite launch date: February 11, 2010
Courtesy of Harvard-Smithsonian Center
for Astrophysics

(above left) *Solar loop structures, seen most clearly at one million degrees Kelvin, are a constant source of beauty and wonder. These loops, still not well understood, are the subject of intense scientific scrutiny.* (above right) *Violent eruptions of solar prominences, such as the one shown here, occur frequently during the peak of the Sun's eleven-year activity cycle. If aimed Earthward, the resulting coronal mass ejections (CMEs) can interact with the Earth's magnetic field to cause a variety of effects such as auroras, cell-phone and GPS service outages and, in extreme cases, power blackouts.*

LIFE ON EARTH DEPENDS on the Sun for its energy, so it is not surprising that humanity has spent millennia studying our local star, using special tools to observe and understand the Sun's behaviors and mysteries. Solar energy can ignite spectacular light shows on Earth, such as the aurora borealis and aurora australis, but it can also cause power outages, disrupt communications, and pose a serious danger to astronauts in space.

On February 11, 2010, NASA launched an advanced suite of solar telescopes into orbit on board the Solar Dynamics Observatory (SDO). The Atmospheric Imaging Assembly (AIA) is the first instrument that allows us to see the entire Sun at twice the resolution of a standard high-definition television. Observers can now investigate small- and large-scale structures on the Sun such as the shape of a coronal hole, which is determined by magnetic fields and is not random.

The AIA consists of four telescopes, each designed to study the Sun in very specific wavelengths of light. Each telescope has two mirrors, and each mirror is coated with a thin, technologically cutting-edge film that reflects a particular wavelength of light. The AIA had to be launched into space, since it studies the Sun in ultraviolet (UV) and extreme ultraviolet (EUV) wavelengths, which are absorbed by the Earth's atmosphere.

While the AIA itself is a remarkable tool, it requires many more innovative tools to use it. On average, its telescopes take eight 4096 x 4096 pixel images every twelve seconds. Uncompressed, this yields about three terabytes of data per day, or three times more than a high-end desktop's

Launch of Solar Dynamics Observatory onboard Atlas V, February 11, 2010

hard drive. To communicate that much data, there is a dedicated radio station that does nothing but receive data from the SDO. This data is then distributed to archives across the world for scientists and the general public to access. Because our eyes cannot see UV and EUV, the images initially have no color—they are just a set of numbers. To create images that our eyes and brains can comprehend, a color is assigned to each number, which not only renders the solar activity visible, but also makes the images visually appealing. Because the AIA images are far too large to be seen on a single computer screen, scientists have built video-display walls that can accommodate a full view of the Sun, while allowing viewers to zoom in on specific areas to study new phenomena in amazing detail.

The AIA can help scientists answer questions about how the Sun stores, transmits, and releases energy, and ultimately how this affects life on Earth. The images are awe-inspiring, representing that point where art and science meet. They also stand for thousands of years of contemplating the Sun—from observation by the unaided eye to the use of telescopes by astronomers like Galileo Galilei and George Ellery Hale.[2] It makes one wonder what tools we will build in the future and what we will learn from them, a thousand years from now. **HTW**

---

[2] In 1908, George Ellery Hale invented the spectroheliograph, which splits light from the Sun into different colors or wavelengths.

View of the SDO being placed in the payload fairing that will protect it during its journey into space

Solar Wall:
Color Bands
2013

THESE VIEWS OF THE SUN demonstrate how new tools can provide new perspectives. The SDO satellite monitors the movement and heating of elements in the solar atmosphere by detecting light emitted in several wavelengths. These layers of data have been given arbitrary colors to accentuate details. The yellowish imagery shows the light we see on a sunny day emitted from the Sun's surface. The other data layers reveal details not visible to human eyes. The red imagery shows light radiated by a form of helium above the surface of the Sun at about 50,000 °C (90,000 °F). Gold-colored imagery shows light emitted by a form of iron in the Sun's atmosphere at even higher temperatures. The magnetic arcs known as "coronal loops" are visible. Purple and blue images reveal magnetically active regions in the Sun's corona that are hotter than 2,000,000 °C (3,600,000 °F). AJ

1. This image shows the chromosphere, a layer of the solar atmosphere. It is located just above the visible portion of the Sun. The heated, ionized gas, called a plasma, is at a temperature of 100,000 degrees Kelvin. This picture was taken by the AIA on the SDO satellite. Telescopes to view the chromosphere and other layers of the solar atmosphere have to be placed on satellites in orbit around the Earth. The atmosphere of the Sun emits UV and EUV light, which is effectively blocked by the Earth's atmosphere.

2. This is the solar corona at one million degrees Kelvin. Active regions on the east and west limbs of the Sun cause a spectacular display of loops and solar activity.

3. An image taken at nearly the same time as no. 2, but looking at the material in the corona that is at 1.2 million degrees Kelvin. There are many similarities between the two images, but also striking differences. The loops here appear more diffuse than their one million degrees Kelvin counterparts. Also, very distinct dark patches, called "coronal holes," are clearly visible at 1.2 million degrees Kelvin.

4. A third image taken at the same time as nos. 1 and 2, but at two million degrees Kelvin. The loops are now so diffuse it is difficult to make out individual structures. The coronal holes are also different in size and shape, but it is still possible to track them back to no. 3. The sequence of images nos. 2–4 highlights how different the Sun appears depending on the temperature. The Sun also varies strongly in time and in spatial scale.

5. The photosphere, or "surface" of the Sun, which is visible to the naked eye (never look directly at the Sun!) is a relatively cool 6,000 degrees Kelvin. While this view of the Sun is mainly used for coalignment with ground-based telescopes, it still provides insight into the corona above it. The dark blemishes on the left and right of the image are sunspots, regions of intense magnetic field. These sunspots are underneath regions that show the most activity in the images of the hotter corona above them.

6. A composite image combining the information from nos. 2, 3, and 4. Examining images like this one provides insight on how coronal materials at different temperatures interact with one another.

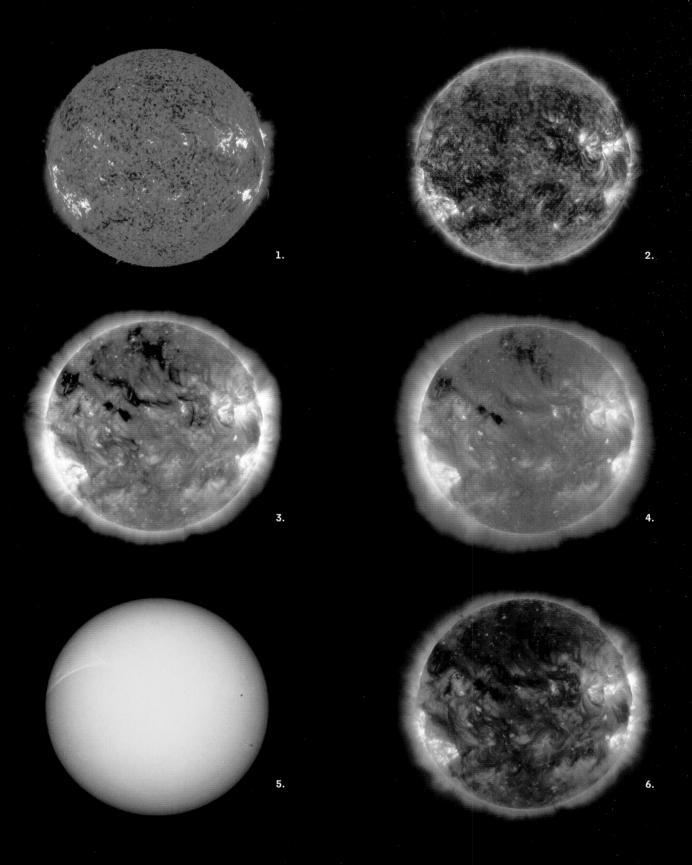

1.

2.

3.

4.

5.

6.

pages 6–7
Joseph B. Friedman, Sketch on Envelope for Pocket Brush

2/3/36
New pocket brush
Lays flat
Moves to vertical position to use

page 193
Orla E. Watson, Telescope Shopping Cart Drawing on Letterhead

-Hinged
-Nested position
-Position when in use

Hinged bottom for lower frame work on single basket telescopic grocery cart. To be used for a supplemental basket.

Dated Monday Nov. 22, 1948

(image not shown)
Earl S. Tupper, Page from Tupper's Notebook "My Purpose in Life"

To live widely and fully. To contact and try to understand the true purpose and intent of everything that has interest or usefulness to humanity and posterity.

To take each thing as I find it and "put it on the spot," so to speak and see how I can improve it, practically to better serve its present purpose, or to serve a better purpose. To try to combine two separate functions on articles to better serve their present purpose, or a better purpose.

To consider myself as a super-coordinator, with observatory and workshop high above this world, where I can look down and take in many things, at once see the blind chases, then coordinate and improve.

To so study all things and put myself in the positions of the different persons and people that I can design and invent so as to both appeal to them and aid them.

To observe general trends i.e. form, stream-lining; music, jazz; health, food, exercise, sunlight, etc. Then invent, not too radically to be accepted by a conservative people, but the next logical step in each trend. Sometimes a revolutionary change may be made and then disguised as just a step forward from the previous standard, in this way people may be weaned much as from breast to a bottle with oatmeal gruel.

Note: An invention may be distinctly more convenient and all that, but if it interferes too much with our set habits, it will be regarded as a nuisance to bother with, and will not be accepted. Everything must progress by steps so as not to be in too jarring harmony with our habits and things around us.

page 195
Charles F. Brannock, Sketch for Mechanism for Measuring Width of Foot

-Heelpiece movable along slot to measure toe at the same time the action of moving the piece would activate the width measurement.

-Same indicator

1) It could move the width slide same as now which would permit narrower device as slide could cut off just outside at the EE line

2) Heel piece action could move a scale of width letter in correct u-letter and an abutment could be brought up to the foot.

- The piece connected by mechanism

page 196
Joseph B. Friedman, Sketch of New Idea for Ice-cream Scoop

New idea 4/9/26
Joseph Friedman
Scoop Ice cream

When handles are pressed band x becomes larger – stretching rubber cup y + ejecting ice cream cake. Edge of wire is sharpened I say wire band; can be narrow metal band on which rubber cup is mounted. Rubber cup is semi-rigid form yet stretchable. Instead of rubber can be metal movable halves.

page 197
Joseph B. Friedman, Sketch for a Safety Razor with Notes
[Left side of page]
State of California
County of San Francisco
Joseph B. Friedman and Albert E. Friedman
December 25, 1927

Being First Duly Sworn, depose and say that they are the inventors of an improvement in safety-razors the following being a description in substance of the basic idea:

An improvement in a safety-razor which consists of combining with the handle or holding means of said razor, a container for safety razor blades. One purpose is a convenient

and readily accessible place for carrying additional blades; another to combine in one article the razor and the blade container box; and a further purpose is to provide a large comfortable handle which is very easy to grasp and effects a good grip and perfect control of the movements of the razor-head. A diagram of the device follows:

—See page 2.—
[Right side of page]
A is an external view of the device. A1 the razor head containing blade and A2 a cylindrical handle containing the extra blades. A3 is a knurled screw cap. When this cap is removed B is exposed (cross-sectional view on horizontal axis). C is a cross-sectional view on a vertical axis. X is the blades. Y is the bent tips of a thin metal strip shown flat in D and bent on dotted lines (E) and to be inserted in the handle A2. C4 is a spring to keep C2 pressed against cap when closed + prevent rattling. C1 is the screw-cap A3 –C2 is the bent strip E. –C3 is the cylinder A2 – The above sketches show the preferred form of the inventions. There can be of course be modifications such as a square or rectangular handle but which would not alter the general and basic idea as described and further deponents saith not.

Signed Joseph B. Friedman
Albert E. Friedman

Subscribed and sworn to before me this 29th day of Dec. 1927
Eleanor A. Simkins, Notary Public

page 198
Joseph B. Friedman, Sketch for Inflatable Umbrella

New Invention
January 19, 1954
A plastic inflated umbrella (no ribs)

X = inflatable tubes or integral sections to a common point (center) of inflation. Inflation can be by mouth or by small air pump in handle of umbrella with release valve to deflate to carry umbrella could be stowed in hollow handle.

-Piston
-Cylinder
-Handle

Lightweight. Wind can't turn inside out. No rust

**Joseph B. Friedman, Pocket Notebook
of Inventions**

[Top]
Rem: Toy spinning top
Stroboscopic

Rem: Bullet

Rem: TV - 3-D
Describes your method–grid

Rem: Jello [xxx]

Rem: air service station

Rem: Pro-carbon paper

Self sealing carton

Rem: Portable minute-minder

W/shield wiper 3/21/58
air supply short tube + present
reciprocating wiper

[Bottom]
Rem: Rent gum soles (shoe-attachable)
for fairs expositions, trade shows, etc.

3-21-58 water keeps A moist
steam-generated by ordinary iron

Rem: Barbecue spit
Selfautomation

Air camp tent
Plastic blow up
Elec. blower + (suction to collapse easily)
Connect to cigarette lighter socket.
Use for air mattress also

Rem: disposable aluminum foil
Broiler
A = perforated foil in a roll
B = Pan – shallow

(image not shown)
**Earl S. Tupper, Sketch for Dental Floss
Cleaning Fork**

Earl S. Tupper
Shirley Mass
April 7, 1939

Yesterday I made drawings, and the rough
frame of my dental floss cleaning fork. Today I
completed the sample and cleaned my teeth
with it. Such things are quickly made and I
should have made it when I first conceived
the idea.

Fig 1. shows cut-away view of hollow handle
holding spool of dental floss with stopper
to hold it in. A groove in the side of stopper
allows the floss to thread it thru and unwind
freely as required.

Fig 3. shows top and bottom view of handle,
forks, and reinforcements with floss stretched
across from points of forks. The forks straddle
the row of teeth and the floss is thus forced
down between the teeth and worked (sawed)
back + forth to clean between teeth. This
dental fork easily reaches + cleans even the
teeth furthest back in the mouth.

Fig 2. shows side view of this cleaner and
shows the general downward curve of the
forks. I showed this to Mike Toto, Alice Dan-
forth, Nelson Benedict, Marie Tupper.

(image not shown)
**Earl S. Tupper, Page from Tupper's
Notebook "How to Invent"**

1. Take any substance and see how many
present things can be made with it. Many
improvements will develop that way. –Tupper

2. Take any object or problem and figure
out ways to overcome present objections to
it. –Tupper

3. Focus your effort on the problem, and not
entirely on the device, that I think, solves the
problem (—extract from article in *Popular
Mechanics*)

4. Take moving sound pictures of my inventions in their various stages of development-
-showing them being demonstrated when-
ever possible. – Tupper

5. Order record searches on the idea in mind.
Then go on developing where past patents
have left off. Or find ways to get around
present ones.

page 200
**Earl S. Tupper, Sketch for "Corsets
with Cross Muscles"**
August 14, 1935
Corsets with Cross Muscles

Wide flat stripes of wood, metal, or other
material. They may or may not be flexible.
They would be made to bend or hinge at
places located similarly to the vertical and
horizontal lines shown in the sketch.

These strips might be flat and straight on
the body side, or they might curve from

end to end, and be convex or concave on
the body side.

Some or all of the strips may be built up in
various ways on the insides (or body side)
to force the body contacting them into any
desired positions--which may easily prove
to advantage in corrective treatments.

Preceeding [sic] are some end view cross
sections of possible cross strips.

The strips of material are hinged to bend
as the powerful front muscles of the body
do. This is more comfortable than the vertical
strips which jab the abdomen and up under
the ribs when bending or stooping.

This corset offers the further advantage of
preventing the flat appearance so much
desired in the abdomen, – and the advantage
of moulding the body to that shape-- the vertical stayed, nor no other corset on the market
offers such advantage.

page 200
**Earl S. Tupper, Sketch for "Adjustable
Lens Sun Glasses or Sun Shade"**

Conceived June 16, 1937
Earl S. Tupper
Adjustable Lens
Sun Glasses or Sun Shade

Fig. 1. Frame (without ear hooks attached)

Fig. 2. Lenses mounted rigidly to round
plastic rod—or they may be hinged.

Lenses may be set into groove of round
plastic rod, or may attach rigidly or loosely
in some other manner. The rod with lenses
attached then snaps into raised groove
over nose bridge on frame.

This same lens hook up might be attached
to a wide variety of frames—including a very
simple one to fit over and use in conjunction
with regular eye adjusting glasses.

A raised piece may be provided on frame at
each end of groove, this piece to have notches
where inner edge of each lens may catch to
provide more positive opening adjustment than
friction of hinge alone would provide.

page 200
**Earl S. Tupper, Sketch for "Water
Motor Cycle"**

Water Motor Cycle
Provided by Outboard Motor

The keel weight may be adjustable (up and down) and the body of the boat may be built high so as to give thrills on leans and curves, or afford absolute sea worthiness under worst sea conditions.

page 200
Earl S. Tupper, Sketch for "Cork or Stopper to Measure Pills from Bottle"

Earl S. Tupper
Shirley, Mass.
Sept 10, 1937

Cork or Stopper to Measure pills from bottle

Bottle of pills with stopper in place ready for pill to roll into hole. When pill is in hole, withdraw stopper far enough to hold it, then tip bottle right side up and pull stopper clean out and deposit pill in hand.

Stopper with hole to receive pill.

page 201
Earl S. Tupper, Sketch of "Adjustable Lens Glasses"

June 16, 1937
Adjustable Lens Glasses

Lenses attach to plastic rod running thru nose bridge. Lenses attach solidly to rod and depend on rod turning in nose bridge; or they may hinge on rod to provide raising for eye shades.

Notches on side of nose rest provide dog-like adjustment for holding lenses in various partly raised positions.

page 202
Earl S. Tupper, Sketches for Comb Designs

Earl Tupper
Shirley, Mass.

No.4 Comb with mirror + ruler
May have clip. Makes good bookmark.
Clip should be on same side as ruler so ruler will lie flat on paper. Mirror may be counter-sunk, cemented on the smoothe [sic] surface or have molding or case or frame around it.

No.5 Comb with ruler and spring clamps to hold compact and lipstick.
Picture or monogram may be pasted or cut on back, opposite mirror.

No.6 Comb with mirror; and having ruler + clip on back side

No.7 Back view, of No. 6. Showing ruler and clip

page 203
Earl S. Tupper, Sketches for Comb Designs

No.8 Comb with ruler having sharp edge + counter-sunk compact with mirror + place for lipstick. Clip should be on same side as ruler, so ruler will lie flat against paper.

No.9 Left handed persons comb, other-wise duplicate of above.

No.10 Dagger type comb with mirror set in handle + clip of celluloid or metal on back. Mirror may be counter-sunk, cemented on top, or have frame or molding around it.

No.11 Dagger type comb that carries curved blade outline into the teeth. Oblong compact with powder, rouge, lipstick, fits into hole cut in handle and adds thickness to both sides. Mirror inside. Clip on back of handle.

page 203
Earl S. Tupper, Sketches for Comb Designs

Earl S. Tupper
Shirley, Mass
Molded comb with thick handle and molded–in compact with water proof sealing ring of rubber. Having mirror in cover and clip on back.

No.1 Pocket comb + with or without clip or fastener to hold in pocket, on belt, or clothes. Mirror may be countersunk, cemented on flat surface, or be set within a frame or molding.

No.2 Comb for pocket pocketbook, book mark, dresser, or to attach to clothes by clip or fastener. Place on back of mirror, on other side of comb, to paste on picture or clamp on compact + lipstick. Mirror may be counter-sunk, cemented on the flat surface, or be set within a frame or molding then fastened by frame or molding or by itself, or both.

No.3 Same as No.2 but having cemented-on compact + lipstick in place of plain mirror. Plain back, picture, monogram.

Ackerman, Lillian A. *A Necessary Balance: Gender and Power Among Indians of the Columbia Plateau*. Norman: University of Oklahoma Press, 2003.

Adams, Vivian M. "In a Spiritual Way: A Portrait of Plateau Spirituality in Traditional Art," In *Native Arts of the Columbia Plateau: The Doris Swayze Bounds Collection*. Edited by Susan E. Harless. Seattle: University of Washington Press, 1998.

Amiotte, Arthur, and Janet Catherine Berlo. *Arthur Amiotte: Collages, 1988–2006*. Santa Fe, NM: Wheelwright Museum of the American Indian, 2006.

Antonelli, Paola, and the Museum of Modern Art. *Objects of Design, from the Museum of Modern Art*. New York: Museum of Modern Art, 2003.

Bailey, J. W. as quoted in C. R. Gilman. "An Account of a Compound Achromatic Microscope, Made by Charles A. Spencer of Canastrota, N.Y." *The American Journal of Science and Arts* V, 2nd ser., (1848): 239.

Beasley, Harry G. *Pacific Island Records: Fish Hooks*. London: John Hewett, 1980.

Bell, Joshua A. "The Sorcery of Sugar: Intersecting Agencies within Collections made by the 1928 USDA Sugarcane Expedition to New Guinea." In *Reassembling the Collection: Ethnographic Museums and Indigenous Agency*. Edited by Rodney Harrison, Sarah Byrne, and Anne Clark, Santa Fe, NM: School of Advanced Research, 2013.

Bigelow, Henry Jacob. "Insensibility During Surgical Operations Produced by Inhalation." *Boston Medical and Surgical Journal* 35, no. 16 (1846): 309–17.

Blum, Andrew. *Tubes: A Journey to the Center of the Internet*. New York: HarperCollins, 2012.

Cebula, Larry. *Plateau Indians and the Quest for Spiritual Power, 1700–1850*. Lincoln: University of Nebraska Press, 2003.

Conn, Richard G. "The Plateau Culture Area and Its Art: Toward an Understanding of Plateau Aesthetics." In *Native Arts of the Columbia Plateau: The Doris Swayze Bounds Collection*. Edited by Susan E. Harless. Seattle: University of Washington Press, 1998.

Corliss, William R. *Scientific Satellites*. NASA SP-133. Washington, DC: Scientific and Technical Information Division, National Aeronautics and Space Administration, 1967.

Curtis, Anthony R., ed. *Space Satellite Handbook*. 3rd ed. Houston: Gulf Publishing Company, 1994.

"Cusp 2011 Van Phillips." YouTube video, 22:55. Posted by "Cusp-Conference," March 23, 2012. http://youtu.be/4d7O8UxFJt4.

Davenport, William H. "Sculpture of the Eastern Solomons." *Expedition* 10 (1968): 4–25.

Diamond, Jared. *Guns, Germs, and Steel: The Fates of Human Societies*. New York: W.W. Norton & Company, 1997.

Eames Office. "*Powers of Ten*. Based on the film by Charles and Ray Eames." http://www.powersof10.com/film.

Eames Office. "Tenth Annual International Powers of Ten Day." MultiVu. Published August 27, 2010. http://multivu.prnewswire.com/mnr/powersof10/45841/.

Harold Evans, with Gail Buckland and David Lefer, *They Made America: From the Steam Engine to the Search Engine: Two Centuries of Innovators* (New York: Little Brown and Company, 2004), 75

Featherstonhaugh, George W. *Excursion Through the Slave States, from Washington on the Potomac*. New York: Harper & Brothers, 1844.

Fienup-Riordan, Ann. "Cenami Up'nerkam Nalini (On the Coast During Spring)." In *The Way We Genuinely Live: Yuungnaqpiallerput: Masterworks of Yup'ik Science and Survival*. Seattle: University of Washington Press, 2007.

Fiore, Quentin, and Marshall McLuhan. *The Medium Is the Message: An Inventory of Effects*. New York: Bantam Books, 1967.

Fisher, Andrew H. *Shadow Tribe: The Making of Columbia River Indian Identity*. Seattle: University of Washington Press, 2010.

Foulkes, Imogen. "From Humble Tool to Global Icon." BBC News. Last modified July 30, 2009. http://news.bbc.co.uk/2/hi/europe/8172917.stm.

Fox, C. E. *The Threshold of the Pacific: An Account of the Social Organization Magic and Religion of the People of San Cristoval in the Solomon Islands*. New York: Alfred A. Knopf, 1925.

Galison, Peter. *Einstein's Clocks and Poincaré's Maps: Empires of Time*. New York: W. W. Norton & Company, 2003.

Giedion, Siegfried. *Mechanization Takes Command, a Contribution to Anonymous History*. New York: Oxford University Press, 1948.

Herzfeld, Ernst. Correspondence, September 23, 1933. Ernst Herzfeld Papers, Freer Sackler Archives.

Herzfeld, Ernst. Unpublished note, N-84, November 22, 1923. Ernst Herzfeld Papers, Freer Sackler Archives.

Jobs, Steve. Commencement address at Stanford University, Stanford, California, June 12, 2005.

Kepes, Gyorgy. *Sign, Image, Symbol*. New York: George Braziller, 1966.

Houchins, Chang-su. *Artifacts of Diplomacy: Smithsonian Collections from Commodore Matthew Perry's Japan Expedition (1853–1854)*. Washington, DC: Smithsonian Institution Press, 1995.

ICanFixThat. "Victorinox Signature Slim." SAKWiki. Last modified January 15, 2013. http://www.sakwiki.com/tiki-index.php?page=Victorinox+Signature+Slim.

Irie, Horishi. "Apprenticeship Training in Tokugawa Japan." *Acta Asiatica* 54 (1988): 1–23.

Ivens, W. G. *Melanesians of the South-East Solomon Islands*. London: Kegan Paul, 1927.

Ivens, Walter G. *A Dictionary of the Language of Sa`a (Mala) and Ulawa, South-East Solomon Islands*. London: Oxford University Press, 1929.

Jackson, Derek. *Swiss Army Knives: A Collector's Companion*. London: Compendium, 2007.

Janssen, Barbara Suit. *Patent Models Index: Guide to the Collections of the National Museum of American History, Smithsonian Institution*. 2 vols. Washington, DC: Smithsonian Institution Scholar Press, 2010.

Kaschko, M. W. "An Archaeological Consideration of the Ethnographic Fishhook Set on Uki Island, Southeast Solomon Islands." In *Southeast Solomon Islands Cultural History: A Preliminary Survey*. Edited by R. C. Green and M. M. Cresswell. Wellington: Royal Society of New Zealand, 1976.

Knott, Cargill G. "The Abacus, in Its Historic and Scientific Aspects." In *Handbook of the Napier Tercentenary Celebration, or, Modern Instruments and Methods of Calculation*. Edited by E. M. Horsburgh. London: G. Bell, 1914. Originally published in *Transactions of the Asiatic Society of Japan* 14, pt. 1 (1886): 18–72.

Kojima, Takashi. *The Japanese Abacus: Its Use and Theory*. Rutland, VT: Charles E. Tuttle Company, 1954.

Leechman, Douglas and M. R. Harrington. *String Records of the Northwest*. New York: Museum of the American Indian, Heye Foundation, 1921.

Levy, Joel. "Swiss Army Knife." In *Really Useful: The Origins of Everyday Things*. Buffalo, NY: Firefly Books, 2002.

Lilley, Sam. *Men, Machines, and History: The Story of Tools and Machines in Relation to Social Progress*. New York: International Publishers, 1966.

Lucas, Alfred. *Antiques, Their Restoration and Preservation*. London: Arnold, 1924.

Mallery, Garrick. "Pictographs of the North American Indians: A Preliminary Paper." In *Fourth Annual Report of the Bureau of American Ethnology to the Secretary of the Smithsonian Institution 1882–'83*. Edited by J. W. Powell. Washington, DC: Government Printing Office, 1886.

Massey, Sir Harrie Stewart Wilson, and M. O. Robins, *History of British Space Science*, Cambridge: Cambridge University Press, 1986.

McKee, W. J. E. "A Controlled Study of the Effects of Tonsillectomy and Adenoidectomy in Children." *British Journal of Preventive and Social Medicine* 17, no. 2 (1963): 49-69. http://www.jstor.org/stable/25565329.

Mead, Sidney M. *Material Culture and Art in the Star Harbour Region, Eastern Solomon Islands*. Toronto: Royal Ontario Museum, 1973.

Meredith, Martin. *Born in Africa: The Quest for the Origins of Human Life*. New York: PublicAffairs, 2011.

Mikami, Yoshio, and David Eugene Smith. *A History of Japanese Mathematics*. Chicago: Open Court Publishing Company, 1914.

Miller, Dayton Clarence. "Rudolph Koenig." In *Anecdotal History of the Science of Sound: To the Beginning of the 20th Century*. New York: Macmillan, 1935.

Ministry of Economy, Trade and Industry of Japan. "*Dentō-teki Kōgei-hin Sangyō wo Meguru Genjō to Kongo no Shinkō Shisaku ni tsuite*" 伝統的工芸品産業をめぐる現状と今後の振興施策について (The Present Conditions and Future Promotion Measures of Traditional Craft Industries). Tokyo: Ministry of Economy, Trade and Industry, 2009.

Nagel, Alexander. "Ernst Herzfeld." In *Tehran 50: ein halbes Jahrhundert deutsche Archäologen in Iran: eine Ausstellung des Deutschen Archäologischen Instituts in Zusammenarbeit mit dem Museum für Islamische Kunst, Staatliche Museen Berlin*. . . . Edited by Barbara Helwing et al. Mainz, Germany: von Zabern, 2011.

National Aeronautics and Space Administration and Goddard Space Flight Center, *ARIEL 1: The First International Satellite, The Project Summary*, NASA SP-43. Washington, DC: Office of Scientific and Technical Information, National Aeronautics and Space Administration, 1963.

Ōdate, Toshio. *Japanese Woodworking Tools: Their Tradition, Spirit, and Use*. Newtown, CT: Taunton Press, 1984.

Ortega, Damián, and Jessica Morgan. *Do it Yourself: Damián Ortega*. New York: Skira Rizzoli, 2009.

Össur International. "Feet." http://www.ossur.com/prosthetic-solutions/products/feet.

Pantalony, David. *Altered Sensations: Rudolph Koenig's Acoustical Workshop in Nineteenth-Century Paris*. Dordrecht, Netherlands: Springer, 2009.

Pogash, Carol. "A Personal Call to a Prosthetic Invention." *New York Times*, July 2, 2008. www.nytimes.com/2008/07/02/sports/olympics/02cheetah.html.

Richmond, Alison, and Alison Lee Bracker, eds. *Conservation: Principles, Dilemmas and Uncomfortable Truths*. Oxford: Butterworth-Heinemann, 2009.

Robert Brookes. "Victorinox Wins Contract for New Army Knife." swissinfo. Published September 8, 2008. http://www.swissinfo.ch/eng/victorinox-wins-contract-for-new-army-knife/993870.

Rousselot, Jean-Loup, William W. Fitzhugh, and Aron Crowell. "Maritime Economies of the North Pacific Rim." In *Crossroads of Continents: Cultures of Siberia and Alaska*. Edited by William W. Fitzhugh and Aron Crowell. Washington, DC: Smithsonian Institution Press, 1988.

Saluskin, Alex. "Old Days and the Present." In *Treaty Centennial, 1855–1955, the Yakimas: Dedicated to the Treaty Chiefs and Yakimas Yet Unborn*. Yakima, WA: Republic Press, 1955.

Schick, Kathy Diane, and Nicholas Patrick Toth. "The Role of Rock: Uses of Early Stone Tools." In *Making Silent Stones Speak: Human Evolution and the Dawn of Technology*. New York: Simon & Schuster, 1993.

Sennett, Richard. *The Craftsman*. New Haven, CT: Yale University Press, 2008.

Smithsonian Institution. "Does Double-Amputee Oscar Pistorius Have an Unfair Advantage at the 2012 Olympic Games?" http://www.smithsonianmag.com/summerolympics/does-double-amputee-oscar-pistorius-have-an-unfair-advantage-at-the-2012-olympic-games-2655123/.

Smithsonian Institution. "Powers of Ten Theater." http://www.si.edu/Exhibitions/Details/Powers-of-Ten-Theater-3485.

Smithsonian National Museum of American History. "Van Phillips :: Inventing Ourselves :: Smithsonian Lemelson Center." http://invention.smithsonian.org/centerpieces/inventingourselves/pop-ups/van-pop-up.htm.

Sobel, Dava. *Longitude: The True Story of a Lone Genius Who Solved the Greatest Scientific Problem of His Time*. London: Harper Perennial, 2011.

"Swiss Army Knife." In *Phaidon Design Classics. Vol. 1*. London: Phaidon, 2006.

Tupper, Earl S. "My Purpose in Life." Notebook, ca. 1935. Earl S. Tupper Papers, Series 2: Early Business, Paper and Scientific notes, Invention Diary and Sketchbook, Box 4, Folder 2, Archives Center, National Museum of American History.

Turner, Fred. From *Counterculture to Cyberculture: Stewart Brand, the Whole Earth Network, and the Rise of Digital Utopianism*. Chicago: University of Chicago Press, 2006.

Turner, Lucien M. *An Aleutian Ethnography*. Edited by Raymond L. Hudson. Fairbanks: University of Alaska Press, 2008.

Uebelacker, Morris Leo, and Jeffery S. Wilson. *Time Ball: A Story of the Yakima People and the Land: A Cultural Resource Overview*. Yakima, WA: Yakima Nation, 1984.

"Victorinox @ work, signature slim 4.6125.TG16GB review." YouTube video, 7:56. Posted by "Pawel eR," September 23, 2013. http://youtu.be/5BwKF_C1SkE.

Victorinox. "SwissChamp SOS Kit." https://www.swissarmy.com/us/app/product/Swiss-Army-Knives/Category/Do-It-Yourself/Swiss-Champ-SOS-Kit/53511.

"Victorinox Swiss Army Knife - History & Factory Tour." YouTube video, 2:55. Posted by "MultiToolTube," January 9, 2010. http://youtu.be/ICIy4-pKR7k.

"Victorinox Swiss Army Knife Commercial - Aboard Every Space Shuttle Mission." YouTube video, 0:30. Posted by "MultiToolTube," January 9, 2010. http://youtu.be/HdVar6FYM9M.

Weber, Robert J. "Stone Age Knife to Swiss Army Knife: An Invention Prototype." In *Inventive Minds: Creativity in Technology*. Edited by Robert J. Weber and David N. Perkins. New York: Oxford University Press, 1992.

Woodford, C. M. "Fish-hooks from the Solomon Islands." *Man* 18 (1918): 130–32.

Zapata-Aubé, Nicole, ed. *Lottin de Laval: archéologue et peintre orientaliste, 1810–1903*. Bernay, France: Éditions de l'Association pour la promotion de la culture, 1997.

All photos not credited here are in the public domain. Any errors or omissions will be corrected in subsequent editions.

Courtesy of the Alfred T. Palmer Collection: page 153. Courtesy of the American Foundation for the Blind Archives: page 112 (bottom). © James H. Barker 1980: page 123 (middle). B.F. Goodrich Collection, Archival Services, University Libraries, The University Akron: page 125 (right). Canadian Museum of History, 39026: page 129. Courtesy of the Choueke Family Residence: page 66. "Controlled Flight of a Biologically Inspired, Insect-Scale Robot," Kevin Y. Ma, Pakpong Chirarattananon, Sawyer B. Fuller, and Robert J. Wood, Science 3 (May 2013): 340 (6132), 603–607. [DOI: 10.1126/science.1231806]. Reprinted with permission from AAAS.: page 245. Cooper Hewitt, Smithsonian Design Museum; Photo by Matt Flynn © Smithsonian Institution: pages 45 (bottom), 75, 91, 93 (top & bottom), 120, 127, 130 (right), 148, 149 (right), 158, 218, 228. Cooper Hewitt, Smithsonian Design Museum; Photo by Ellen McDermott © Smithsonian Institution: pages 29, 80–81, 82, 87 (left, middle, right), 168, 225, 226, 227, 234 (right). Cooper Hewitt, Smithsonian Design Museum; © Smithsonian Institution: pages 174, 175, 211. Courtesy of CyArk, www.CyArk.org: page 171 (top, bottom left, bottom right). Department of Anthropology, Smithsonian Institution; Photo by Donald E. Hurlbert © Smithsonian Institution: pages 26 (E11043), 27 (E3513), 43 (left & right, E29847), 46–7 (E45990), 48 (top & bottom, E257827), 49 (E399982), 50 (E399972), 51 (top & bottom, E399972), 52 (E257801), 53 (left & right, E257801), 54–5 (E244858), 62 (left, E322652), 63 (left, E322652-11), 64 (left, E378), 64 (right, E380), 65 (left, E385), 65 (right, E376), 67 (left, E385), 74 (left, A581650), 74 (right, A581651), 76 (2065648, Field No. I-EgMK), 78 (No. 2065648, Field No. Loc. 77-IIV), 79 (A146025), 84 (A365240), 86 (left, A365240), 88–90 (A207910), 97 (A315235), 110 (E3790), 117 (E316756), 150 (top & bottom, E432083), 220 (E36240), 221 (E65272). Dowling Studios Inc. 2009: page 139. Ami Drach and Dov Ganchrow, Photo: Moti Fishbain: page 44 (top left, bottom left, & right). © Eames Office, LLC: pages 230, 242–43. Ernst Herzfeld Papers, Freer Gallery of Art and Arthur M. Sackler Gallery Archives: pages 100, 101. Courtesy of General Electric: page 140. Getty Images: page 130 (left). Courtesy of Given Imaging Ltd.: page 235. Courtesy of Glass Foundation and WIRED magazine: pages 142, 143. Google, Inc.; Photo by Andrew Meredith: page 205. Courtesy Michael Hanz, aafradio.org: page 161. Courtesy of Harvard School of Engineering and Applied Science and Wyss Institute for Biologically Inspired Engineering: page 244. Hawaii State Archives: page 28 (top & bottom). International Organization for Standardization: page 103. The J. Paul Getty Museum, Los Angeles: pages 2, 34 (all), 35–42. Karen Carr Studio, courtesy of Human Origins Program, Smithsonian Institution: page 77. Courtesy of Karten Design: page 234 (left). Kentucky Historical Society: page 118. Klassik Stiftung Weimar, Goethe and Schiller Archive, GSA 71/234, Bl, 31: page 180. Jason Lee: pages 62 (right), 63 (right). The LIFE Premium Collection/Getty Images: page 92. Ruggero Lorenzi, Target Communication SRL: page 45 (top). Courtesy of Made In Space, Inc.: pages 206, 207. MicroSystems Laboratory of the University of California, Irvine: pages 144, 146, 147.

Courtesy of Nanobiosym: page 138. NASA/Tony Gray and Sandra Joseph, February 11, 2010: page 252 (bottom). NASA/Jim Grossman, January 21, 2010: page 253. Photo by Mark Avino, Smithsonian National Air and Space Museum: pages 56–58 (NASM Acc. 2012-0026), 102 (NASM 2014-01646), 124 (NASM 2003-27315), 125 (left, NASM 2008-8613). Photo by Mark Avino and Ron Cunningham, Smithsonian National Air and Space Museum: page 22 (NASM 2008-1856). Photo by Eric Long, National Air and Space Museum, Smithsonian Institution: pages 246–47 (NASM 2007-29725). Photo by Dane A. Penland, Smithsonian National Air and Space Museum: page 248 (NASM 2014-02554). Photo by Benjamin G. Sullivan, Smithsonian National Air and Space Museum, Smithsonian Institution: pages 24, 214. National Anthropological Archives, Smithsonian Institution: pages 90 [INV 0863110], 98 (08633800). National Anthropological Archives, Smithsonian Institution; Photo by John A. Anderson: page 99 (NAA INV 03494000). National Museum of African Art, Smithsonian Institution; Photo by Franko Khoury: page 126. Archives Center, National Museum of American History, Smithsonian Institution: pages 19, 176, 191, 192, 193, 194, 195 (top left, top right, bottom right), 196 (1, 3, 4), 197 (top & bottom), 198 (left & right), 199 (left & right), 200, 201, 202, 203. Joseph B. Friedman Papers, Archives Center, National Museum of American History: pages 4–5. Harold Dorwin, National Museum of American History, Smithsonian Institution: page 183 (bottom). Jaclyn Nash, National Museum of American History, Smithsonian Institution: pages 156 (right), 166–67, 169, 186–87 (left to right), 237 (right). Richard W. Strauss, National Museum of American History, Smithsonian Institution: pages 160, 182, 189. Hugh Talman, National Museum of American History, Smithsonian Institution: pages 8, 58, 60–61, 104–5, 106, 107, 111, 112 (top), 131, 132, 134, 135 (top & bottom), 136, 152 (top & bottom), 164 (left & right), 170, 172, 179, 184, 185 (left), 189 (left), 208, 212, 213 (top & bottom), 216, 217 (top & bottom), 232, 233, 236, 238 (left & right), 240, 241. National Museum of American History & Smithsonian Institution Archives: pages 162, 210. National Museum of the American Indian; Photo by Roger Whiteside © Smithsonian Institution: pages 94 (100297.000), 95 (100297.000), 128 (227435.000), 222 (21/800), 223 (4/8457), 224 (3/6271). National Museum of the American Indian; Photo by Ernest Amoroso © Smithsonian Institution: pages 122 (22/7435), 123 (top, 22/7435). National Museum of the American Indian; Photo by Leuman M. Waugh © Smithsonian Institution: page 123 (bottom, L02290). © Damián Ortega: pages 30 (top & bottom), 32–33. Photograph by Robert Pontsioen: page 66 (right). The Royal Library – Copenhagen: page 86 (right). © The Royal Society: page 237 (left). Smithsonian American Art Museum: page 219. Smithsonian Libraries: pages 113–15, 154, 155, 156 (left), 157, 190. Smithsonian National Postal Museum: pages 108, 109. Solar Dynamics Observatory/NASA: pages 250–51, 252 (top left & right), 255. Tangible Media Group and MIT Media Lab: page 204. Courtesy of the University of Illinois at Urbana-Champaign: page 141. The William Dunn School of Pathology: page 137 (top). © WSDOT: pages 68–73. Courtesy of the Yakima Valley Museum: page 96.

Index Notes: Page numbers in *italics* indicate featured tools. Where photographs and related captions are on opposite or subsequent pages, page references indicate captions.